Göttinger Wirtschaftsinformatik

Herausgeber: J. Biethahn · L. M. Kolbe · M. Schumann

Band 64

Nils-Holger Schmidt

Environmentally Sustainable Information Management

Theories and Concepts for Sustainability, Green IS, and Green IT

CUVILLIER VERLAG

Herausgeber

Prof. Dr. J. Biethahn   L. M. Kolbe   Prof. Dr. M. Schumann

Georg-August-Universität
Wirtschaftsinformatik
Platz der Göttinger Sieben 5
37073 Göttingen

Bibliografische Information der Deutschen Nationalbibliothek
Die Deutsche Nationalbibliothek verzeichnet diese Publikation in der Deutschen
Nationalbibliografie; detaillierte bibliografische Daten sind im Internet über
http://dnb.d-nb.de abrufbar.
1. Aufl. - Göttingen : Cuvillier, 2011
  Zugl.: Göttingen, Univ., Diss., 2011

ISBN 978-3-86955-825-7

© CUVILLIER VERLAG, Göttingen 2011
  Nonnenstieg 8, 37075 Göttingen
  Telefon: 0551-54724-0
  Telefax: 0551-54724-21

Alle Rechte vorbehalten. Ohne ausdrückliche Genehmigung
des Verlages ist es nicht gestattet, das Buch oder Teile
daraus auf fotomechanischem Weg (Fotokopie, Mikrokopie)
zu vervielfältigen.
1. Auflage, 2011
Gedruckt auf säurefreiem Papier

ISBN 978-3-86955-825-7

Environmentally Sustainable Information Management
Theories and Concepts for Sustainability, Green IS, and Green IT

Dissertation

zur Erlangung des wirtschaftswissenschaftlichen Doktorgrades
der Wirtschaftswissenschaftlichen Fakultät der Georg-August-Universität Göttingen

vorgelegt von

Dipl.-Wirtsch.-Inf. Nils-Holger Schmidt

aus Hanau

Göttingen, 2011

Erstgutachter:	Prof. Dr. Lutz M. Kolbe
Zweitgutachter:	Prof. Dr. Matthias Schumann
Tag der mündlichen Prüfung:	08. Juli 2011

Preface

In the 21st century, environmental protection is a very important issue. As a result of the growing global population, increasing demands, and limited resources, as well as the effects of global warming, and a societal shift, there is an urgent need for management reorientation. Therefore, information technology (IT) must minimize its environmental impact and facilitate new, smart solutions to provide more with less. In this context, the information systems (IS) research discipline can play an important role by developing theories and concepts whereby IT can contribute to environmental sustainability.

This cumulative dissertation "Environmentally Sustainable Information Management - Theories and Concepts for Sustainability, Green IS, and Green IT" provides initial findings related to environmental protection and IT. Its primary focus is on IT organizations' strategic and organizational issues. The dissertation was developed at the Chair of Information Management at the Georg-August-Universität Göttingen in close cooperation with the Chair of Information and Communication Management at the Technische Universität Berlin. It consists of 10 publications that were published between 2009 and 2011 in international conference proceedings or in renowned IS research journals. The publications are framed by background information regarding environmental sustainability and IT, as well as a comprehensive summary of the main findings and further research topics.

This type of study is not possible without the support and help of many people. Therefore, I would like to thank everyone who contributed to my thesis and supported me throughout the process.

First, I thank Prof. Dr. Lutz M. Kolbe for providing an excellent, practice oriented research environment. I thank him for his pleasant, friendly cooperation, and the critical and constructive discussions. I learned much from his proactive and communicative management approach.

My sincere thanks also go to our close research partners, Koray Erek and Prof. Dr. Rüdiger Zarnekow, from the Technische Universität Berlin. Without their support, the research on Green IS and Green IT, and this dissertation would not have been possible.

The publications are the core of this thesis. Therefore, I thank all co-authors, namely Prof. Dr. Jutta Geldermann, Tobias Langkau, Thierry Ruch, Meike Schmehl, Timo Schmidtchen, and Florian Thies for their contributions.

My thanks also go to Prof. Dr. Matthias Schumann for providing important hints in the doctoral colloquium and for being the second examiner of this work.

I thank my colleagues for the encouraging and motivating work atmosphere. I will miss their humor in and outside working hours and the challenging fights at the soccer table. My special thanks go to Matthias Kießling, Stefan Bitzer, and Lars Thoroe for being poco poco. I thank Arne Frerichs for showing up in my office late at night to provide inspiration and motivation just before important deadlines. Furthermore, I thank my colleagues Janis Kossahl, Mauricio Marrone, Nicky Opitz, and Carla Sanchez for many fruitful discussions. I also thank our graduate assistants, especially Yvonne Bernhardt, Benjamin Brauer, and Katja Kusiak. Without their support, many activities would not have been possible. Regarding this thesis, I thank Renette Pickering for helping me with the English.

A great workplace is nothing without a great environment. Therefore, I thank my flat mates who always reminded me about the most important things in life, and taught me some valuable lessons about cooking and relaxation. My thanks go to Schrissi, Karo, Anschu, Lili, Silu, Klaus, Bianka, Wiebke, Robert, Joanna, Schluki, and Schruben. You are the greatest. The Goldgraben is the best place on earth and it will always have a special place in my heart.

For their great scientific input from a different economic perspective – often until sunrise – I thank my friends Felix, Tobi, Dimi, and Knut from the Chair of Development Economics.

With all my heart I thank Theda for always being there. Her understanding, support, and the great tennis matches helped me enormously during the entire dissertation process.

For her scientific input and critical mind, I express my greatest thanks to Christina, whose integrity always provided a benchmark. Convincing her often promoted deeper reflection.

Finally, I thank my family. My parents motivated me throughout my education; they encouraged me and provided valuable guidance. Without my parents, this thesis would never have been written. To them I dedicate this work.

Göttingen, July 2011   *Nils-Holger Schmidt*

Table of Contents

Abstract ix
List of Figures xi
List of Tables xii
Acronyms xv

A.   Foundations 1

1   Introduction 1

    1.1   Motivation 1
    1.2   Research Questions 4
    1.3   Structure of the Thesis 7
    1.4   Addressees and Anticipated Contributions 8

2   Research Methodology 10

    2.1   General Research Approach 10
    2.2   Applied Methodologies 13

3   Related Research on Sustainability and Information Systems 16

    3.1   Beginning and Emergence of Research 16
    3.2   Overview of Applied Theories and Concepts 18
    3.3   Terminology and Relationships of Key Terms 19
         3.3.1   Sustainability and IS 19
         3.3.2   Green IS as an Environmental Enabler 21
               3.3.2.1   Distinction Between Green IS and Green IT 21
               3.3.2.2   Potentials and Examples of Green IS 22
         3.3.3   Green IT for the Environmental Alignment of IT Organizations 25
               3.3.3.1   Environmental Impact of IT 26
               3.3.3.2   Perspectives and Categories to Describe Green IT 27
               3.3.3.3   Exemplary Measures 31
               3.3.3.4   Performance Metrics 37
    3.4   Industrialized Information Management 41

B.   Sustainability and Information Systems 44

1   Sustainable Information Systems Management 46

    1.1   The Ecological and Social Dimension of Information Systems Management ... 47
    1.2   Sustainability and Resource Orientation 47
         1.2.1   History and Concept of Sustainability 47
         1.2.2   Resource-based View on IS Management 48
    1.3   Framework of Sustainable IS Management 49
         1.3.1   Principles and Characteristics 49
         1.3.2   Management Cycle 49
         1.3.3   Measures and Implementation on the Process Level 51
    1.4   Importance for Business and Information Systems Engineering Research 52

2 Towards a Procedural Model for Sustainable Information Systems Management 53

- 2.1 Introduction 54
- 2.2 Towards Sustainable IS Management 55
  - 2.2.1 The Value Chain of IS Business 55
  - 2.2.2 Understanding the Concept of Sustainability 57
  - 2.2.3 Sustainability within the Resources of IS 58
- 2.3 Theoretical Foundation of Sustainable IS Management 59
- 2.4 Implementing Sustainability in IS – A Procedural Model 61
  - 2.4.1 Resource Identification 61
  - 2.4.2 Assessment of IS Resources 62
  - 2.4.3 Identification of Measures 64
  - 2.4.4 Prioritization and Implementation 64
  - 2.4.5 Monitor and Evaluate 65
  - 2.4.6 Case of an IS Service Provider 66
- 2.5 Conclusion and Future Research 67

3 Influence of Green IT on Consumers' Buying Behavior of Personal Computers 69

- 3.1 Introduction 70
- 3.2 Theoretical Background and Research Questions 71
- 3.3 Methodology 72
- 3.4 Findings 73
- 3.5 Implications 77
- 3.6 Conclusion and Future Research 78

4 Search Engines and Social Business – Implications from the Case of Ecosia 80

- 4.1 Introduction 81
- 4.2 Related Research 82
  - 4.2.1 Traditional Business Models 82
  - 4.2.2 Characteristics of Social Businesses 83
- 4.3 Methodology 84
- 4.4 Ecosia's Social Business Model 85
  - 4.4.1 Company Overview 85
  - 4.4.2 Mechanics of the Social Business Model 86
- 4.5 Findings 88
  - 4.5.1 Market Potential 88
  - 4.5.2 Competitive Potential 89
- 4.6 Business and Research Implications 90
- 4.7 Conclusion and Discussion 91

5 Ökobilanzierung in der Informationstechnik 93

- 5.1 Ökobilanzierung und Informationstechnik 94
- 5.2 Grundlagen der Ökobilanzierung 95
- 5.3 Zwei Distributionsformen der Musikindustrie im ökobilanziellen Vergleich 96
  - 5.3.1 Zielsetzung 96
  - 5.3.2 Untersuchungsrahmen: CD-Album 97
  - 5.3.3 Sachbilanz: CD-Album 98
  - 5.3.4 Untersuchungsrahmen: MP3-Album 99
  - 5.3.5 Sachbilanz: MP3-Album 99
- 5.4 Wirkungsabschätzung und Auswertung 100
- 5.5 Handlungsempfehlungen und Ausblick 102

6	**Sustainability in Information Systems: Assortment of Current Practices in IS Organizations**	**103**
6.1	Introduction	104
6.2	Related Research	105
6.2.1	The Principle of Corporate Sustainability	105
6.2.2	The Value Chain of IS Management	106
6.3	Expected Outcomes and Data Collection	107
6.3.1	Expected Connections Between Sustainability Objectives, Green Measures and Their Benefits	107
6.4	Data Collection and Assessment of Current Measures	110
6.5	Analysis: Insights from IS Organizations	112
6.5.1	CO_2 Targets are Gaining Ground but Electricity Consumption of IT is Hard to Measure	112
6.5.2	The Main Area of Interest: The Data Center	112
6.5.3	Behavioral Challenges in the Office Environment	113
6.5.4	Stakeholder Dialogs and Green IT	114
6.6	Conclusion and Further Research	114
7	**Examining the Contribution of Green IT to the Objectives of IT Departments**	**116**
7.1	Introduction	117
7.2	Theoretical Background	117
7.2.1	The Principle of Corporate Sustainability	117
7.2.2	The Value Chain of IT Departments	118
7.2.3	Comparison of benefits from CSR and Green IT	120
7.3	Methodology	121
7.3.1	Research Model	121
7.3.2	Questionnaire and Statistical Analysis	121
7.3.3	Sample Profile	122
7.4	Results from the Empirical Analysis	123
7.4.1	Importance and Implementation	123
7.4.2	Benefits and Objectives	124
7.4.3	Domains and Objectives	126
7.5	Implications	127
7.6	Limitations and Conclusion	127
8	**Predictors of Green IT Adoption: Implications from an Empirical Investigation**	**129**
8.1	Introduction	130
8.2	Theoretical Background of Green IT	130
8.3	Conceptual Framework	131
8.4	Methodology	133
8.5	Findings	136
8.5.1	Importance of Green IT (Research question 1)	137
8.5.2	Uncertainty about Green IT (Research question 2)	138
8.5.3	Planning and Implementation of Green IT Measures (Research question 3)	140
8.6	Implications and Limitations	141
8.7	Conclusion and Further Research	143
9	**Towards a Contingency Model for Green IT Governance**	**144**
9.1	Introduction	145
9.2	Developing a Contingency Model for Green IT Governance	146
9.2.1	IT Governance and Contingency Theory	146

9.2.2	Green IT	147
9.2.3	Archetypes of Green IT Governance	147
9.2.4	A Contingency Model of Green IT Governance	149
9.3	Case Study Research Design	152
9.4	Findings from Case Studies	153
9.5	Theoretical and Practical Implications	154
9.6	Conclusion and Further Research	155

10   Strategic Green IT Planning: Lessons from a Financial Services Case ... 157

10.1	Introduction	158
10.2	Developing a Strategic Green IT Framework	159
10.2.1	Green IT	159
10.2.2	Strategic Planning	159
10.2.3	A Framework for Strategic Green IT Planning	160
10.3	Methodology	162
10.4	The Case	163
10.5	Strategic Green IT Planning at the CSD Bank	165
10.5.1	Defining the Strategic Objectives	165
10.5.2	Analysis of Current Situation	166
10.5.3	Development and Identification of Measures	169
10.5.4	Prioritization of Measures	171
10.6	Business and Research Implications	173
10.7	Conclusion and Limitations	174

C.   Contributions ... 175

1   Findings ... 175

1.1	Findings Regarding Sustainability and IS	175
1.2	Findings Regarding Green IS	176
1.3	Findings Regarding Green IT	177
1.4	Towards Environmentally Sustainable Information Management	180

2   Implications ... 184

2.1	Policy Implications	184
2.2	Managerial Implications	185
2.3	Research Implications	187

3   Conclusion and Further Research ... 189

3.1	Limitations	189
3.2	Further Research	190
3.2.1	Further Research on Sustainability and IS	190
3.2.2	Further Research on Green IS	191
3.2.3	Further Research on Green IT	193
3.3	Concluding Statements	194

References ... 195

Appendix ... 219

Abstract

The aim of this study is to provide decision-makers and researchers with an understanding of the positive role that information systems (IS) and information technologies (IT) can play in the struggle against climate change.

Owing to its extensive use of resources and energy, IT is part of the global environmental problem. However, IT also enables new IS, which help to solve the global environmental crisis. Theories and concepts that support environmentally sustainable information management and provide scientists with a starting point for further research in this field are the main contributions of this thesis.

Environmental protection is commonly classified under the overarching sustainability concept. Sustainability covers economical, ecological, and social dimensions, providing a solid basis for this research. Although sustainability has been researched in general management, it has not been studied in terms of IS. Drawing from the resource-based view, stakeholder theory and transaction cost theory, this thesis provides two contributions to incorporate and manage sustainability in IS, for which a procedural model for sustainable IS management is developed.

After describing sustainability in IS, the potential for IT-enabled environmental initiatives is highlighted, which is called "Green IS".

A survey in which 500 people participated indicates that the market share for IT with green features could be 26.6%. The findings show that the marketing mix should emphasize disposal attributes, rather than energy attributes, and it should focus more on female rather than on male customers. This example demonstrates the overall market relevance of environmentally sustainable IT.

IT can, furthermore, enable green business models. The example provided is that of the environmentally friendly search engine Ecosia. This search engine follows the social business concept. At least 80% of its revenues are donated to the World Wildlife Fund, leading to a constant increase in users. Ecosia also exerts an influence on its competitors regarding their environmental engagement.

IT's greatest environmental contribution might be that it can change physical processes into digital processes. This dematerialization is said to lead to lower emissions. The thesis investigates this claim by comparing physical music distribution with digital music distribution via life cycle assessment. Owing to IT's energy consumption, the results indicate that digital music distribution only has a very small advantage.

Besides highlighting IT's environmental opportunities, this thesis also focuses on IT's environmental challenges, due to its resource and energy consumption. Endeavors aimed at mitigating IT's environmental impact are subsumed under the term "Green IT". Interviews with 15

IT executives from major companies provide an expert's overview and indicate Green IT's relevance in practice. Related measures are implemented in the value chain of IT organizations, covering: source, make, delivery, return, and governance. Green IT pursues similar objectives as corporate social responsibility. A survey of 116 IT executives confirms that Green IT contributes to more efficient internal operations, higher reputational management, and greater market competitiveness. Furthermore, it illustrates that the factors that determine the adoption of Green IT are importance and uncertainty. Importance derives from corporate management, environmental engagement, and experience, while uncertainty relates to a lack of experience, measurements, standards, and IT staff support.

After describing and explaining how IT managers perceive and apply Green IT, recommendations and artifacts for managing Green IT are developed.

Although companies have begun to implement Green IT, its governance varies significantly. Building on contingency theory and IT governance, a contingency model for Green IT governance is developed. This model demonstrates the fit between contingencies and the company-specific configuration. The model is then validated by the insights gained in five case studies. With the enhanced understanding of how Green IT governance is shaped by contingency factors, IT organizations can select the most successful form of Green IT governance.

Included in the set of management concepts is a strategic Green IT planning framework that was developed and validated by means of a banking industry case study. The framework provides concepts, procedures, and tools that can be applied by executives and IT managers. Concrete Green IT measures and performance metrics complement the findings.

Finally, the thesis consolidates the findings from sustainability and IS, Green IS, and Green IT in a model for environmentally sustainable information management. The model shows the IT organizations' tasks, roles and responsibilities for pursuing environmental protection. This model supports IT executives in their daily work, and provides IS scientists with a theoretical basis for further research in this emerging field.

The conclusion summarizes the limitations of the thesis and provides new ideas for further research regarding sustainability and IS, Green IS, Green IT, and environmentally sustainable information management.

The thesis contributes to a better understanding of the relevance and benefits of sustainability, Green IS, and Green IT. The knowledge and tools enable practitioners and researchers to engage in the global struggle against climate change within the scope of IT, and to make a positive contribution to environmental protection.

List of Figures

Figure A.1: Structure of the Thesis ... 7
Figure A.2: Research Process of the Thesis (Developed from Dubé and Paré (2003), March and Storey (2008), as well as Österle et al. (1992)) ... 11
Figure A.3: Complementary Research Cycle of Design and Behavioral Science Research in the Scope of Environmental Sustainability and IS (Adopted from Winter (2009)) ... 12
Figure A.4: Aggregated PUE Development of Ten Large-scale Google Data Centers (Google Inc., 2011) ... 40
Figure A.5: Model of Industrialized Information Management (Hochstein et al., 2006; Zarnekow et al., 2005) ... 43
Figure B.1: Management Cycle of Sustainable IS Management ... 50
Figure B.2: Value Chain of Information Systems Product and Service Provision ... 56
Figure B.3: The Connection Between Sustainability and Stakeholder Risks ... 60
Figure B.4: Procedural Model for Sustainable Information Systems Management ... 62
Figure B.5: Assessment of Resources ... 63
Figure B.6: Clusters of Respondents According to Their Preferred Attribute ... 75
Figure B.7: Web Interface of Ecosia's Search Service ... 85
Figure B.8: Social Business Model of Ecosia ... 86
Abbildung B.9: Vorgehen der Ökobilanzierung, in Anlehnung an: (Deutsches Institut für Normung e.V., 2009) ... 95
Abbildung B.10: Untersuchungsrahmen der CD-Distribution ... 97
Abbildung B.11: CO_2-Emissionen der Distributionswege im Vergleich ... 101
Figure B.13: Value Chain of the IT Department (Source: Erek et al. 2009) ... 119
Figure B.14: The Connection Between Green IT, Value Chain, Benefits, and Objectives ... 121
Figure B.15: Proposed Research Framework of Predictors for Green IT Adoption ... 133
Figure B.16: Contingency Model (Adapted from Weber et al. (2009b) and Umanath (2003)) ... 147
Figure B.17: Archetypes of Green IT Governance Patterns ... 148
Figure B.18: Contingency Model of Green IT Governance ... 150
Figure B.19: Strategic Green IT Framework (Developed from Schmidt et al. (2009a) and Ward and Peppard (2002)) ... 161
Figure B.20: Interviewees and Organizational Structure of the CSD Bank's COO Division ... 164
Figure B.21: Strategic Direction of the CSD Bank in the Green IT Reach-Richness Framework (Adapted from Molla (2009)) ... 166
Figure B.22: Evaluation of Green IT Measures in a Business Case-Environment Framework ... 172
Figure B.23: Prioritization of Green IT Measures by a Cost Saving-Complexity Portfolio ... 172
Figure C.1: Environmentally Sustainable Information Management Between Enabling and Alignment Using Green IS and Green IT (Adapted from Krcmar (2005)) ... 180
Figure C.2: Model of Environmentally Sustainable Information Management Consolidated from the Individual Findings ... 181

List of Tables

Table A.1:	Overview of Research Questions and Applied Methodologies	14
Table A.2:	Numbers of Published Papers that Relate to Sustainability and IS (Extension of the Work from Bengtsson and Agerfalk (2011))	17
Table A.3:	Theories and Concepts Applied to Research on Environmental Sustainability and IS	18
Table A.4:	Estimations of Green IS enabled Energy Efficiency Effects Up to 2020 (Climate Group and Global eSustainability Initiative, 2008)	23
Table A.5:	Selection of Software Applications for Environmental Management in Enterprises	23
Table A.6:	Comparison of a Traditional Business Model and an IT-enabled Green Business Model	24
Table A.7:	Examples of IT-enabled Green Business Models from Various Industries	24
Table A.8:	Estimated Compound Annual Growth Rates of Power Consumption by IT	27
Table A.9:	Perspectives and Categories for Describing Green IT	28
Table A.10:	General Green IT Metrics	38
Table A.11:	Green IT Metrics in the Office Environment	38
Table A.12:	Green IT Metrics for the Data Center	39
Table B.1:	Summary of Presented Publications	44
Table B.2:	Fact Sheet of Publication No. 1	46
Table B.3:	Typology of IS Resources (According to Wade & Hulland, 2004)	48
Table B.4:	Characteristics of Sustainable IS Management	49
Table B.5:	Exemplary Measures and Their Contribution to the Social and Ecological Dimension of Sustainability (According to Schmidt et al., 2009b)	51
Table B.6:	Fact Sheet of Publication No. 2	53
Table B.7:	Objectives and Exemplary ICT Sustainability Measures	65
Table B.8:	Fact Sheet of Publication No. 3	69
Table B.9:	Preference Order of the First Choice PC Concepts for the Respondents	73
Table B.10:	Partial Utility Estimates for Each of the PC Specifications from the Consumers' Perspective	74
Table B.11:	Relative Importance of PC Attributes for the Clusters	76
Table B.12:	Characteristics of the Clusters	76
Table B.13:	Fact Sheet of Publication No. 4	80
Table B.14:	Comparison of Traditional and Social Business Models	83
Table B.15:	Overview of Ecosia	86
Table B.16:	Selection of Social Business Web Search Services	90
Table B.17:	Fact Sheet of Publication No. 5	93
Tabelle B.18:	Auswahl durchgeführter Ökobilanzen im Bereich der Informationstechnik	94

List of Tables

Table B.19:	Fact Sheet of Publication No. 6	103
Table B.20:	Expected Connections in the Scope of Sustainable IS Management	108
Table B.21:	Implementation Scale of Green IT Measures	110
Table B.22:	Scope of Green IT Measures and Their Implementation	111
Table B.23:	Fact Sheet of Publication No. 7	116
Table B.24:	Comparison of CSR and Green IT Value Drivers and Their Possible Categorization	120
Table B.25:	Turnover and Employees of the Responding Companies	122
Table B.26:	Size and Target Markets of the IT Departments	123
Table B.27:	Implementation and Domains of Green IT	123
Table B.28:	Benefits of Green IT and Related Objectives	125
Table B.29:	Correlations Between Green IT Domains and Objectives of the IT Department	126
Table B.30:	Fact Sheet of Publication No.8	129
Table B.31:	Questionnaire Response Formats and Sample Items	134
Table B.32:	Turnover and Employees of the Enterprises	136
Table B.33:	Importance of Green IT	137
Table B.34:	Parameter Estimates for the Importance of Green IT	137
Table B.35:	Uncertainty about Green IT	138
Table B.36:	Parameter Estimates for the Uncertainty about Green IT	139
Table B.37:	Planning and Implementation of Green IT	140
Table B.38:	Parameter Estimates for Planning and Implementation of Green IT	141
Table B.39:	Fact Sheet of Publication No. 9	144
Table B.40:	Description of Green IT Governance Archetypes	149
Table B.41:	Contingency Factors and Their Assumed Influence on Green IT Governance	151
Table B.42:	Description of Case Studies	153
Table B.43:	Influence of Contingency Factors on the Green IT Governance Design of Company A	153
Table B.44:	Summary of Findings (Trends Towards: (c) Centralized, (f) Federal, (d) Decentralized)	154
Table B.45:	Fact Sheet of Publication No. 10	157
Table B.46:	Summary of the Data Collection Analysis Process at the CSD Bank	162
Table B.47:	Company Overview	164
Table B.48:	Priority Ranking of Green IT Objectives and Stakeholders	165
Table B.49:	Consumption of Basic Resources at the CSD Bank	167
Table B.50:	IT-related Electricity Consumption and Environmental Impact	167
Table B.51:	Estimations for the Energy Consumption of Data Centers	168
Table B.52:	IT in the Office Environment and Its Estimated Environmental Impact	168
Table B.53:	Assessment of Possible Green IT Measures	170

Table B.54:	Overview and Ranking of the Proposed Green IT Measures	171
Table C.1:	Roles and Responsibilities of the ESIM Model	182
Table C.2:	Policy Implications	184
Table C.3:	Managerial Implications	186
Table C.4:	Research Implications	187

Acronyms

ACIS	Australasian Conference on Information Systems
AMCIS	Americas Conference on Information Systems
CEO	Chief Executive Officer
CIO	Chief Information Officer
CO_2	Carbon Dioxide
CO_2e	Carbon Dioxide Equivalent
COO	Chief Operating Officer
CPU	Central Processing Unit
CSR	Corporate Social Responsibility
DC	Data Center
ECIS	European Conference on Information Systems
EJIS	European Journal of Information Systems
EMIS	Environmental Management Information System
EPEAT	Electronic Product Environmental Assessment Tool
ESIM	Environmentally Sustainable Information Management
E-waste	Electronic Waste
FLOPS	FLoating Point OPerations per Second
FTE	Full-time Equivalent
GWh	Gigawatt Hour
ICIS	International Conference on Information Systems
ICT	Information and Communication Technology
IPS	Instructions per Second
IS	Information Systems
ISJ	Information Systems Journal
ISO	International Organization for Standardization
ISR	Information Systems Research
IT	Information Technology
ITIL	Information Technology Infrastructure Library
JAIS	Journal of the Association of Information Systems
JIT	Journal of Information Technology
JMIS	Journal of Management Information Systems
JSIS	Journal of Strategic Information Systems
kW	Kilowatt
kWh	Kilowatt Hour
LCA	Life Cycle Assessment
MISQ	MIS Quarterly
OE	Office Environment
PACIS	Pacific Asia Conference on Information Systems
PC	Personal Computer
PT	Production Theory
PUE	Power Usage Effectiveness
RBV	Resource-based View
SCOR	Supply Chain Operations Reference Model
ST	Stakeholder Theory

TCT   Transaction Cost Theory
UPS   Uninterruptible Power Supply

A. Foundations

This part provides the reader with background information of this cumulative dissertation. The introduction in Section A.1 highlights the relevance of the research topic. The methodology in Section A.2 describes the pursued research approaches. Finally, Section A.3 provides insights from related research.

1 Introduction

In the following sections, the motivation for this work (Section A.1.1), the derived research questions (Section A.1.2), the structure (Section A.1.3) and the anticipated contributions (Section A.1.4) are presented.

1.1 Motivation

"Green is worth it," stated Peter Löscher (2011) Chief Executive Officer (CEO) of Siemens AG at the annual shareholders' meeting. The German engineering giant plans a radical restructuring to attain a better position in the growing green technology market, especially in the world's expanding urban areas (Fuhrmanns & Crawford, 2011). This example shows how important the green factor has become in the economy. Until recently, managers associated "green" with chaos, costs and campfires. Today, managers and legislators realize that environmental sustainability is a key driver of economies and businesses.

The global market for green[1] technologies has become a multi-billion euro business with enormous growth potential. The sector reached about €1.6 trillion in spending at the end of 2010, with a projected €3.0 trillion by 2020 (Roland Berger Strategy Consultants GmbH, 2011). The job markets also reflect this trend. Since 2004, the number of green jobs in Germany has more than doubled to 340,000, and is expected to increase by at least 31% by 2030 (Lehr et al., 2010). In the USA, 750,000 green jobs account for less than half a percent of total jobs. Estimations are that 4.2 million new green jobs will be added to the US economy over the next 30 years (Diaz et al., 2008).

This development is the result of the global population's expansion, which is characterized by rising demands, scarcity of natural resources, global warming's effects and a political and societal shift regarding environmental protection. Worldwide, governments have agreed to work towards

---

[1] In this thesis, the term "green" is used as a synonym for environmental sustainability, environmentally friendly, and eco-friendly, which refer to goods and services, laws, organizations, technologies, behaviors, guidelines and policies aimed at inflicting minimal or no harm on the environment.

environmental sustainability, especially by reducing greenhouse gas emissions, such as carbon dioxide (CO_2), to keep the rise in global temperature below 2° C (United Nations Environment Programme, 2011). Employers are challenged by young professionals, who expect eco-awareness and social consciousness, even in office energy use. Nearly one quarter of young professionals consider it very important to work in a green, environmentally conscious workplace (Hewlett et al., 2009). Therefore, the private sector has responded with green products, services, processes, investments, and technologies.

Global environmental consciousness also affects the information technology[2] (IT) industry. In terms of sustainability, IT plays two conflicting roles: Owing to its use of resources and energy, it is part of the problem but IT also contributes to the global environmental solution (Chen et al., 2009b; Elliot, 2011).

IT-enabled information systems that aim for environmental sustainability are referred to as green information systems (Green IS). Green IS enables environmentally oriented business models, processes, reporting systems, and communication strategies. It is estimated that by the year 2020, Green IS applications in business functions such as energy, manufacturing, buildings, and transportation will globally have saved about 7.8 billion tons of CO_2 emissions and €600 billion of costs (Climate Group and Global eSustainability Initiative, 2008).

This thesis mainly focuses on IT's environmental impact and Green IT's ability to mitigate this impact. In 2007, IT's energy use accounted for about two percent of the global CO_2 emissions[3] (Buhl & Laartz, 2008; Climate Group and Global eSustainability Initiative, 2008; Gartner Inc., 2007). IT's global CO_2 emissions are expected to grow each year by 6% until 2020, regardless of potential technological developments (Climate Group and Global eSustainability Initiative, 2008). Owing to economic growth, rising incomes and growing affordability, especially in developing countries such as China and India, the demand for IT-related goods and services will increase. The share of the global population that owns a PC is expected to grow from 2% in 2008 to 33% in 2020. By then, 50% will own a mobile phone and 5% will have broadband connection (Climate Group and Global eSustainability Initiative, 2008). Manufacturing and disposal of IT also have other environmental effects. Manufacturing requires energy, as well as valuable and rare resources, such as gold, copper, tantalum, and coltan. Furthermore, the disposal of IT equipment containing

---

[2] Here, the term "information technology" (IT) is synonymous with the broader term "information and communication technologies" (ICT).

[3] In this thesis, CO_2 generally refers to the carbon dioxide equivalent CO_2e. CO_2e represents, for a given mixture of greenhouse gas, the amount of CO_2 that would have the same global warming potential.

toxic substances, such as mercury or lead, represents a severe environmental threat (Chen et al., 2008).

Green IT is not only important for reducing IT's environmental impact, but also for decreasing resource consumption and thereby cutting costs. Symantec (2009) conducted a global survey of 1,052 companies in 2009, and consequently showed that 16% to 20% of the IT budget is being spent on electricity for data centers. It is estimated that in 2020 an average data center will consume as much power as 25,000 US households (Nguyen et al., 2009).

> **Examples of the environmental impact of IT services**
>
> *Facebook.com:* The social networking site Facebook has come under public pressure from Greenpeace International, due to Facebook's construction of a data center in Prineville in the US that will be powered by PacifiCorp, a company that gets 58% of its energy from burning coal (Ross, 2010).
>
> *Google.com:* The search engine Google operates about 450,000 servers, which consume approximately 800 GWh of electricity per year, and is therefore indirectly responsible for tremendous amounts of CO_2 emissions (Chou, 2008). Controversial estimates of the CO_2 emissions caused by one search request are between 1g and 10g (Glass, 2009; Leake & Woods, 2009).

Market estimations highlight this topic's practical future relevance. Pike Research's market analysts forecast that by 2015, Green IT in data centers will provide a market opportunity in excess of US$40 billion worldwide (Woods & Wheelock, 2010). The consulting company Experton Group expects the German Green IT market to grow from €12.1 billion in 2010 to €19.3 billion in 2012 (Schwab, 2011), at an annual growth rate of approximately 26%. These figures must be treated with caution, because many authors are active in the Green IT market and therefore might be biased. Nevertheless, the figures confirm that Green IT's importance will continue to rise.

Despite the practical relevance, not much academic research explains and describes phenomena related to sustainability and IS, Green IS, and Green IT (Bengtsson & Agerfalk, 2011; Jenkin et al., 2011). The implications of sustainability and corporate social responsibility (CSR) has primarily been researched in the general management literature (see for example Elkington, 1997; Esty & Winston, 2006; Marrewijk, 2003; Porter & Kramer, 2006; Porter & van der Linde, 1995; Porter & Reinhardt, 2007). Regarding technical issues, research primarily focuses on single IT practices, such as cloud computing (Weinhardt et al., 2009) or virtualization (Gibbs, 2008), without linking them clearly to sustainability, Green IS or Green IT. A holistic view that connects the conceptual level with the technical level is absent in IS research. Such research would enable integrated environmental management at all company levels, down to the IT department.

In summary, the following research gaps can be identified:

- descriptions of the connections and differences between sustainability, Green IS, and Green IT;
- models, concepts, and methods that illustrate how sustainability can be incorporated and managed in IT organizations;
- demonstrations of how IS can contribute to environmental sustainability;
- theories that explain IT organizations' behavior regarding Green IT; and
- models, concepts, and methods that illustrate how Green IS and Green IT can be managed in IT organizations.

Although in the past twenty years sustainability has occasionally been explored in IS research, the issue has gained considerable momentum in the academic community since 2007 (Section A.3.1).

Given the above facts, the motivation for this thesis becomes apparent when following Benbasat and Zmud (1999) who recommended: "The foremost criterion to be applied in selecting research topics should be directly related to the future interest that key stakeholders (journals, colleagues, and practitioners) are likely to hold in a topic." Owing to the global development and the social, practical, and theoretical interest in environmental protection, it seems that sustainability, Green IS, and Green IT will remain a long term issue in IS research, providing substantial motivation for this thesis.

Based on the identified research gaps, specific research questions are derived in the next section, which are answered throughout the thesis.

1.2 Research Questions

This thesis aims to bridge the identified research gaps and to contribute to the emerging knowledge base on sustainability and IS by developing a model for environmentally sustainable information management (ESIM). The central research question of this thesis is therefore:

How should ESIM be incorporated into IT organizations?

To answer this research question, two major research objectives are pursued. First it is necessary to gain an understanding of the research area and the practical relevance of sustainability, Green IS, and Green IT. Second, practical solutions need to be developed.

These two objectives correspond with the objectives of behavioral and design science research (Section A.2), and can be formulated as follows:

- describing theories that explain why and how sustainability, Green IS, and Green IT are perceived, implemented, and managed by IT organizations (behavioral oriented);

- developing and evaluating concepts to incorporate, implement, and manage sustainability, Green IS, and Green IT by IT organizations (design oriented).

From the central research question and the outlined objectives, twelve partial research questions are derived. These research questions are answered in ten corresponding articles in Part B, and in two sections in Part A. The research questions are ordered according to the outside-inside approach, starting with the all-encompassing sustainability concept, then Green IS, and ending with the concrete measurement of Green IT success in the IT department. The central research question is answered in Section C.1.4 by consolidating the findings from all research questions in a model for environmentally sustainable information management.

The understanding of sustainability was predominantly shaped by the Brundtland Commission's definition in 1987, which described sustainable development as "development that meets the needs of the present without compromising the ability of future generations to meet their own needs" (Hauff, 1987). Although the sustainability topic has been discussed in terms of general management, it still lacks a theoretical foundation in IS management. Porter and Reinhardt (2007) argue that the question concerning sustainability has moved from *whether* to *how* corporate sustainability can be integrated into day-to-day management decisions. This also applies to the IS field. When these thoughts are considered in the context of IS, the following questions emerge:

1. What theories and concepts provide a foundation for incorporating sustainability into IS?
2. How can sustainability be managed in IS?

Regarding the three dimensions of sustainability, practitioners and researchers particularly emphasize the environmental aspect. IS can play a critical role in enabling environmental sustainability (Jenkin et al., 2011; Watson et al., 2010). Various applications in different business functions and industries can facilitate such initiatives. To emphasize the importance of IS as an environmental enabler, three cases are investigated. These cases belong to the fields of marketing, processes, and business models, and are considered in order to answer the following research questions:

3. What is the market potential of IT with green features?
4. What is the potential of IT-enabled green business models?
5. What is the green advantage of IT-enabled processes?

This thesis especially focuses on the environmental impact of IT organizations and IT departments, and their endeavors to reduce IT's environmental impact. Practices that address energy and resource consumption, as well as waste and emissions associated with the use of hardware and software, are referred to in this thesis as Green IT (Jenkin et al., 2011). Green IT denotes IT departments' activities and efforts to incorporate green technologies and processes into the entire

IT life cycle in order to align itself with the corporate objectives, environmental strategy, and relevant stakeholders. Owing to limited scientific knowledge of Green IT, descriptive and explanatory research is needed for theory building. Therefore, the following questions need to be answered:

6. What is Green IT's scope in practice?
7. What Green IT objectives are pursued by IT departments?
8. Why is Green IT adopted by IT departments?

This behaviorally oriented research is complemented by design science research, as suggested by Hevner et al. (2004). Design science aims to develop and evaluate new innovative artifacts to attain practically relevant objectives. Accordingly, the thesis aims to develop methods to support practitioners in their Green IT management. This is highlighted by the following research questions:

9. How should Green IT governance be designed?
10. How should Green IT planning be conducted?

To provide useful information for Green IT management, a summary of possible Green IT practices and metrics, based on a literature research, is provided. This summary aims to answer the last research questions, namely:

11. What Green IT measures are applicable?
12. What metrics are available to evaluate Green IT success?

Research questions 1 and 2 highlight sustainability's relevance and possible inclusion in IS. These two questions are investigated in Publications B.1 and B.2. Research questions 3 to 5 investigate exemplary potentials of Green IS (Publications B.3, B.4, and B.5). The research focus of this thesis is on Green IT; therefore, research questions 6 to 8 analyze Green IT, mainly from a behavioral perspective (Publications B.6, B.7, and B.8). Thereafter, research questions 9 and 10 consider the development of artifacts for managing Green IT (Publications B.9 and B.10). To complete the analysis, research questions 11 and 12 describe concrete Green IT practices and metrics (Sections A.3.3.3.3 and A.3.3.3.4).

All the research questions' findings are used to design a reference model for environmentally sustainable information management in Section C.1.4 and to answer the central research question of this thesis.

1.3 Structure of the Thesis

The work is a cumulative dissertation, and is divided into an introduction (Part A), a main publication section (Part B) and a conclusion (Part C). An overview of the structure and approach of the thesis is provided in Figure A.1.

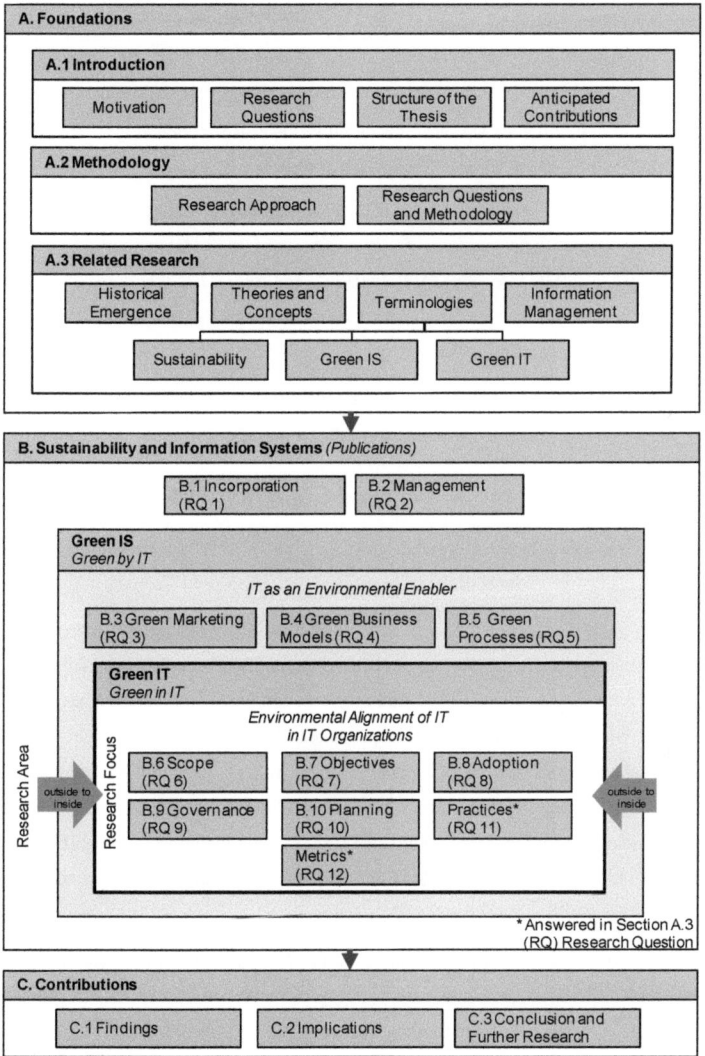

Figure A.1: Structure of the Thesis

Part A provides an impression of the existing knowledge base related to sustainability and IS. The aim of this part is to provide the reader with a comprehensive overview of the topic in order to enable the assessment of each publication's contributions, in Part B and in the rest of the thesis. To understand the topic's relevance in terms of IS research, its emergence is described. Thereafter, popular IS theories' application is illustrated. In the terminology section, key terms, namely sustainability, Green IS, and Green IT are described, and more background information is provided. The answers to research question 11 and 12 are found in this part of the thesis, in Section A.3.3.3.3 and A.3.3.3.4. Part A concludes with the description of industrialized information management, which is the conceptual foundation to most of the publications and to the model of environmentally sustainable information management in C.1.4.

Part B consists of 10 publications, which were published between 2009 and 2011 in the proceedings of international conferences or in renowned IS research journals. The publications provide deeper insights into Part A's contents, and represent the core of this thesis. The publications are ordered in three levels: sustainability, Green IS, and Green IT. Each publication aligns with a research question in Section A.1.2.

Part C summarizes the findings and draws implications for research and practice. Finally, the limitations of this work and further research needs are outlined.

1.4 Addressees and Anticipated Contributions

The work addresses companies' decision-makers, scholars of IS and the environment, legislators, as well as teachers and students of the IS discipline.

Organization's IT decision-makers and sustainability managers are given concrete recommendations for sustainability, Green IS, and Green IT. The developed methods and concepts help introducing these topics into organizations, managing them and avoiding errors. A management model for sustainability is presented. The research on Green IS illustrates the environmental potentials that can be exploited by using IT. This should stimulate more ideas. Concrete recommendations and information about Green IT are provided to IT departments. Recommendations concerning the governance and strategic planning of Green IT, as well as key performance indicators can increase the IT department's contribution to the business value.

Researchers are provided with a sound knowledge base and starting points for further research. The conceptualization of IS sustainability enables researchers to connect their work to the economic, environmental and social branch of this evolving phenomenon. Green IS can potentially enable environmental sustainability in marketing, business models, and processes, which illustrates the many research opportunities in IT-enabled environmental sustainability. Regarding Green IT, the theories concerning its scope, adoption, and objectives provide explanations but also demand further refinement and validation.

Policy-makers will find a comprehensive knowledge base that they can consult regarding legislative processes. Furthermore, the findings help managing IT in the public administration. In contrast to private companies' or industry associations' publications, this thesis provides an unbiased, scientific view on sustainability issues, Green IS issues, and Green IT issues. It provides a knowledge base to critically evaluate industry recommendations and results.

Teachers can base their sustainability and IS lectures on this thesis, thereby enhancing their course offerings with a green component. This dissertation's logical outside-in approach could provide the common thread for a series of lectures that lead from sustainability to the concrete level of Green IT in the IT department.

Students can expand their environmental protection knowledge to the IS field and thereby enhance their green profile. Thus, this work is of particular interest to students who would like to work at the interface between environmental protection and IT.

2 Research Methodology

This thesis primarily draws on two established IS research paradigms: design science research and behavioral science research, as described by Hevner et al. (2004). In this section, these two paradigms are described in detail. They are also assigned to a general research process, which has been developed from the work of Dubé and Paré (2003), March and Storey (2008), as well as Österle et al. (1992). The research process (Figure A.2) provides the methodological basis for answering the research questions outlined in Section A.1.2. After explaining the process elements in this section, the applied methodology of each research question is described and characterized in Section A.2.2.

2.1 General Research Approach

The thesis belongs to the IS research discipline. This discipline aims to generate knowledge that aids IT's productive application to organizations and their management (Hevner et al., 2004). Demand for IS research arises when the existing knowledge base is unable to answer practical questions and challenges. The knowledge base provides the raw materials from and through which IS research is accomplished, and includes theories, frameworks, instruments, constructs, models, methods, instantiations from prior IS research, and results from reference disciplines (Hevner et al., 2004).

With regard to environmental sustainability and IS, the practical relevance of the research and the attention that it receives is high, but due to the novelty of the research area, the related knowledge base is small and is still being collated (Figure A.2). Therefore, foundations must be combined with other research fields related to sustainability and IS.

Rigorous IS research provides the template for conducting studies. Design science research requires that rigorous methods be applied in a study's construction and evaluation phases (Hevner et al., 2004). Rigor differentiates a research project from a routine design (Winter, 2009). In behavioral science research, rigor is often associated with appropriate data collection and analysis techniques in the justification and evaluation phase (Hevner et al., 2004).

A close interaction with the practical context ensures that IS research results have high relevance. In this practical context, IT-related usage and management behaviors appear (Benbasat & Zmud, 1999). IS research findings inform new practical concepts, which then alter practitioners' perspectives and concepts in their daily work (Benbasat & Zmud, 1999).

A.2 Research Methodology

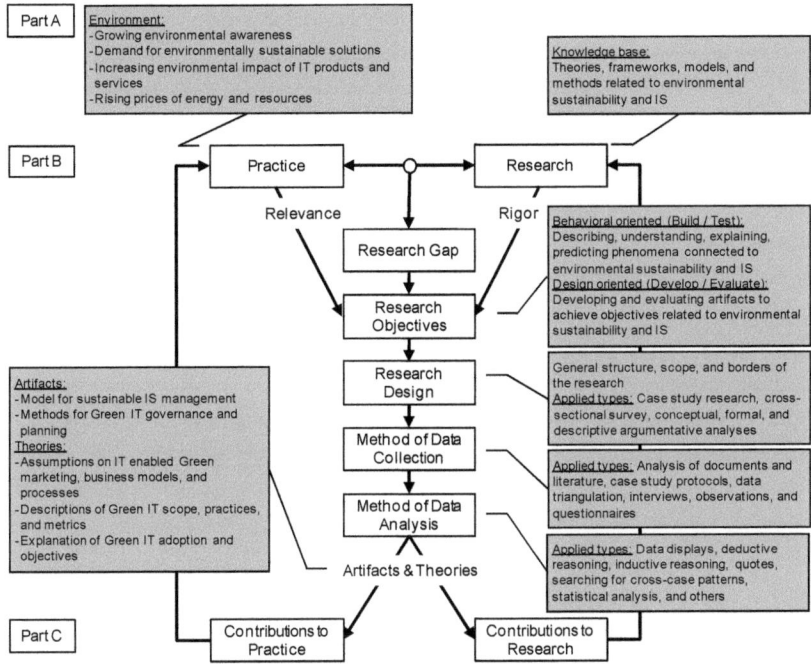

Figure A.2: Research Process of the Thesis (Developed from Dubé and Paré (2003), March and Storey (2008), as well as Österle et al. (1992))

This study's research objectives originate from the identified research gaps (Section A.1.1). There are two distinct types of research objectives, which relate to behavioral sciences and design sciences.

Behavioral science research aims to understand, explain, and predict behavior by building and testing suitable theories. Behavioral science research is indebted to natural science research methods. It builds and tests theories that explain or predict organizational and human behavior with regard to the analysis, design, implementation, management, and use of information systems. Behavioral science aims to describe *what is going on*, by descriptive or positivistic research, and *why things are going on*, by explanatory research. Descriptive research, also referred to as positivistic research, describes data about a phenomenon being studied, as well as its characteristics. Descriptive research answers questions concerning who, what, where, when and how. Explanatory research answers questions concerning why, by developing and evaluating causal theories. These theories vary in their complexity, abstraction, and scope. Theory building can be done in two ways: The first option is to derive a theory from observations, using inductive reasoning. The second option is to develop a theory by deductive reasoning from other accepted theories that are considered to be true. A theory is tested by subjecting it to deductive reasoning: observations should provide a test of the theory's worth (De Vaus, 2001; Hevner et al., 2004; March & Smith, 1995).

Design science research aims to develop and evaluate new innovative artifacts to attain practically relevant objectives. Design science research builds and evaluates artifacts, based on existing ideas that are drawn from the knowledge base. IT artifacts are defined as constructs (vocabulary and symbols), models (abstractions and representations), methods (algorithms, guidelines, and practices), and instantiations (implemented and prototype systems). Design science answers *how can* and *how should*-type of research questions, while *how should*-type of questions are related to normative research. Normative research assumes that one type of artifact is better than another. This is assessed by describing and demonstrating the utility of an artifact. The normative strand is concerned with how organizations can act in ways that bring them closer to an ideal. Similar to behavioral science, an artifact can be developed by inductive reasoning from observations, or by deductive reasoning from other artifacts that have proved utility. The evaluation is done using deductive reasoning, in which observations provide a test of the artifact's worth (Gregor, 2006; Hevner et al., 2004; March & Smith, 1995; Winter, 2009).

Since design science creates artifacts that must be tested against actual behavior, the two fields are closely linked (Hevner et al., 2004). A green artifact's design must be supported by appropriate theories that explain or predict human behaviors. In an ideal research cycle within the scope of environmental sustainability and IS, design and behavioral science research will be applied jointly, as illustrated in Figure A.3. Effective IS artifacts that provide environmental utility and justified theories that provide truth are complementary (Winter, 2009). Behavioral research results drive innovative design, and design research leads to the search for new behavioral theories (Winter, 2009).

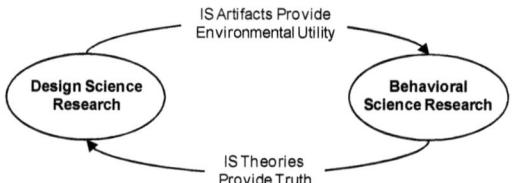

Figure A.3: Complementary Research Cycle of Design and Behavioral Science Research in the Scope of Environmental Sustainability and IS (Adopted from Winter (2009))

The research design depends on the type of type of the pursued objectives. The research design differs from data collection methods and data analysis methods (De Vaus, 2001). In its most elementary sense, the research design defines the study's general structure, scope and borders. Its function is to ensure that the evidence obtained enables unambiguous answering of the initial question, as much as possible (De Vaus, 2001). There are many established IS research designs, including action research, case study research, conceptual argumentative analysis, cross-sectional survey, descriptive argumentative analysis, field experiment, formal argumentative analysis, laboratory experiment, longitudinal survey, prototyping, and simulation (Dubé & Paré, 2003; Gable, 1994; Galliers & Land, 1987; Palvia et al., 2003; Wilde & Hess, 2007). It is also possible to combine different designs, such as case study research and prototyping, to increase the validity of derived results.

The data collection method determines the overall quality of the data collection process. It considers the choice of data collection methods, both qualitative and quantitative, and how they are applied, as well as the measures for enhancing reliability and validity. A particular research design should not be associated with only quantitative or only qualitative methods. Data collection methods include document analysis, literature analysis, case study protocols, data triangulation (multiple data sources), documentations, interviews (structured or loosely structured), observations, and questionnaires (De Vaus, 2001; Dubé & Paré, 2003).

The data analysis method describes the analysis process and the preliminary techniques for preparing the data. Analysis methods include coding, comparing with extant literature, displaying data, deductive reasoning, explanation building, inductive reasoning, quoting, searching for cross-case patterns, analyzing statistics, and analyzing time series (Dubé & Paré, 2003). The chosen data collection method limits the availability of possible data analysis methods. For example, during exploratory research, data might be collected by interviewing, but it would be inappropriate to apply statistical procedures, such as linear regression, to analyze the data.

2.2 Applied Methodologies

This section describes the research design, data collection, and data analysis methods that are applied in this thesis. Table A.1 describes the methodological characteristics, in line with the research process described in Section A.2.1, for each research question from Section A.1.2.

Every research question refers to one corresponding research paper in Part B. In each publication, multiple research questions are answered; the research questions outlined below represent only the core intention of each publication.

Due to the plurality of research questions, all contributions pursue design science and behavioral science oriented aspects. Nevertheless, it is possible to identify each contribution's primary objective with regard to one of the two paradigms.

The knowledge base framing outlines the most important theories, models, concepts and methods, which served as a base to investigate the research question.

Scope	Section	Core Research Question	Research Objective	Knowledge Base Framing	Research Design	Dominant Method of Data Collection	Method of Data Analysis	Main Contribution
Sustainability	B.1	1. What theories and concepts provide a foundation for incorporating sustainability into IS?	Behavioral oriented	Resource-based view	Conceptual argumentative analysis	Analysis of literature	Deductive reasoning	Theoretical and conceptual foundations for IS research on sustainability
Sustainability	B.2	2. How can sustainability be managed in IS?	Design oriented	Resource-based view, transaction cost theory, IT value chain	Conceptual argumentative analysis	Analysis of literature	Deductive reasoning	Model to structure IS sustainability measures / Method for implementing sustainability in IT organizations
Green IS	B.3	3. What is the market potential of IT with green features?	Behavioral oriented	Marketing mix, conjoint analysis	Cross-sectional survey and simulation (N = 500)	Questionnaires	Statistical analyses (cluster analysis, discriminant analysis)	Theoretical assumptions on the market potential of IT with green features / Design of adequate marketing mix
Green IS	B.4	4. What is the potential of IT-enabled green business models?	Behavioral oriented	Social business	Case study (N = 1)	Data triangulation	Inductive reasoning	Theoretical assumptions on the market influence of IT-enabled green business models
Green IS	B.5	5. What is the green advantage of IT-enabled processes?	Behavioral oriented	Life cycle assessment	Formal argumentative analysis	Observations, interviews	Data displays, inductive reasoning, estimations	Theoretical assumptions on the green advantage of IT-enabled distribution processes
Green IT	B.6	6. What is Green IT's scope in practice?	Behavioral oriented	IT value chain, sustainable IS management	Expert Interviews (N = 15)	Structured interviews	Data displays, inductive reasoning	Overview of implemented Green IT measures in IT organizations
Green IT	B.7	7. What Green IT objectives are pursued by IT departments?	Behavioral oriented	Corporate social responsibility, IT value chain	Cross-sectional survey (N = 116)	Questionnaires	Statistical analyses (factor and correlation analysis)	Theoretical verification that Green IT pursues equal objectives as corporate social responsibility
Green IT	B.8	8. Why is Green IT adopted by IT departments?	Behavioral oriented	Adoption research	Cross-sectional survey (N = 116)	Questionnaires	Statistical analysis (multinomial logistic regression)	Theoretical framework on why IT departments adopt Green IT
Green IT	B.9	9. How should Green IT governance be designed?	Design oriented	Contingency theory	Case studies (N = 5)	Structured interviews, analysis of documents	Searching for cross-case patterns	Method to determine the ideal form of Green IT governance
Green IT	B.10	10. How should Green IT planning be conducted?	Design oriented	Procedural model for sustainable IS management	Case study (N = 1)	Data triangulation	Data displays, quotes, inductive reasoning	Method for planning and management of Green IT
Green IT	A.3.3.3.3	11. What Green IT measures are applicable?	Behavioral oriented	Green IT literature	Descriptive argumentative analysis	Analysis of literature	Summarizing of data	Overview of applicable Green IT practices
Green IT	A.3.3.3.4	12. What metrics are available to evaluate Green IT success?	Behavioral oriented	Green IT and performance measurement literature	Descriptive argumentative analysis	Analysis of literature	Summarizing of data	Overview of applicable Green IT performance metrics
Σ	C.1.4	How should ESIM be incorporated into IT organizations?	Design oriented	IT value chain	Descriptive argumentative analysis	Analysis of publications	Deductive reasoning	ESIM Model

Table A.1: Overview of Research Questions and Applied Methodologies

A.2 Research Methodology

Each paper, and indeed the entire thesis, is based on thorough literature review (Section A.3). Additionally, empirical data was gathered for this thesis from:

- 116 surveyed CIOs and IT managers;
- 7 case studies with companies;
- 15 expert interviews with CIOs and IT managers; and
- 500 surveyed IT equipment end-users.

Owing to the research area's novelty, the knowledge base of sustainability and IS, Green IS, and Green IT is limited, and theory building is therefore needed. Accordingly, most of the work focuses on descriptive and explanatory research. Three publications (B.2, B.9, and B.10) and Section C.1.4 focus on the development of artifacts, and have concrete practical relevance. The presented results' test and verification should be subject to future research in this field.

3 Related Research on Sustainability and Information Systems

This section describes the emergence of research on sustainability and IS (Section A.3.1), provides an overview of applied theories and concepts (Section A.3.2), and defines and differentiates the most important terms, including sustainability, Green IS, and Green IT (Section A.3.3). Sections A.3.3.3.3 and A.3.3.3.4 present measures and performance metrics that relate to Green IT; focusing on research questions 11 and 12. The part concludes with Section A.3.4, which provides an introduction on industrialized information management.

3.1 Beginning and Emergence of Research

Environmental sustainability in IS has been researched for almost 20 years. Early publications deal with toxic substances, radiation, and energy consumption of PCs (Eder, 1994), energy policies for office equipment (Dandridge et al., 1994), energy consumption and energy efficiency of office equipment (Kawamoto et al., 2002; 2004; Mungwititkul & Mohanty, 1997; Smerdon, 2000), and the global environmental impact of ICT (Berkhout & Hertin, 2001). Later research extends to data centers, particularly with regard to energy efficiency (Mitchell-Jackson et al., 2003; Rasmussen, 2006a; 2006b).

Until 2007, there were not many publications about environmental sustainability and IS. However, in 2007, four key publications emerged. These publications, which had a significant impact on practice and research, were from:

- Jonathan G. Koomey (2007), who estimated the total power consumption by servers in the US and the world;
- The Environmental Protection Agency (2007), which reported to the US congress on the power consumption of data centers and servers, and estimated an exceptionally high compound annual growth rate of 15.48%;
- Simon Mingay (2007) from Gartner Inc., who stated that ICT accounts for two percent of the global CO_2 emission; and
- Steve Elliot (2007), who described environmentally sustainable ICT as a critical topic for IS research.

The key messages of these publications spread in practice and research, initiating the topic's upswing. This development is illustrated by the historical research trend shown in Table A.2.

A.3 Related Research on Sustainability and Information Systems

Melville's (2010) literature research on environmental sustainability, covering the period from 2000 to 2007, showed that until then only one article, by Heng and de Moor (2003), had been published in an IS journal. Bengtsson and Agerfalk (2011) added to this literature research, including IS conferences and extending the covered period to May 2010. For this thesis, a complementary search was conducted for material published in 2010 in AIS Senior Scholars' basket of journals (EJIS, ISJ, ISR, JAIS, JIT, JMIS, JSIS, and MISQ) and in the Proceedings of AIS associated conferences (ACIS, AMCIS, ECIS, ICIS, and PACIS). Using a similar procedure to Bengtsson and Agerfalk (2011), all papers containing the words "green", "sustainable", "sustainability", "environmental", or "environment" in the title, abstract, or keywords were selected. Their content was also examined to confirm that they belong to the research area of environmental sustainability and IS. An overview of the added publications can be found in the Appendix.

Year	2000	2001	2002	2003	2004	2005	2006	2007	2008	2009	2010	Total
AIS Basket												
EJIS												
ISJ			1									1
ISR												
JAIS												
JIT												
JMIS												
JSIS											1	1
MISQ											2	2
AIS Conferences												
ACIS			1					1	2		2	6
AMCIS	1		1				3		3	5	18	31
ECIS									1	1	3	5
ICIS			1							6	4	11
PACIS								1	2	3	3	9
Total	1		3	1			3	2	8	16	32	66

Table A.2: Numbers of Published Papers that Relate to Sustainability and IS (Extension of the Work from Bengtsson and Agerfalk (2011))

Table A.2 provides a synopsis of the identified publications by source and year. It shows that 66 research contributions on environmental sustainability in premier IS conferences and the AIS basket of journals were published between 2000 and 2010.

The literature analysis on environmental sustainability and IS shows that:

- 85% of all publications appeared in the last three years;
- the number of publications has at least doubled each year since 2007; and
- IS conferences account for 94% of all publications.

From these findings, it can be concluded that substantial research on sustainability and IS commenced in 2007. Academic discussions on this topic take place particularly at IS conferences. Until 2010, very few papers were published in the AIS basket of journals. In the beginning of 2011, the MISQ published a third paper on environmental sustainability in IS, written by Steve Elliot (2011).

The exponential growth of publications in the last three years, especially due to IS conferences, highlights the topic's increasing importance for the IS research community. However, this development is unlikely to continue forever. The "peak of inflated expectations", referred to in Gartner's (2009) hype cycle, could soon be reached. Nevertheless, at this stage environmental sustainability and IS is an important topic for academia, and is likely to receive more future attention.

3.2 Overview of Applied Theories and Concepts

Theories and concepts that are applied in the research on environmental sustainability and IS provide the context of this thesis. This section offers researchers an overview and starting point for their work. It shows theoretical and conceptual gaps, and helps to assess the contribution made by the publications in Part B and the entire thesis.

Underlying IS Theories and Concepts	References
Actor Network Theory	Bengtsson & Agerfalk, 2011
Belief-Action-Outcome Framework	Melville, 2010; Mithas et al., 2010
Contingency Theory	Schmidt & Kolbe, 2011 (Publication B.9)
Corporate Social Responsibility	Pozzebon et al., 2006; Schmidt et al., 2010a (Publication B.7)
Diffusion of Innovations Theory	Bose & Luo, 2011
Energy Informatics Framework	Watson et al., 2010
Embeddedness Perspective	Corbett, 2010
E-Readiness	Molla et al., 2009; Molla et al., 2008
Industrialized Information Management (IT Value Chain)	Cater-Steel & Tan, 2010; Erek et al., 2009; Schmidt et al., 2009a; 2010a (Publications B.2, B.6, B.7)
Institutional Theory	Butler & Daly, 2008; Chen et al., 2008; Chen et al., 2009b
IT Service Management	Cater-Steel & Tan, 2010
Life Cycle Assessment	Schmidt et al., 2010c (Publication B.5); Tenhunen & Penttinen, 2010
Marketing Mix	Schmidt et al., 2010d (Publication B.3)
Precautionary Principle	Som et al., 2009
Process Virtualization Theory	Bose & Luo, 2011
Resource-based View of the Firm	Chen et al., 2009a; Corbett, 2010; Schmidt et al., 2009a; 2009b (Publications B.1, B.2); Vykoukal et al., 2009
Social Business	Schmidt, 2011 (Publication B.4)
Stakeholder Theory	Bengtsson & Agerfalk, 2011; Schmidt et al., 2009a; 2009b (Publications B.1, B.2); Watson et al., 2010
Technology Acceptance Model	Molla, 2008
Technology Organization Environment Theory	Bose & Luo, 2011
Tragedy of the Commons	DesAutels & Berthon, 2011
Transaction Cost Theory	Bose & Luo, 2011; Schmidt et al., 2009a (Publication B.2)

Table A.3: Theories and Concepts Applied to Research on Environmental Sustainability and IS

Table A.3 provides an overview of applied theories and concepts related to environmental sustainability and IS. A more detailed description of the listed theories and concepts can be found in the referred publications or in the "Theories Used in IS Research Wiki" from the York University (2011).

While most of the theories and concepts have only been applied once or twice, a few of them are referred to more often. The more established theories and concepts are particularly "institutional theory", "stakeholder theory", "the resource-based view of the firm", and "the IT value chain".

Most of the research, theories and concepts that were only used once or twice need further validation and enhancement. The absence of other popular IS theories, such as the DeLone and McLean (2003) information systems success model, the organizational culture theory (Pettigrew, 1979), and the principal agent theory (Alchian & Demsetz, 1972; Eisenhardt, 1989b) represents a research gap. These theories can provide a starting point for novel theory-driven research on environmental sustainability and IS.

3.3 Terminology and Relationships of Key Terms

A number of terms, such as "sustainable IS", "Green IS", "Green IT", "environmental sustainability of IT", "Green ICT", and "Green IT/IS" are used in scientific literature (sometimes interchangeably) to describe responsible behavior towards the natural environment within the IS scope (Ijab et al., 2010). These terms need clarification. In this section, the relevant terms are defined and linked to each other to provide a better understanding of the topic.

3.3.1 Sustainability and IS

The term "sustainability" is widely used and has acquired many overlapping definitions (Russo, 2003). A generally accepted definition was formulated by the World Commission on Environment and Development (1987), suggesting that sustainability is "development that meets the needs of the present without compromising the ability of future generations to meet their own needs." On the corporate level, sustainability is usually equated with corporate social responsibility (CSR) (Montiel, 2008).

Dyllick and Hockerts (2002) identify three key elements of sustainability: economic, ecological, and social aspects. This implies that, contrary to the opinion of some authors, sustainability is not equivalent to environmental protection. Instead, sustainability is broader, as highlighted by Watson et al. (2010), who propose that "seeking sustainability does not mean abandoning economic thinking".

Sustainability has a fundamental impact on key issues of business strategy, such as production economics, cost competitiveness, investment decisions, and the value of different types of assets

(Enkvist et al., 2007). Consequently, sustainability should be extended towards IS and IT (Molla et al., 2009).

IS can play two roles: It can be subject to sustainability, or it can enable sustainability. Regardless of the role it plays, the objectives of sustainability depend on the internal and external stakeholders' demands (Schmidt et al., 2009b; Watson et al., 2010). A stakeholder is any group or individual who can affect or is affected by the achievement of the organization's objectives (Freeman, 1984). From these demands, short and long-term objectives are developed and weighted according to stakeholders' relevance. The objectives can be classified as economical, ecological, or social (Schmidt et al., 2009b). These sustainability objectives need to be incorporated in IT's technical, human, and managerial resources to solve both IT and non IT-related sustainability problems (Molla et al., 2009).

Based on the above finding, the following definitions regarding sustainability and IS are developed:

> **Sustainability and IS** can have two meanings, namely sustainability by IS and sustainability in IS.
>
> **Sustainability by IS** refers to IS application to enable activities aimed at achieving long-term economical, ecological, and social objectives.
>
> **Sustainability in IS** refers to an economical, ecological, and socially long-term compliant application of IS.
>
> *In both cases, the objective function depends on internal and external stakeholders' demands and their relevance for the organization.*

Research on sustainability by IS investigates how IS can mitigate or eliminate problems related to economical issues, as well as social issues such as inequalities in education, or environmental issues such as inefficiencies in energy networks. The environmental perspective also includes Green IS, as described in this thesis.

Similarly, research on sustainability in IS covers the economical, environmental, and social aspect of IS, including, for example, ethical issues surrounding IT's utilization (Mingers & Walsham, 2010), as well as challenges and practices related to Green IT (Section A.3.3.3).

3.3.2 Green IS as an Environmental Enabler

Of the three central aspects of sustainability, the environmental issue is clearly dominant in IS research publications (Bengtsson & Agerfalk, 2011). This domain has been labeled as:

- Green IS (Watson et al., 2010);
- Green IT (Butler & Daly, 2008; Hedwig et al., 2009; Mann et al., 2009; Molla, 2008; 2009; Murugesan, 2008; Schmidt et al., 2010b);
- environmental sustainability of IT (Elliot, 2007; 2011; Elliot & Binney, 2008);
- Green ICT (Fuchs, 2006; Hilty et al., 2009); and
- Green IT/IS (Chen et al., 2009a; Jenkin et al., 2011).

There is consensus about the dual role of IS and IT, as both pose a problem but also offer a solution for the natural environment (Elliot, 2011; Melville, 2010; Molla et al., 2009). However, views regarding the terminology, especially in terms of Green IS and Green IT, differ. Although Green IT could be considered a narrower field than Green IS, the terms are often used interchangeably (Mithas et al., 2010). Therefore, a distinction between Green IS and Green IT is needed.

3.3.2.1 Distinction Between Green IS and Green IT

Watson et al. (2010) provide the clearest definition of Green IS and its relationship to IT. They propose that Green IS is inclusive of Green IT. In their opinion, Green IT is too narrow and should be extended to IS, which they define as an "... *integrated and cooperating set of people, processes, software, and information technologies to support individual, organizational, or societal goals*" (Watson et al., 2010). IT refers to the technologies that provide information systems' technological foundation (Melville, 2010).

Other researchers support this perspective. They argue that Green IT primarily focuses on activities and efforts that incorporate ecologically friendly technologies and processes into the entire hardware life cycle, particularly IT's energy efficient use in data centers (Bengtsson & Agerfalk, 2011; Elliot, 2011; Hedwig et al., 2009).

Conversely, Molla et al. (2009) argue that Green IT does not only refer to greening of the IT infrastructure but also to IT usage to achieve sustainability in business and supply chain processes.

Ijab et al. (2010) state that the IT industry and IT managers are responsible for Green IT. From this point of view, Green IT is an important issue for IT organizations such as IT hardware manufacturers and IT departments.

The terms "Green ICT" and "environmental sustainability of IT" are similar to Green IT. Fuchs (2006) relates Green ICT to the greening of production and energy consumption of ICT.

According to Elliot (2011), the term "environmental sustainability of IT" covers:

"activities to minimize the negative impacts and maximize the positive impacts of human behavior on the environment through the design, production, application, operation, and disposal of IT and IT-enabled products and services throughout their life cycle."

One way to get around the definition problem is to unite the terms "Green IS" and "Green IT". For example, Chen et al. (2009a) suggest that:

"Green IS & IT refers to IS & IT products (e.g., software that manages an organization's overall emissions) and practices (e.g., disposal of IT equipment in an environmentally friendly way) that aims to achieve pollution prevention, product stewardship, or sustainable development."

Jenkin et al. (2011) also use the term "Green IT/IS", referring to information technology and system initiatives and programs that address environmental sustainability. However, in contrast to other authors, they distinguish between the two concepts in terms of their focus and impact on the environment.

From Jenkin et al.'s (2011) perspective, Green IS refers to the development and use of information systems to enable environmental sustainability initiatives and, thus, tends to have a positive impact on the environment.

Based on Jenkin et al.'s (2011) definition, as well as Butler and Daly (2008), the following definition of Green IS applies to this thesis:

> **Green IS** is understood as **green by IT**. It refers to the application of IT-enabled information systems in organizations, to support and enable green business activities, reporting, and processes. It distinguishes from Green IT by emphasizing its role as an environmental enabler in general business functions.

3.3.2.2 Potentials and Examples of Green IS

Green IS investigates the potential of using IS to support business initiatives in reducing their negative environmental impacts (Jenkin et al., 2010; Watson et al., 2010). The possible scope of Green IS is vast; only its some potentials and practices can be outlined in this thesis.

From an industry oriented perspective, Green IS can potentially reduce emissions and costs in different sectors, such as production, logistics, buildings, and energy provision. Table A.4 illustrates estimated global benefits up to 2020. This ability of Green IS is also called "smart" (Climate Group and Global eSustainability Initiative, 2008). Terms such as "smart grid" or "smart power" (Fox-Penner, 2010) refer to Green IS for specific business sectors.

A.3 Related Research on Sustainability and Information Systems

Sector	Global Emissions Savings in Billion of Tons of CO_2 up to 2020	Global Cost Savings in Billion of Euros up to 2020
Motor Systems	0.97	68
Logistics	1.52	280
Buildings	1.68	216
Energy Grids	2.03	79
Total	6.2	643

Table A.4: Estimations of Green IS enabled Energy Efficiency Effects Up to 2020 (Climate Group and Global eSustainability Initiative, 2008)

Green IS can also be structured from a business functions perspective. Porter (1998) distinguishes between primary functions (inbound logistics, operations, outbound logistics, marketing, and service) and support functions (infrastructure, human resource management, technology development, and procurement). Each of these functions can apply Green IS, thereby improving the related processes with regard to environmental effectiveness, efficiency, control, and compliance.

Examples of Green IS initiatives include dematerialization practices (substituting digital goods for physical goods), improvements in supply chain efficiency, and increasing capacity utilization (Melville, 2010). Furthermore, systems that monitor, evaluate and communicate the environmental impact belong to Green IS (Elliot, 2011). In IS research, these systems are referred to as environmental management information systems (EMIS) (El-Gayar & Fritz, 2006; Teuteberg & Straßenburg, 2009).

The topic has also a market relevance to companies. Table A.5 illustrates a selection of providers and software applications that support environmental management.

Software	Provider	Functions
City Cockpit	Siemens IT Solutions and Services	Visualization of a city's CO_2 emissions, electricity and water consumption
Eco-footprint	IFS	Measurement of costs related to lead and CO_2 emissions. Assignment of transportation methods to life cycle assessments
Environment Sustainability Dashboard	Microsoft	Supplement to the Dynamics AX ERP suite. Portal application to generate reports on emissions and energy usage from business data
Maximo Asset Management	IBM	Facility management software, which can identify the energy costs and CO_2 consumption of buildings
Sofi-Software	PE International	Measurement of energy consumption and emissions by companies
Sustainability Management	SAS	Software to measure and predict the environmental, social and economic effects of a company's activity

Table A.5: Selection of Software Applications for Environmental Management in Enterprises

The successful implementation of Green IS can eventually enable a green marketing strategy, which must be treated cautiously. Marketing of environmental initiatives is always under threat of being called greenwashing, which occurs when significantly more resources are channeled into claims about being green rather than into actual environmentally sound practices (Watson et al., 2010). Greenwashing also includes disclosing false information, deliberately misleading, or failing to fully disclose all information regarding environmental impacts (Melville, 2010).

The competences and resources related to Green IS can give an enterprise a competitive advantage. Green IS might even become the key enabler of entire business models, which are termed as "IT-enabled green business model" (Schmidt, 2011).

The business model describes a path from basic human needs to continuous financial success (Magretta, 2002). Green business has grown into an important management concept (Starik & Rands, 1995). Although its economic dimension is often highlighted, green business is based on ethical considerations (Schendler, 2002). A business model can be interpreted as green if it primarily pursues environmental objectives under the minimum constraint of cost-coverage.

Attribute	Traditional Business Model	IT-enabled Green Business Model
Objective	Profit maximization	Maximization of environmental benefits / at least full cost recovery
Role of IT/IS	Green IT aligns to the business model	Green IS enables the business model
Main Stakeholders	Investors, shareholders	Society, legislation, investors, shareholders
Appropriation of Profits	Dividends to investors and shareholders, reinvestment	Reinvestment, extension of activities, payback of investors
Objectives of Investors	Added financial value (one-dimensional)	Contribution to the environment, conservation of value (multi-dimensional)
Potential Customers	Price / performance oriented	Quality / environment oriented

Table A.6: *Comparison of a Traditional Business Model and an IT-enabled Green Business Model*

An IT-enabled green business model distinguishes itself clearly from traditional business models. An initial comparison between the two types is outlined in Table A.6.

Name	Homepage	Type of Service	Customers	Environmental Benefits
car2go (2011)	car2go.com	Transportation	City residents	IT-enabled car sharing concept, using web mapping. Reduces traffic jams, emissions, stress, and noise.
Cyber Rain (2011)	cyber-rain.com	Software	Home owners	Cyber Rain uses wireless technology to check the local weather forecast and to adjust sprinkler watering schedules to match daily conditions, which saves up to 40% of water.
Ecosia (2010a)	ecosia.org	Internet search engine	Internet users	Ecosia is a green search engine that donates at least 80% of its advertising revenue to a rainforest protection program run by the WWF.
GreenQloud (2011)	greenqloud.com	IT services	IT departments	GreenQloud operates data centers that are 100% powered by renewable geothermal and hydropower energy.
ifu Hamburg (2011)	umberto.de	Software	Manufacturers	Umberto is the software tool for material and energy flow analysis and life cycle assessment.
Metrolight (2011)	metrolight.com	Electronic ballasts / Software	Organizations with major lighting	Metrolight manufactures electronic ballasts that power energy efficient lighting systems, saving up to 65% of lighting costs.
Verdiem (2011)	verdiem.com	Software	IT departments	Verdiem provides enterprise software solutions to reduce energy consumption of PC networks.
Zonzoo (2011)	zonzoo.co.uk	Service	Mobile phone users	Zonzoo buys old mobile phones and recycles them, and plants a tree for every old phone.

Table A.7: *Examples of IT-enabled Green Business Models from Various Industries*

The condition that must be in place for an IT-enabled green business model to succeed is that the firm must operate at or beyond the cost recovery point. Therefore, donations or grants can play a significant role as a source of revenue (Emerson, 2003).

In practice, there are examples of IT-enabled green business models in various industries (Table A.7). They are all enabled by Green IS and use resources efficiently, avoid harmful waste, create transparency or invest their revenues to support environmental initiatives.

IS's strategic role in enabling environmental sustainability has not been explored in great depth (Thambusamy & Salam, 2010). Therefore, Green IS's full potential cannot be estimated yet. Green IS provides a mostly undiscovered IS research area and countless opportunities for practitioners. Given the environmental topic's relevance, further research is needed to develop this area.

3.3.3 Green IT for the Environmental Alignment of IT Organizations

In contrast to Green IS, Green IT addresses energy and resource consumption, as well as waste and emissions associated with hardware and software use. Green IT tends to have a direct and positive impact (Jenkin et al., 2011), for example, improving the energy efficiency of hardware and data centers, consolidating servers using virtualization software, and reducing waste associated with obsolete equipment (Jenkin et al., 2011).

Based on the definitions developed by Jenkin et al. (2011), Hedwig et al. (2009) and Ijab et al. (2010), the following definition of Green IT applies to this thesis:

> **Green IT** is understood as **green in IT**. It denotes all activities and efforts of IT organizations (hardware manufacturers, IT departments, and IT service providers) to incorporate green technologies and processes into IT's entire life cycle to achieve alignment with the corporate objectives, environmental strategy, and relevant stakeholders.

The term "Green IT" is subject to criticism. For example, Elliot (2011) states that Green IT is an oxymoron; as it focuses on technology rather than its application; and there is "inherent lack of greenness in the technology". Heng (2009) makes the same criticism, stating "IT is not green and never ever will be!" These statements are even supported by theory. The Margolus-Levitin theorem states that any physical system needs energy to commute information, based on the laws of quantum physics (Margolus & Levitin, 1998).

Although this criticism has some merit and terms such as "Greener IT" or "Greening IT" might describe the phenomenon better, the term "Green IT" is widely accepted and used in research and practice. Therefore, the term "Green IT" is used in this study, without negating its true meaning.

3.3.3.1 Environmental Impact of IT

In addition to the information provided earlier on (Section A.1.1), this section aims to provide details on IT's environmental impact, consisting of material and energetic effects.

The material impact derives from mining the necessary materials to build IT and from disposing old equipment at the end of its life cycle.

A good example to illustrate the negative impact of IT induced mining is found in coltan, which is referred to as a digital mineral (Smith, 2011). It is used to make capacitors for most IT devices (Schlager, 2009). Over 50% of coltan comes from Africa, especially from the Democratic Republic of the Congo. Besides social problems, the coltan mining endangers the lowland gorillas, and causes deforestation and water pollution (Dürr, 2010; Lin, 2011).

When IT equipment reaches the end of its life cycle, it contributes to tremendous amounts of e-waste. About 5 million tons of IT-related e-waste is generated each year on a global scale (Schmidt et al., 2009a). IDC (2010) forecasts PC sales in 2011 of 380 million units worldwide of which 250 million units (66%) will be portable. With an estimated lifespan of 3 years, these units will have to be disposed of or recycled by 2014 with obvious environmental impact.

Obsolete IT does not just pose a threat to the environment; the materials used during manufacturing also have a monetary value. In 2008, the material used for IT equipment in 53,000 German data centers was estimated to contain approximately 12,000 t of electronics, 17,000 t of copper, 7,000 t of aluminum, 11,000 t of plastics and 58,000 t of iron. The electronics contain 1.8 t of gold, 7.5 t of silver and 0.8 t of palladium. Almost 30% of the materials are used in the 50 major data centers (Hintemann & Fichter, 2010).

IT's impact on energy stems from its manufacturing and utilization, which are processes that consume energy generated by different energy sources (e.g., nuclear, coal, oil, gas, wind, and sun). Each energy source has a specific carbon emission factor. This is expressed by the unit $kgCO_2/kWh$, with which a carbon footprint can be calculated. The CO_2 emissions generated during manufacturing is about one quarter of the overall IT footprint; the rest is produced during usage (Climate Group and Global eSustainability Initiative, 2008).

Many studies estimate IT utilization's energy consumption. The expected annual increases vary, depending on the domain, country, sector, and period (Table A.8). The Green IT scenario assumes that always the most energy efficient IT will be implemented in data centers and the office environment. The business as usual scenario expects a regular efficiency increase of IT hardware due to miniaturization and Moore's law (Moore, 1998), but no further efforts regarding energy efficiency. The estimations indicate that energy consumption in the data centers is likely to increase further despite possible Green IT measures. In contrast, IT energy consumption in the office environment will probably decline.

IT Domain	Country / Sector	Period	Compound Annual Increase in Rates of Power Consumption		Authors
			Green IT Scenario	Business as Usual Scenario	
Data Centers and Servers	USA	2007-2011	-6.68%	+15.48%	Environmental Protection Agency, 2007
All IT	EU-25	2005-2020	+3.04%	+4.98%	European Commission, 2008a
Data Centers	EU-25	2005-2020	+6.01%	+8.28%	European Commission, 2008a
PCs and Monitors	EU-25	2005-2020	+0.56%	+2.24%	European Commission, 2008a
Data Centers and Servers	Western Europe	2007-2020	+4.88%		European Commission, 2009
All IT	Germany / Businesses	2007-2020	+0.36%	+1.45%	Fraunhofer IZM & Fraunhofer ISI, 2009
Data Centers	Germany / Businesses	2007-2020	+1.15%	+2.34%	Fraunhofer IZM & Fraunhofer ISI, 2009
Data Centers	Germany / Public administration	2007-2020	+0.12%	+1.30%	Fraunhofer IZM & Fraunhofer ISI, 2009
IT-end-user Devices	Germany / Businesses	2007-2020	-1.15%	+0.24%	Fraunhofer IZM & Fraunhofer ISI, 2009
IT-end-user Devices	Germany / Public administration	2007-2020	-3.04%	-1.87%	Fraunhofer IZM & Fraunhofer ISI, 2009
Data Centers	Germany	2008-2015	-7.17%	+4.99%	Hintemann & Fichter, 2010

Table A.8: Estimated Compound Annual Growth Rates of Power Consumption by IT

In summary, this section illustrates that IT causes environmental impacts throughout its entire life cycle. Structured in line with the Greenhouse Gas Protocol, these emissions consist of direct emissions (Scope 1), emissions from the generation of purchased electricity (Scope 2), and other related emissions (Scope 3) (WBCSD and WRI, 2004).

After this practical perspective, the following section provides a scientific view on Green IT.

3.3.3.2 Perspectives and Categories to Describe Green IT

The Green IT phenomenon can be described from many different perspectives. In this section, Green IT categories, based on literature review findings, are presented. These categories are structured into perspectives that aim to answer specific questions. These perspectives are:

- Drivers - Why do IT organizations apply Green IT?
- Fields - Where do IT organizations apply Green IT?
- Measures - How do IT organizations apply Green IT?
- Benefits - For what do IT organizations apply Green IT?

The summary in Table A.9 provides a comprehensive overview of academic Green IT research. The perspectives and related categories that are presented help to describe Green IT and to structure the existent knowledge base. The presented perspectives and categories provide guidance and reference points for further Green IT research.

	Criteria	Categories					
Drivers (Why?)	Drivers of Green IT initialization (Bose & Luo, 2011)	Technological context		Organizational context		Environmental context	
	Adoption due to pressures (Chen et al., 2009a; Chen et al., 2008)	Mimetic pressures		Normative pressures		Coercive pressures	
	Motivating forces (Jenkin et al., 2011)	Ecological		Organizational	Political-economic	Socio-cultural	
	Extension of Green IT (Kuo & Dick, 2010)	Motivational pressures		Organizational factors		Technological constraints	
	Objectives of IT department (Schmidt et al., 2010a) (B.7)	Efficient internal operation		Market competitiveness		Reputation management	
	Extension of Green IT adoption (Schmidt et al., 2010b) (B.8)	Uncertainty			Importance		
Fields (Where?)	Types of IT products and services (Erek et al., 2009; Schmidt et al., 2009a) (B.2, B.6)	Hardware		Software		Services	
	Value chain of IT organizations (Erek et al., 2009; Schmidt et al., 2009a) (B.2, B.6)	Source	Make	Deliver		Return	Govern
	Related impacts of IT (Forge, 2007)	First order effects		Second order effects		Third order effects	
	Fields of Green IT operation (Hedwig et al., 2009)	Data center location	Data center layout	Hardware		Software	Management
	Green IT reach (Molla, 2009)	Creation		Sourcing		Operations	Disposal
	Addressed problems of IT (Murugesan, 2008)	Design		Manufacturing		Use	Disposal
Measures (How?)	Green IT changes (Bose & Luo, 2011)	Technology changes			Behavioral changes		
	Types of Green IT (Corbett, 2010)	Information to support decision-making	Direct IT assets and infrastructure	Collaboration		Sustainable products and services	
	Environmental friendliness (Eder, 2009)	Avoidance or reduction of materials and radiation		Use of materials and packaging that facilitate recycling		Economical use of energy and resources	
	Green IT richness (Molla, 2009)	Policies		Practices		Technologies and systems	
	Green IT readiness (Molla et al., 2009)	Policies	Practices	Technologies		Attitude	Governance
Benefits (For what?)	Green IT benefits (Bose & Luo, 2011)	Reduced power consumption	Lower costs	Lower environmental impact	Improved systems performance	Space savings	Increased interaction amid constituents	Agile workforce
	Associated benefits (Erek et al., 2009) (B.6)	Cost reduction		Risk reduction		Higher flexibility	Improved reputation
	Green IT potentials (Molla, 2008)	Competitive opportunities	Reduced carbon emissions	Improved overall business efficiency	Positive brand image	Positive mindset of customers and investors	Mitigated environmental liabilities
	Benefits of Green IT (Murugesan, 2008)	Reduced power consumption	Lower costs	Lower environmental impact	Improved systems performance	Space savings	

Table A.9: Perspectives and Categories for Describing Green IT

A.3 Related Research on Sustainability and Information Systems

The drivers show that internal and external factors determine the initiation of Green IT within the technological context's limitations.

Bose and Luo (2011) develop a conceptual model for capturing factors from the organizational, technological and environmental context that influence Green IT initialization.

Building on institutional theory, Chen et al. (2008) explain why organizations adopt Green IS and Green IT practices. They refer to mimetic, normative and coercive pressures (Chen et al., 2009a): Mimetic pressures occur when organizations model other organizations' behaviors in pursuit of legitimacy or generally accepted practices. Normative pressures arise when organizations feel compelled to recognize certain cultural expectations of professional circles or the larger society. Coercive pressures come from organizations' interconnectedness or from important stakeholders upon whom an organization depends. Mimetic pressure is a particularly important determinant of organizational adoption of Green IS and Green IT (Chen et al., 2009a).

Jenkin et al. (2011) describe certain motivating forces that could influence an organization's environmental strategy. Among these are ecological forces, organizational forces, political-economic forces, and socio-cultural forces. These forces can motivate or constrain environmental strategies (Jenkin et al., 2011).

Kuo and Dick (2010) propose that the level of Green IT that is adopted is likely to be influenced by motivational pressures. These consist of competitive, legitimation, and social responsibility pressures, as well as organizational factors and technological constraints.

Schmidt et al. (2010a) investigates why IT departments adopt Green IT. After an empirical investigation with CIOs, they conclude that IT departments pursue one of three categories of objectives when they apply Green IT. These objectives are: efficient internal operations, market competitiveness, and reputation management, which lead to concrete benefits for the IT department.

In another study, Schmidt et al. (2010b) develop predictors of Green IT planning and implementation activities. In their investigation, Green IT's importance and an organization's uncertainty about Green IT affect its adoption level.

After evaluating the drivers of Green IT initialization, the possible fields in which Green IT can be applied are described. The question answered is "where can Green IT be applied?"

Erek et al. (2009) and Schmidt et al. (2009b) provide a product and service oriented perspective, as well as a process oriented perspective on Green IT. They subdivide Green IT into the categories hardware, software and service. Furthermore, they structure IT organizations according to the supply chain operations reference (SCOR) model (Supply-Chain Council Inc., 2006) into the processes "source", "make", "deliver", "return" and "govern". They also link Green IT measures to these phases.

Forge (2007) takes an emission oriented standpoint. He distinguishes between three environmental impact types of IT to which Green IT activities can be assigned: First order impacts evolve from the IT manufacturing and its physical existence. Second order effects come from ongoing IT use and its application. It includes the power consumed and the power saved by using IT. Third order effects cover the rebound impacts created when IT is being used over the medium to long term. For example, telecommunication could substitute travelling's physical effects.

Hedwig et al. (2009) emphasize the importance of data centers for Green IT. Their "fields of Green IT operation" consist of data center location, data center layout, hardware, software, and management tasks.

Similar to Erek et al. (2009) and Schmidt et al. (2009b), Molla (2009) describes IT's phases of environmental considerations which are made during creation, sourcing, then operation, and finally disposal.

Murugesan (2008) shares this life-cycle perspective and highlights the role of hardware manufacturers in Green IT more strongly. He describes the start of the IT process by referring to the IT product design phase first. The process then continues with manufacturing, use, and disposal.

Green IT can also be categorized in terms of measures. The question answered is, "how can Green IT be applied?"

Bose and Luo (2011) divide Green IT measures into two categories: changes in technology, and changes in behavior. This simple but reasonable perspective is applied in Section A.3.3.3.3 to structure Green IT measures.

Corbett (2010) develops four groups of Green IT measures. The first group supports decision-making by informing relevant stakeholders, and includes, for example, business intelligence applications or carbon footprint calculators. The second group, labeled "direct IT assets and infrastructure", deals with measures for efficient computing, especially in the data center. The third group, "collaboration", contains communication and workflow measures such as video conferencing or document sharing. Finally, "sustainable products and services" is a group of measures that describes market related activities towards customers, such as new online services.

Eder (2009) emphasizes the hardware aspect and categorizes Green IT measures according to their environmental objectives. These objectives are: avoiding or reducing materials and radiation that are harmful to the environment and dangerous to health, using materials and packaging that facilitate recycling, and economical energy and resource consumption.

Molla (2009) describes three categories of Green IT activities: policy, practice, and technology. In another study, Molla et al. (2009) add two more dimensions: attitude and governance. The model offers a common platform against which practitioners can benchmark their Green IT initiatives and progress (Molla et al., 2009).

The final group of categories explains Green IT from the perspective of achievable benefits. The question answered is "for what is Green IT applied?"

Bose and Luo (2011) present increased interaction amid constituents and an agile workforce as benefits of Green IT. Erek et al. (2009) include risk and reputation as additional benefit dimensions, besides cost reduction and higher flexibility.

Molla (2008) mentions competitive opportunities, reduced carbon emissions, improved overall business efficiency, positive brand image, customers' and investors' positive mindset, as well as mitigated environmental liabilities, as Green IT potentials.

Murugesan's (2008) list of Green IT benefits includes reduced power consumption, lower costs, lower carbon emissions and lower environmental impact, improved systems performance and use, and space savings.

The findings of the papers in Part B informed the description of Green IT drivers, fields and benefits, as shown in this section. However, no publication directly relates to detailed Green IT practices or metrics. The following two additional sections fill this gap.

3.3.3.3 Exemplary Measures

This section answers research question 11 by outlining possible Green IT measures. The selection of measures is especially pertinent to IT departments and IT service providers. Measures were collected by studying the work of Mann et al. (2009), Nguyen et al. (2009), Hintemann and Pfahl (2008), Velte et al. (2008), and Woods (2010).

According to Bose and Luo (2011), all measures fall into the following two categories:

- behavioral changes; or
- technology changes.

Each measure relates to a phase of IT organizations' value chain process, which includes the activities of sourcing, making, delivery, return, and governing (Erek et al., 2009; Schmidt et al., 2009a).

3.3.3.3.1 Behavioral Measures

Behavioral measures include changes in the organizational processes, in IT usage, or in the IT organization's relationships.

The following are behavioral measures for the *sourcing process*:

- *Use of renewable energy:* The easiest way to decrease the environmental impact of IT usage is to rely on solar, wind, water, geothermal or other renewable energy sources. This can instantly reduce IT's carbon footprint and improve the IT organization's reputation. However, unavailability and high costs are the main obstacles to using renewable energy sources.

- *Procurement of hardware and software that are energy efficient and environmentally friendly:* The procurement of IT hard- and software determines how much energy the IT equipment will consume during its utilization, the environmental footprint, and the waste that will be disposed of at the end of its life cycle. Therefore, it is recommended that energy and environment related procurement policies be put in place. IT eco-labels could, for example, be made mandatory during procurement, for example, by considering EPEAT, Energy Star, EcoLogo, Blue Angel, TCO, Nordic swan, Eco mark, Green seal or Climate savers (DesAutels & Berthon, 2011). Companies can also evaluate the environmental product information provided by the manufacturer and developers, or they can carry out own tests and measurements.

- *Audits of hardware, software, and service suppliers:* Supplier audits provide valuable information about their environmental behavior, and can serve as quality indicators. The audits can lead to reduced asymmetric information and behavioral risk. The criteria that can indicate Green IT include certification after ISO 14001, ranking in the Guide to Greener Electronics (Greenpeace International, 2009), size of carbon footprint, and compliance with the Code of Conduct on Data Center Energy Efficiency (European Commission, 2008b). However, most suppliers can only estimate their own environmental impact because until now it is impossible to exactly measure the environmental impact of the hundreds and thousands of parts used in their products and services.

The following are behavioral measures of the *production process* (the phase of the value chain process labeled "making"), and covers the data center and the office environment:

- *Optimization of the data center layout:* An efficient data center layout decreases energy consumption. The most commonly used strategy for cooling computer rooms with air is a layout of alternating hot and cold aisles. This optimizes the airflow to cool down the servers and extract heat from them. The advantages of the hot aisle / cold aisle configuration can be maximized by containing the air in the aisles, keeping hot and cold air from mixing. Holes, through which cold air and hot air escape, should be plugged. The under floor cavity should be cleaned out so that cold air can circulate. Cabling should be routed in such a way that it does not impede the cool air flow, and should possibly be placed in the hot aisles to ensure a free flow of air in the cold aisles. Surplus cables should also be removed.

- *Optimization of the printer layout:* Printers consume electricity, paper and cartridges. Printer optimization leads to lower electricity and paper consumption, as well as less waste. Printer rooms and card readers aid the printing effort and deter unnecessary printing.

- *Introduction of guidelines for IT utilization, data management, and printing:* Many employees keep their PCs turned on when they leave the workplace during business hours. Even at night, computers often stay active (Publication B.10). This energy wastage can easily be avoided if employees act more consciously or if they use the power management tools provided by the operating system. Employees should extend this awareness to data management, keeping in mind that less data results in less backup, which leads to lower demands for disk space, thereby cutting down on the energy costs from constantly spinning disks, network transmissions and cooling. Employees can also save paper and cartridges by reducing printing and by doing double-sided printing.

The following are behavioral measures for the *delivery process*:

- *Communication of efforts towards stakeholders:* In order to improve the IT organization's reputation regarding its use of Green IT, it is necessary to convey news of efforts and achievements to stakeholders, including employees, other business units, investors, and customers. Communication can take the form of forums, employee publications, workshops, practitioner magazines, and newspapers. Achievements can be measured by Green IT metrics (Section A.3.3.3.4) and can be certified by external organizations such as TÜV Rheinland (2011).

- *Marketing of Green IT services and products:* If Green IT knowledge, skills, and achievements are significant, marketing of Green IT services (e.g., Green IT consulting) and products (e.g., Green IT e-mail service) is possible. Attention must be paid to credibility and greenwashing must be avoided.

The following are behavioral measures for the *return process*:

- *Hardware reuse:* By reusing old servers and PCs, companies can reduce the need for new hardware. The savings from the reuse must, however, be compared with the potential energy reduction represented by new, more efficient hardware.
- *Audits of disposal companies:* Disposal companies' audits mitigate externally induced risk by ensuring that the IT hardware is disposed in a socially and environmentally responsible manner. There is a global market for e-waste business, involving international waste brokers and carriers. These actors sometimes neglect appropriate environmental and social standards when they deal with e-waste, for example by transferring the waste to countries with lower environmental standards.

The following are behavioral measures for the governing process:

- *Collection, distribution, and standardization of Green IT best practices:* Particularly in large companies, the IT organization is often decentralized over multiple locations. Green IT measures that work well in one place could be equally effective elsewhere. A standardization of good working measures should be considered. Therefore, a structured collection and distribution of Green IT best practices throughout the IT organization can leverage related benefits.
- *Strategic Green IT planning:* The Green IT strategy should align with the entire corporate strategy. The organization's objectives should therefore be refined at Green IT level to influence certain measures' implementation. This process needs to be structured and comprehensible. An example of a strategic Green IT planning process is presented in Publication B.10.
- *Green IT performance metrics:* Metrics help monitor the achievement level and establish objectives. Furthermore, they enable to benchmark practices, locations, and organizations. A selection of Green IT metrics is provided in Section A.3.3.3.4.

Behavioral measures are generally less expensive than technological measures. However, it is difficult to ensure their success because they depend on employee support.

3.3.3.3.2 Technological Measures

Technological measures include changes in infrastructure, as well as in the organization's IT applications, to make them environmental friendly. Most technological measures apply to production ("making" in the data center and office environment). In the other processes, applications can support behavioral measures.

A.3 Related Research on Sustainability and Information Systems

The following are technological measures for *sourcing, making, delivery, return and governing processes*:

- *Green IT applications for data exchange and decision support:* All relevant data (e.g., power consumption and performance indicators) must be collected and shared throughout the organization to support decision-making and other efforts at all levels. This data can be used to generate Green IT reports that make specific recommendations. Software applications for data exchange and reporting can support these tasks.

The following are technological measures of *production* in the office environment (the "making" process):

- *Use of thin clients:* Thin clients use client-server architectures and rely on servers for their processing capabilities. They act as localized input and output locations for users and use much less energy than PCs. They have multiple advantages such as lower IT administration costs, easy application deployment, lower energy consumption, lower hardware costs, more efficient computing resource usage, and lower hardware upgrade costs. When thin clients are used, the energy savings in the office environment must be compared with the higher utilization of servers in the data center. Furthermore, organizations must consider the implications of employees rejecting the decision to "downgrade" to a thin client.

- *Communication, collaboration, and workflow applications:* Communication, collaboration, and workflow applications enable users to digitally interact via videoconferencing, content management systems, document management systems, portals, and other applications. This could lead to less travel, lower paper consumption, and less people in the office, which would in turn lead to reduced resource consumption and lower CO_2 emissions. However, organizations must pay attention to rebound effects; for example, easier communication and collaboration could enable new opportunities, which could lead to more travel and more emissions.

- *Use of multifunction printers:* Multifunction printers that replace multiple devices (printer, scanner, and fax) use less energy. Some modern devices demand employee IDs before starting a print job, thereby saving paper and enabling a cause-based allocation of printing costs, which creates additional incentives.

- *Automatic default settings for PCs and printers:* Instead of relying on a behavioral change in employees' use of IT devices, environmentally friendly default settings can automatically be applied to PCs and printers (e.g., automatic shut-down and double-sided printing). These settings help to save energy and paper. However, organizations should monitor employees' responses, as they might perceive these kinds of measures as interfering in their work processes.

The following are technological measures of *production* (the "making" process) in the data center:

- *Using data compression:* Data compression (e.g., by de-duplication) reduces the storage needed for files, resulting in lower demands for physical disk space, which cuts down on the energy costs that result from constantly spinning disks, network transmissions and cooling.

- *Virtualization of servers, storage and memory:* Virtualization abstracts the logical device from the physical device. Physical devices work in a non-dedicated manner, making it possible to run multiple logical devices on the hardware, which increases utilization rate and hardware flexibility. Therefore, less hardware devices are needed, which results in lower power consumption and cooling demands.

- *Efficient uninterrupted power supplies (UPS):* UPS consume a lot of power to remain in a state of readiness. A more efficient UPS system decreases energy consumption, reduces cost, and lowers carbon emissions.

- *Consolidation of data centers, servers, storage, and workload:* Consolidation occurs when many things are merged into one. This means that the overall physical number of locations and devices is reduced. From a Green IT perspective, consolidation should result in an overall reduction of resource consumption, because when fewer units are used, lowered transactional and frictional losses follow.

- *Energy efficient software:* The energy consumed by a processor depends on the computational steps, which are determined by related software. Capra and Merlo (2009) argue that software applications' energy consumption is amplified by all the IT layers (servers, storage, networks, and cooling). Therefore, energy efficient software can have a great impact on the data center's total energy consumption.

- *Inter-organizational collaboration concepts:* Cloud and grid computing are flexible inter-organizational collaboration concepts that promote consecutive performance of computing tasks by using a connected IT infrastructure. The concept is similar to virtualization and consolidation, but on a higher organizational level. Environmental benefits result, assuming that a large-scale centralized IT infrastructure is more energy efficient than a decentralized, fragmented IT infrastructure.

- *Efficient cooling:* Inefficient cooling lowers the data center's energy efficiency. Old air conditioning units use a lot of power and should be replaced, although the organization needs to weigh up advantages. Alternative cooling methods often provide much more efficient cooling of the data center. If external air can be sucked directly into the data center, then the heat exchange can be simplified (Woods, 2010). In many data centers, the temperature can be increased to 27 C°, producing energy savings.

Ideally, behavioral measures and technological measures are combined to achieve the greatest possible Green IT benefit. The success of Green IT measures is monitored and controlled by Green IT performance metrics.

3.3.3.4 Performance Metrics

Peter Drucker's famous adage "if you can't measure it, you can't manage it" (Singleton et al., 1988) also applies to Green IT initiatives. Green IT pursues metrics-based improvements (Cater-Steel & Tan, 2010). Metrics help to establish objectives and monitor the achievement level. Furthermore, they enable to benchmark practices, locations, and organizations.

A Green IT metric should meet three requirements to be practically relevant, namely, it should be:

- meaningful;
- understandable; and
- easy to measure.

A metric is meaningful if it delivers information about an object or situation of interest. It is understandable if it is intersubjectively verifiable and easy to grasp. It is easy to measure if the effort required for data collection and data analysis is low.

Green IT metrics can be drilled down to the technical level of single circuits and CPUs. Based on the objectives of this thesis, the indicators are intended to help IT managers in their daily work; therefore, Green IT metrics are presented for an organizational level.

Green IT metrics fall into three categories: general environmental metrics (Table A.10), metrics for the office environment (Table A.11), and metrics for the data center (Table A.12). Some metrics were gathered from sources; others were developed for this thesis. Many indicators are interrelated. The range determines the possible span of the metric's values. The optimum describes the metric's ideal value from an environmental perspective.

Table A.10 shows the general environmental metrics. Most of these metrics deal with electricity consumption and related CO_2 emissions. Based on these figures, decision-makers can calculate carbon productivity and IT effectiveness. An additional metric is the Green IT media awareness. This indicator captures Green IT's contribution to the overall marketing strategy of the enterprise.

General Environmental Metrics				
Metric	Calculation / Dimension	Description	Range	Optimum
CEF (Carbon Emission Factor)	CEF ($kgCO_2$/kWh)	CO_2 emissions by the energy supplier for each kWh of electricity delivered (Belady et al., 2010)	0 to ∞	0
CFIO (Carbon Footprint of IT Operations)	CFIO = IEP x CEF ($kgCO_2$)	CO_2 emissions of the entire IT	0 to ∞	0
CUE (Carbon Usage Effectiveness)	CUE = CEF x PUE ($kgCO_2$/kWh)	The product of the carbon emission factor (CEF) and the data center's PUE (Belady et al., 2010)	0 to ∞	0
GMA (Green IT Media Awareness)	GMA = Green IT Announcements in Media / Period	The number of Green IT media reports and announcements for a specified period	0 to ∞	∞
ICP (IT Carbon Productivity)	ICP = IT services / CFIO (IT services / $kgCO_2$)	The number of IT services (e.g., transactions, storage, FLOPS, IPS) per kg CO_2 emissions	0 to ∞	∞
IEP (IT Equipment Power)	IEP = IEP_{DC} + IEP_{OE} (kWh)	The power consumption of the IT equipment in the data center (DC) and the office environment (OE) in kWh	0 to ∞	0

Table A.10: General Green IT Metrics

Table A.11 presents metrics for the office environment. Here, IT equipment, such as PCs, notebooks, and printers, is considered in terms of electricity and paper consumption. In order to obtain a meaningful metric, the consumption of these resources needs to include a consideration of the office staff.

Office Environment Metrics				
Metric	Calculation / Dimension	Description	Range	Optimum
IEP_{OE} (IT Equipment Power in the Office Environment)	IEP_{OE} (kWh)	Power consumption of the IT equipment in the office environment (OE) in kWh	0 to ∞	0
OIPUE (Office IT Power Usage Effectiveness)	OIPUE = IEP_{OE} / Employees in the office environment in FTEs (kWh / FTE)	Power consumption of the IT equipment in office environment (OE) in kWh per full-time office worker	0 to ∞	0
PCC (Paper Consumption per Capita)	PCC = Amount of consumed paper per year / Employees in the office environment in FTEs (Pages / FTE)	Amount of consumed paper in the office environment per year, divided by the number of full-time office workers	0 to ∞	0

Table A.11: Green IT Metrics in the Office Environment

A.3 Related Research on Sustainability and Information Systems

Most of the indicators that are mentioned in practice and research relate to the data center (Table A.12).

Data Center Metrics				
Metric	**Calculation / Dimension**	**Description**	**Range**	**Optimum**
IT-PEW$_{Best}$ (Best Possible IT Productivity per Embedded Watt)	IT-PEW$_{Best}$ = IT services / kWh (IT services / kWh)	IT services (e.g., transactions, storage, FLOPS, IPS), divided by the power consumption of the best available IT equipment (Brill, 2007)	0 to ∞	∞
CADE (Corporate Average Data Center Efficiency)	CADE = DCiE x FAU x ITU x IEE (Number)	CADE identifies the IT and facility efficiency of a data center, examining both energy efficiency and asset utilization (Kaplan et al., 2008)	0 to 1	1
DC-EEP (Data Center Energy Efficiency and Productivity)	DC-EEP = SI-EER x IT-PEW$_{Actual}$ (IT services / kWh)	Composite result at the data center level, attained by multiplying SI-EER and IT-PEW$_{Actual}$ (Brill, 2007)	0 to ∞	∞
DCiE (Data Center Infrastructure Efficiency)	DCiE = 1 / PUE = IEP$_{DC}$ / TFP$_{DC}$ (%)	Inverse of PUE. Ratio of the power delivered to the servers, storage, and networking gear, divided by the power delivered to the facility (Belady et al., 2008)	0 to 1	1
EUE (Energy Usage Effectiveness)	EUE = PUE$_{(year)}$ (Number)	Ratio of the power delivered to the facility, divided by the power delivered to the servers, storage, and networking gear in one year (Sijpheer, 2008)	1 to ∞	1
FAU (Facility Asset Utilization)	FAU = Average facility utilization (server, cooling, storage, network, floor space) / Maximum facility utilization (%)	Describes how much of a facility's capacity is being used (Kaplan et al., 2008)	0 to 1	1
IEE (IT Energy Efficiency)	IEE = IT-PEW$_{Current}$ / IT-PEW$_{Best}$ (%)	Measures how effective current IT equipment transforms energy into IT services compared to the best IT equipment (Kaplan et al., 2008)	0 to 1	1
IEP$_{DC}$ (IT Equipment Power in Datacenter)	IEP$_{DC}$ (kWh)	Power in kWh delivered to the servers, storage, and networking gear (Belady et al., 2008)	0 to ∞	0
IT-PEW$_{Current}$ (IT Productivity per Embedded Watt)	IT-PEW$_{Current}$ = IT services / kWh (IT services / kWh)	IT services (e.g., transactions, storage, FLOPS, IPS), divided by the current power consumption of the IT equipment (Brill, 2007)	0 to ∞	∞
ITU (IT Utilization)	ITU = Average utilization of CPUs / Maximum utilization of CPUs (%)	Measures how much of the total computational asset capacity is being utilized (Kaplan et al., 2008)	0 to 1	1
PUE (Power Usage Effectiveness)	PUE = TFP$_{DC}$ / IEP$_{DC}$ (Number)	Ratio of the power delivered to the facility, divided by the power delivered to the servers, storage, and networking gear (Belady et al., 2008)	1 to ∞	1
SI-EER (Site Infrastructure Energy Efficiency Ratio)	SI-EER = PUE = TFP$_{DC}$ / IEP$_{DC}$ (number)	Ratio of the power delivered to the facility, divided by the power delivered to the servers, storage, and networking gear (Brill, 2007)	1 to ∞	1
TFP$_{DC}$ (Total Facility Power of the Data Center)	TFP$_{DC}$ (kWh)	Power measured by the utility meter of the data center (Belady et al., 2008)	0 to ∞	0
WUE (Water Usage Effectiveness)	WUE = Annual Water Usage$_{DC}$ / IEP$_{DC}$ (L/ kWh)	Water usage in the data center, divided by the power delivered to the servers, storage, and networking gear (Patterson et al., 2011)	0 to ∞	0

Table A.12: Green IT Metrics for the Data Center

Power Usage Effectiveness (PUE) is probably the most widely used metric in IT organizations. This indicator measures data centers' efficiency by relating total energy consumption to useful energy consumption for computing.

An exemplary application of PUE is presented in Figure A.4, based on data from ten Google data centers. The most efficient and the least efficient data center values are shown, and are presented by an unbroken line. The dashed line represents the average. The optimal value would be 1 in which case all power is consumed for computing.

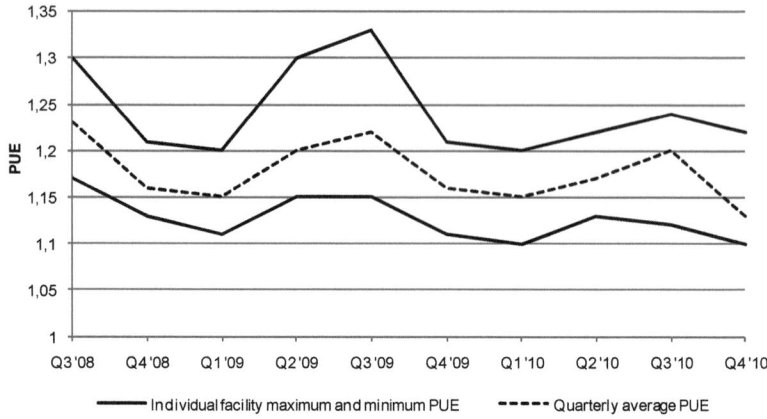

Figure A.4: Aggregated PUE Development of Ten Large-scale Google Data Centers (Google Inc., 2011)

The PUE metric applied to the Google data centers illustrates the following:

- Average efficiency is increasing slightly.
- The most efficient and the least efficient data centers differ vastly.
- Data center efficiency varies during the course of the year.

Based on this information, it can be concluded that Green IT measures contribute to more efficient Google data centers. Unfortunately, Google does not provide any detailed information about the real amount of consumed energy, thus no conclusion about Google's environmental impact can be drawn.

Data centers' differing efficiency levels might point to dissimilar technological practices or management practices. This hints at potential best practices, which should be collected and disseminated throughout the company.

The efficiency fluctuations over the year can be explained by the seasons. Since most of Google's data centers are located in the northern hemisphere, during summer (Q2 and Q3), more energy is needed for cooling. This seasonal variation worsens the PUE value.

Informative value can be enhanced by using multiple measures to further evaluate Green IT performance. It is also possible to apply Green IT metrics as part of a Green IT maturity model, as outlined by Elliot and Binney (2008), as well as Jenkin et al. (2011). Maturity models enable organizations to describe their current Green IT situation and to outline their requirements for achieving greater maturity.

Of the three requirements for Green IT metrics, ease of measurement is probably the most difficult to achieve. Many enterprises don't have sensors and measurement instruments that can determine exact IT resource consumption. Calculations are therefore based on estimates in these companies. When decision-makers consider installing sensors, they must determine the added value of information and ensure that there is a satisfactory ratio to the effort of obtaining the underlying data.

The listed Green IT metrics provide practitioners with a useful controlling instrument to manage their Green IT initiatives. Further research needs to be done to evaluate the utility of the proposed measures, to develop additional measures and to define standardized measurement processes.

3.4 Industrialized Information Management

After defining and describing the key terms, it is necessary to identify the responsible parties for Green IS and Green IT within the company. IS and IT management is generally assigned to information managers. A special variant of information management is industrialized information management, which provides the conceptual basis for this thesis and the Publications B.2, B.6, and B.7. In this section, the key terms of industrialized information management are described.

The term "information management" differs in English-language and German-language IS research publications. In the English literature, information management covers processes related to the production, acquisition, organization, maintenance, storage, retrieval and dissemination of information (Mithas et al., 2011; Stenmark et al., 2010). In contrast to this narrow perspective, the German IS literature defines the term much broader. A widely accepted definition of information management is provided by Krcmar (2009)

> **Information Management** is the management of the information economy, the information systems, the information and communication technology, and the overall executive functions (translated from Krcmar (2009)).

In this context, information management can be equated with corporate information systems management, as described by Applegate et al. (1999). This thesis aligns with the broader perspective and uses information management in the wider sense, as defined by Krcmar (2009).

Information management is part of corporate management (Brenner, 1994). It can be described from a functional and an institutional perspective:

- Information management from a functional perspective comprises tasks related to the management, the development, the design and the application of IS and IT in business and administration (Brenner, 1994; Krcmar, 2009).

- Information management from an institutional perspective describes the organizations and positions that are responsible for the execution of these tasks in businesses and administrations (Brenner, 1994; Krcmar, 2009).

The objective of information management is to ensure the best use of information in relation to the business targets (Krcmar, 2009). Information management's objectives and tasks must be derived from the strategic potential and the given internal situation of IS and IT (Heinrich & Lehner, 2005).

IS literature provides a multitude of information management concepts. Krcmar (2009) classifies these models as problem-oriented (e.g., Applegate et al., 1999; Earl, 1998; Parker et al., 1988), task-oriented (e.g., Brenner, 1994; Heinrich & Lehner, 2005; Zarnekow et al., 2006), process-oriented (e.g., Österle et al., 1992), level-oriented (e.g., Voß & Gutenschwager, 2001), or architecture-oriented (e.g., Scheer, 1992; Zachman, 1987).

Critics note that many information management concepts emphasize applications and technology management, rather than service management. Furthermore, they arrange tasks by strategic, tactical, and operational layers, instead of focusing on the IT value chain (Hochstein et al., 2006). As a result, there is no IT supplier, customer and stakeholder orientation in these concepts.

As a result of this deficit, the model of integrated or industrialized information management evolved (Hochstein et al., 2006; Zarnekow et al., 2005; 2006). Its approach is theoretically based on industrial management and outlines an IT value chain, based on the SCOR model (supply chain operations reference model) (Supply-Chain Council Inc., 2006). Industrialized information management's fundamental idea is to compare IT service provisioning processes with manufacturers' production processes.

From this perspective, all information management tasks and responsibilities can be assigned to a value chain that is made up of the processes sourcing, making, delivery, and governing, as shown in Figure A.5. A detailed description of each of the process steps can be found in the work of Hochstein et al. (2006), Zarnekow et al. (2006) or in Part B of this thesis in Publications B.2, B.6, and B.7.

A.3 Related Research on Sustainability and Information Systems

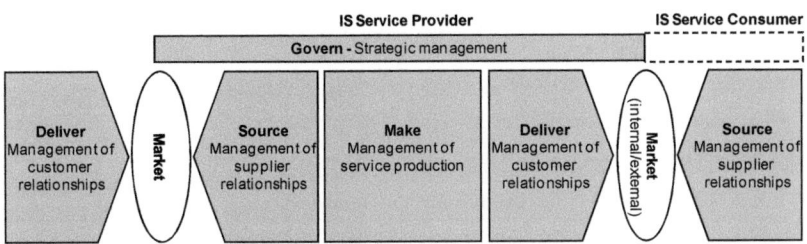

Figure A.5: Model of Industrialized Information Management (Hochstein et al., 2006; Zarnekow et al., 2005)

The industrialized information management concept has been used in research on environmental sustainability and IS (Cater-Steel & Tan, 2010; Erek et al., 2009; Schmidt et al., 2009a; 2010a). It fits this research area perfectly for several reasons.

The environmental impact of IT (Section A.1.1) relates closely to the increasingly industrialized type of IT provision and usage. Enormous data centers that provide IT services for the global market are digital industrialization's modern plants. Therefore, it is compelling to transfer the notion of industrialization to information management.

Traditional business history shows that industrialization also relates to the emergence of environmental problems, such as global warming (Mason, 1997). It is therefore reasonable to expect that when industrialization is transferred to information management, environmental problems related to industrialization will also be transferred to information management.

Thus, an extension to industrialized information management is needed to manage the environmental impacts of IS and IT. This thesis meets this need by providing a model for environmentally sustainable information management (Section C.1.4). This model is developed from the findings of the publications in Part B.

B. Sustainability and Information Systems

This part of the thesis consists of 10 peer-reviewed publications by the author. Table B.1 summarizes all the publications that support the line of reasoning of this thesis. The numbering of the publications complies with the order in which the papers are presented.

	#	Title of Article	Authors	Published	Ranking	Reference
Sustainability	B.1	Sustainable Information Systems Management	Schmidt, Erek, Kolbe, Zarnekow	Business & Information Systems Engineering (BISE)	A	(Schmidt et al., 2009b)
Sustainability	B.2	Towards a Procedural Model for Sustainable Information Systems Management	Schmidt, Erek, Kolbe, Zarnekow	Proceedings of the 42nd Hawaii International Conference on System Sciences (HICSS 2009)	B	(Schmidt et al., 2009a)
Green IS	B.3	Influence of Green IT on Consumers' Buying Behavior of Personal Computers: Implications from a Conjoint Analysis	Schmidt, Schmidtchen, Erek, Kolbe, Zarnekow	Proceedings of the 18th European Conference on Information Systems (ECIS 2010)	A	(Schmidt et al., 2010d)
Green IS	B.4	Search Engines and Social Business – Implications from the Case of Ecosia	Schmidt	Proceedings of the 4th International Conference - Information Systems & Economic Intelligence (SIIE 2010)	-	(Schmidt, 2011)
Green IS	B.5	Ökobilanzierung in der Informationstechnik – Zwei Distributionsformen der Musikindustrie im Vergleich (German)	Schmidt, Schmehl, Thies, Geldermann, Kolbe	HMD - Praxis der Wirtschaftsinformatik	B	(Schmidt et al., 2010c)
Green IT	B.6	Sustainability in Information Systems – Assortment of Current Practices in IS Organizations	Erek, Schmidt, Zarnekow, Kolbe	Proceedings of the 15th Americas Conference on Information Systems (AMCIS 2009)	B	(Erek et al., 2009)
Green IT	B.7	Examining the Contribution of Green IT to the Objectives of IT Departments: Empirical Evidence from German Enterprises	Schmidt, Erek, Kolbe, Zarnekow	Australasian Journal of Information Systems (AJIS)	B	(Schmidt et al., 2010a)
Green IT	B.8	Predictors of Green IT Adoption: Implications from an Empirical Investigation	Schmidt, Erek, Kolbe, Zarnekow	Proceedings of the 16th Americas Conference on Information Systems (AMCIS 2010)	B	(Schmidt et al., 2010b)
Green IT	B.9	Towards a Contingency Model for Green IT Governance	Schmidt, Kolbe	Proceedings of the 19th European Conference on Information Systems (ECIS 2011)	A	(Schmidt & Kolbe, 2011)
Green IT	B.10	Strategic Green IT Planning: Lessons from a Financial Services Case	Schmidt, Langkau, Ruch, Kolbe	Proceedings of the 8th European, Mediterranean and Middle Eastern Conference on Information Systems (EMCIS 2011)	-	(Schmidt et al., 2011)

Table B.1: Summary of Presented Publications

A.3 Sustainability and Information Systems

All papers were published between 2009 and 2011 in the proceedings of international conferences or renowned IS research journals. The publications are ordered according to the levels of sustainability and IS, Green IS, and Green IT. Each publication relates to one key research question in Section A.1.2.

Also listed are the each publication's co-authors, the publication organ, the ranking, and the reference.

The order of the paper's authors corresponds with their contribution. Their share depends on the total number of authors and varies between: 60% to 40% for the first author; 40% to 30% for the second author; and 10% for the third and all following authors. An exact assignment of certain parts of a paper to a specific author is impossible due to the combined work on each paper.

The paper's ranking is based on the recommendations of the scientific commission of information systems within the German association of business and administration (WKWI). The WKWI ranking represents a compilation of the most important journals, conferences, proceedings, and lecture notes for the German-speaking IS research community. The ranking reaches from A (highest) to C (lowest) (WKWI, 2008). Publications in journals, conferences, proceedings, or lecture notes which have yet not been listed in the WKWI ranking are marked with a "-".

Publication B.5 was published in German; therefore, only the abstract is provided in English.

To achieve a homogenous and consistent appearance of this work, all publications were transferred into the current format and citation style. In this process, grammatical, typographical and spelling errors were corrected. Any correction of information or data that alters the meaning of a sentence is highlighted and explained in a footnote. The citation style followed is based on the 6th Edition of the American Psychological Association. Every publication is introduced with a fact sheet that contains meta-information about the authors, affiliation, publication organ, and abstract. The spelling was adapted to American English and the format of graphics and tables were adjusted to achieve a consistent appearance.

1 Sustainable Information Systems Management

Title of Article	Sustainable Information Systems Management
Authors	Nils-Holger Schmidt* nschmid@uni-goettingen.de Koray Erek⁺ koray.erek@tu-berlin.de Lutz M. Kolbe* lkolbe@uni-goettingen.de Rüdiger Zarnekow⁺ ruediger.zarnekow@tu-berlin.de *Georg-August-Universität Göttingen Chair of Information Management Platz der Göttinger Sieben 5 37073 Göttingen ⁺Berlin Institute of Technology (TU Berlin) Chair of Information and Communication Management Strasse des 17. Juni 135 10623 Berlin
Published	Business & Information Systems Engineering (BISE) (English Version of "Wirtschaftsinformatik") (Schmidt et al., 2009b)
Abstract	The increasing dissemination and growing dependency on information technologies and related services create new unconsidered ecological and social challenges for information systems management. Based on the resource-based view, a management cycle of sustainable IS management is developed. Sustainable IS management responds to the demands of stakeholders through a balanced consideration of economic, environmental and social aspects. The explicit consideration of stakeholders, sustainability objectives and resources provides a holistic structural approach and opens up a new research area with a multitude of research questions. By a stronger integration of social science and a renaissance of the resource-based view, Business and Information Systems Engineering research can develop a broad, socially relevant field of research and contribute to its systematic investigation in the future.

Table B.2: Fact Sheet of Publication No. 1

1.1 The Ecological and Social Dimension of Information Systems Management

The increasing dissemination and growing dependency on information technologies (IT) and related services create new, unconsidered ecological and social challenges for information systems (IS) management.

Due to this development, IS management is confronted with new demands from business units, customers and employees. A sustainable IS management covers not only the economical, but also the ecological and social perspective, extending traditional concepts of IS management.

The *ecological impact* of IT through its toxic substances, radiation and energy consumption on humans and nature has been investigated for many years (Eder, 1994). The current discussion about Green IT has brought back the ecological impact of IT into the public and academic focus. IT service providers, such as Google, whose 450,000 operating servers consume approximately 800 gigawatt hours electricity per year, account for tremendous amounts of indirect CO_2 emissions (Chou, 2008). The cumulative energy consumption of all servers worldwide approximately equates to the consumption of the entire Polish economy (Koomey, 2007).

The *social responsibility* of IS management is outlined by the frequent reports about data misuse connected to IT, by which companies, employees or customers are affected. The handling of data within many companies is described as being challenging (Bundesamt für Sicherheit in der Informationstechnik, 2009). Hence, IS management is coming under increasing pressure from external stakeholders. The social dimension of sustainable IS management includes topics of IT utilization by individuals and organizations, but also comprises the challenges of generating, preserving and safeguarding knowledge, information and data.

1.2 Sustainability and Resource Orientation

1.2.1 History and Concept of Sustainability

The predominant understanding of sustainability was shaped by the definition of the Brundtland Commission in 1987, which defined "sustainable development" as a "development that meets the needs of the present without compromising the ability of future generations to meet their own needs" (Hauff, 1987).

At the business level, the concept of sustainability has emerged, based on the objectives of resource conservation and environmental protection, as an equitable and simultaneous consideration of economical, ecological and social objectives, known as the triple bottom line concept of sustainability. In this context, sustainable management can be defined as a concept of long-term simultaneous optimization of economical, ecological and social objectives to generate a lasting superior financial performance for the business (Elkington, 1997). The triple bottom line concept provides a framework against which companies can measure and report their performance and organizational success according to these three pillars.

Addressees of a sustainable management are particularly internal (e. g., departments, employees) and external (e. g., customers, owners, suppliers, investors) stakeholders who exert tangible or intangible influence on the organization through various mechanisms of action; thereby encouraging environmental and social responsible value creation (Freeman, 1984). Sustainable IS management responds to the needs of all these stakeholders through the balanced consideration of economic, environmental and social aspects. By doing so, it contributes to the companies' strategic objectives as well as to IS management's critical resources.

1.2.2 Resource-based View on IS Management

In the scope of corporate sustainability, the resource-based view has proven itself to be an applicable framework for the evaluation of strategically important corporate resources. In this regard, the impulse the resource-based view can provide for the development of a sustainable IS management needs to be investigated. The traditionally limited focus on resources such as information, communication and IT does not cope with today's role of IS management within corporations. From the standpoint of the resourced-based view, the success of IS management results from certain tangible and intangible resources of the organization. Referring to this, Wade and Hulland (2004) identified, from a variety of studies, eight fundamental core resources of IS management. They place these resources into three categories: outside-in, spanning and inside-out resources (Table B.3).

Outside-In	Spanning	Inside-Out
• External relationship management • Market responsiveness	• IS-business partnerships • IS management/planning	• IS infrastructure • IS technical skills • IS development • Cost efficient IS operations

Table B.3: Typology of IS Resources (According to Wade & Hulland, 2004)

The resource-based view states that a competitive advantage and the related success of a corporate function, in this case the IS management, depends on how it is able to obtain, apply and secure valuable resources in the long run (Wade & Hulland, 2004).

1.3 Framework of Sustainable IS Management

1.3.1 Principles and Characteristics

Numerous concepts of IS management have established themselves in the German-speaking world. In general, they can be differentiated into problem oriented, task oriented, process oriented, level oriented and architectural oriented concepts (Krcmar, 2005). These concepts already comprise certain aspects of sustainable IS management without emphasizing them.

Based on the concepts of sustainability and the resource-based view, an ideal model of sustainable IS management can be outlined (Table B.4).

	Characteristics				
	Intention of IS Management	Primary Objectives	Scope of Action *(Resources)*	Primary Stakeholders	Responsibility
Reference Model of Sustainable IS Management	Contribution to the vision and the strategic objectives of the corporation	Weighted, short and long-term economical, ecological and social objectives	Information, knowledge, infrastructure, internal and external relations, market responsiveness	Management board, business divisions, customers, partners, employees, suppliers, investors, NGOs, legislators	CIO/COO

Table B.4: Characteristics of Sustainable IS Management

The purpose of sustainable IS management is to contribute to the vision, the overall strategy and the strategic objectives of the corporation, which do not only inhere economic, but also ecological and social targets.

These objectives do not only apply to information as a resource but also to all other resources identified by the resource-based view. The target groups are all primary stakeholders of IS management. Given the fact that ecological and social topics are integrated tasks of the entire corporation, the main responsibility of IS management might shift to the level of the Chief Operating Officer (COO).

1.3.2 Management Cycle

From the previous sections, the presented aspects of sustainability, the resource-based view, and IS management can be integrated into a management cycle of sustainable IS management (Figure B.1).

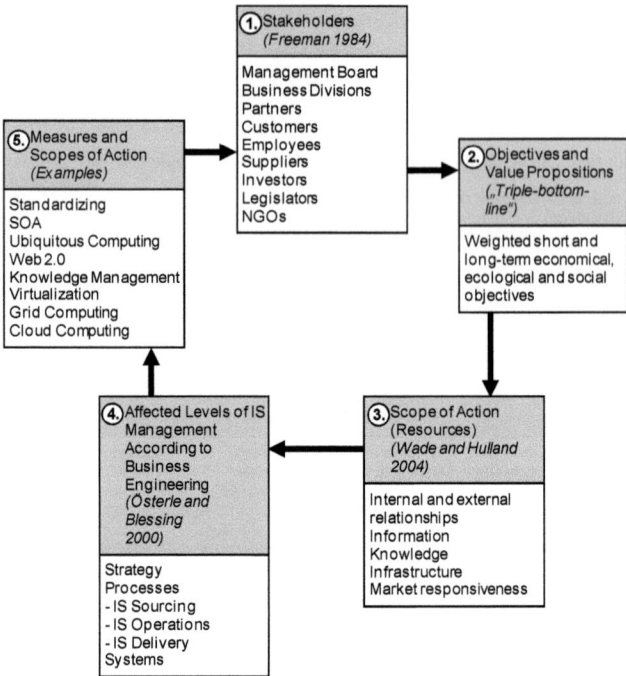

Figure B.1: Management Cycle of Sustainable IS Management

The stakeholders' needs are at the core of all planning considerations by sustainable IS management (Figure B.1[1.]). Depending on their significance and power of influence, weighted short and long-term economical, ecological and social objectives are derived from the triple bottom line concept of sustainable management (Figure B.1[2.]). Sustainable IS management achieves these targets by obtaining, applying and securing its essential resources (Figure B.1[3.]). The implementation is based on the meta-model of Business Engineering on the strategic, process and system level of IS management (Österle & Blessing, 2000) (Figure B.1[4.]). Finally, IS management's concrete measures and different scopes of action meet these stakeholders' demands. Various topics that are currently being discussed, for example service orientation or grid computing, can be motivated by the objectives that sustainable IS management tries to accomplish (Figure B.1[5.]).

Green IT measures, for instance, improve the economic and ecologic impact by cutting energy consumption (Buhl et al., 2009). Thereby demands made by the management boards, the business units and by employees and customers are addressed. The resources that play an important role in this context are primarily infrastructure, internal and external relationships, and market responsiveness. For this reason, the sustainable IS management model can illustrate complex relationships and effects between stakeholders, objectives and measures.

1.3.3 Measures and Implementation on the Process Level

Individual measures can be assigned to the levels of IS management. Server virtualization in the data center, for example, primarily touches the levels of IT operations processes and systems, whereas more complex measures such as grid or cloud computing require change to the overall strategy, the processes and the systems of IS management.

In this way, current measures can be classified. Following Schmidt et al. (2009a), at the process level of sustainable IS management, the ecological and social dimension can be linked within in a portfolio analysis. This approach results in a variety of possible combinations (Table B.5). Thereby, the influence a measure has can be shown, apart from its single-focused economic dimension.

Process Level of IS Management	Key Areas/Dimensions	
	Social Dimension	Ecological Dimension
IS Sourcing	- Employee selection - Software selection - Audits of suppliers - Negotiation of SLAs	- Check for certification - Check for eco-labels (e.g., Energy Star) - TCO analysis
IS Operations	- Compliance to data privacy and data security - Knowledge management (e.g., Web 2.0) - Knowledge generation - Use of standards (e.g., ITIL) - Workstation concepts (Shared Desk) - Communication management (e.g., instant messaging)	- Virtualization concepts - Grid computing - Cloud computing - Thin clients - Cooling concepts in data centers - Wake-on LAN - Compliance to standards and laws
IS Delivery	- Social marketing - Training of customers and employees - Documentation of projects - Stakeholder relationship management	- Eco-marketing - Publication of an ecological balance sheet - Stakeholder relationship management

Table B.5: Exemplary Measures and Their Contribution to the Social and Ecological Dimension of Sustainability (According to Schmidt et al., 2009b)

1.4 Importance for Business and Information Systems Engineering Research

Ecological and social topics related to IS management are likely to gain importance in the future. On the one hand, the global share of IT induced CO_2 emissions will increase to 3% by 2020. On the other hand, IT is an enabler of intelligent business and production processes or environmental software applications and can therefore contribute to responsible resource consumption within corporations (Buhl et al., 2009). These inward-looking and outward-looking perspectives are integrated in the concept of sustainable IS management.

For Business and Information Systems Engineering (BISE) research, the explicit consideration of stakeholders, sustainability objectives and resources provides a holistic structural approach and opens up a new research area with a multitude of research questions. This leads to the question regarding the measures by which IT can contribute to satisfying the specific ecological and social needs of single internal and external stakeholder groups[4]. In this context, opportunities and risks of the increasing interconnectedness need to be evaluated to deduce implications for the companies' IS management. If IT develops like other industries, such as the automotive industry, the importance of ecological and social topics, as well as regulatory conditions, is likely to increase. In many large-scale enterprises, business units already specify quantitative sustainability targets for their IT. Therefore, the complementation of existent IS management models seems reasonable.

By a stronger integration of social science and a renaissance of the resource-based view, BISE research can develop a broad, socially relevant field of research and contribute to its systematic investigation in the future.

---

[4] The sentence has been reformulated for better understanding.

2 Towards a Procedural Model for Sustainable Information Systems Management

Title of Article	Towards a Procedural Model for Sustainable Information Systems Management[5]
Authors	Nils-Holger Schmidt* nschmid@uni-goettingen.de Koray Erek† koray.erek@tu-berlin.de Lutz M. Kolbe* lkolbe@uni-goettingen.de Rüdiger Zarnekow† ruediger.zarnekow@tu-berlin.de *Georg-August-Universität Göttingen Chair of Information Management Platz der Göttinger Sieben 5 37073 Göttingen †Berlin Institute of Technology (TU Berlin) Chair of Information and Communication Management Strasse des 17. Juni 135 10623 Berlin
Published	Proceedings of the 42nd Hawaii International Conference on System Sciences (HICSS 2009) (Schmidt et al., 2009a)
Abstract	The increasing economical, ecological and social significance of information systems (IS) demands reorientation for IS management. Ever-growing energy consumption, waste streams, data amounts, and performance expectations require management that considers these forces. While concepts of corporate social responsibility or sustainability have been applied to other industries, IS still lacks a theoretical and conceptional foundation. The purpose of this paper is to apply the concept of sustainability in the field of IS management. As a contribution to the ongoing discussion of Green IT, we provide a theoretical foundation and justification of sustainable IS management, using the resource-based view. Thereafter, we develop a sustainable IS management procedural model that outlines the most important steps towards the implementation of sustainability within IS organizations. This model should provide IS managers, such as CIOs, with a framework for including sustainability in business operations.

Table B.6: Fact Sheet of Publication No. 2

---

[5] © 2009 IEEE. Reprinted, with permission, from Schmidt, N.-H., Erek, K., Kolbe, L. M., & Zarnekow, R., Towards a Procedural Model for Sustainable Information Systems Management, Proceedings of the 42nd Hawaii International Conference on System Sciences (HICSS 2009)

2.1 Introduction

Owing to the growing global impact of IS[6] on the economy, ecology and society, IS management is increasingly challenged to take sustainability into account. Sustainable management can be understood as a concept of long-term, simultaneous optimization of economical, ecological and social objectives to generate a lasting, superior financial performance for the business (Elkington, 1997; Epstein, 2008).

In 2008, the global information and communication technology (ICT) spending was expected to grow by 10.3% to over US$3.7 trillion, accounting for a share of 6.4% of the World's gross domestic product (GDP) (World Information Technology and Service Alliance, 2008). From the world's 50 most innovative companies, 16 are highly ICT related (Businessweek, 2007).

The ecological impact of the IS business has been discussed under the heading "Green IT", which has been the key topic of the CeBIT 2008, the world's largest ICT trade fair, showing its practical relevance for the ICT business. The global ICT industry is claimed to account for approximately two percent of global carbon dioxide (CO_2), a figure equivalent to the aviation industry (Gartner Inc., 2007). A 2005 study on the global power consumption of servers revealed that worldwide, including related cooling and auxiliary infrastructure, servers used 123,000 Giga Watt hours (GWh) of electricity, an amount comparable to the power consumption of a country such as Poland (Koomey, 2007). Google alone operates about 450,000 servers, consuming nearly 800 GWh a year (Chou, 2008).

Social and ecological problems additionally derive from waste of electronic products (e-waste), which increases by three to five percent each year, making it the fastest growing waste stream in the industrialized world (United Nations Environment Programme, 2007). Information and communication equipment, as well as monitors, make up 25% of the approximately 20 to 50 million tons of e-waste generated each year. This means that a minimum of 5 million tons per year of ICT related waste is produced, an amount comparable to the weight of almost 9000 fully loaded Airbus A380 passenger planes containing dangerous metals, such as lead, mercury and cadmium.

However, sustainability in IS does not only cover Green IT. Further challenges derive from information waste, clogging up IS. Analysts from IDC (International Data Corporation) (Gantz et al., 2008) expect an increase in the amount of digital information produced from 281 exabytes in 2007 to 1,800 exabytes in 2011.

---

[6] Henceforth information systems (IS) are defined as a combination of information and communication technology (ICT), people, processes, and organizational mechanisms, to gather, process, store, use and disseminate information to improve organizational performance (McNurlin & Sprague, 2006).

The above facts not only point to a huge need, but also to a great complexity in sustainable IS management. Porter and Reinhardt (2007) argue that companies have no other choice than to deal with sustainability, and that the challenge has moved from "whether" to "how" to integrate corporate sustainability into day-to-day management decisions. Despite the hype in trade press, especially concerning Green IT, the topic of sustainability in IS management still lacks a theoretical foundation. The research questions arising from this are:

- What is the scope of sustainable IS management?
- Which theoretical foundations can be applied to the concept of sustainability?
- What are the links between sustainable IS management and business value?
- How can sustainability be efficiently implemented in IS management?

In order to address these questions, we need to create a clear view of IS management and the concept of sustainability. The next step is to outline the connection between sustainable IS management and business benefits. For this, we propose using the resource-based view (RBV). We will argue that sustainable IS management helps to accumulate, secure and foster competitive advantage, resulting in superior long-term IS performance. Consequently, we introduce a procedural model for sustainable IS management, which provides a theoretical foundation and a starting point for further research in this field.

2.2 Towards Sustainable IS Management

2.2.1 The Value Chain of IS Business

In order to define the field of research, it is necessary to identify the relevant scope of IS management and to outline the key activities of IS product and service provisioning. The IS business consists of internal (in-house) and external organizations that provide products and services that can be assigned to ICT, including hardware, software and services. These types of enterprises generally follow the processes *source*, *make*, *deliver*, and *return* through which the value creation takes place. The management of these processes defines the scope of IS management.

The foundation for this process oriented concept originated with the supply chain operations reference (SCOR) model (Supply-Chain Council Inc., 2006), a well-known value chain concept in industrial management, which makes it applicable for IS hardware providers. The transfer of the SCOR model to IS software and IS service providers has been done by Zarnekow et al. (2006) by developing the integrated information management (IIM) model. The IIM model focuses on the whole IS value chain, including customer and supplier relationships, while traditional IS management concepts focus on the management of applications (Hochstein et al., 2006). Figure B.2 illustrates the value chain of IS business, including a *return* process and *stakeholders' interests*:

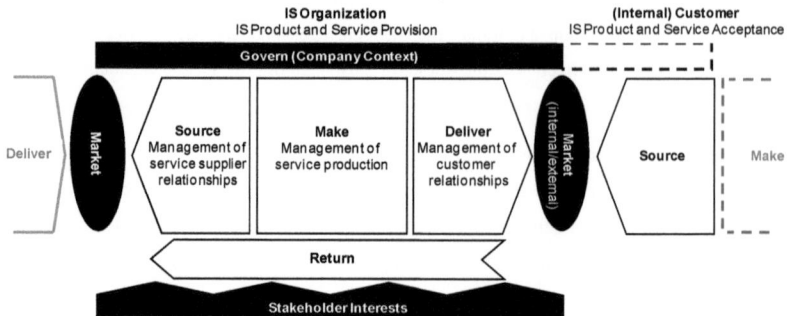

Figure B.2: Value Chain of Information Systems Product and Service Provision

The *govern* process encompasses the strategic functions, procedures, and measures that ensure that allocated IS products and services contribute to the business goal achievements. In particular, IS governance determines the supervisory functions, organizational structures, and processes. The core tasks are divided into strategic alignment, value delivery, risk management, controlling, and resource management.

The *source* process covers all tasks that form part of supplier relationships management. Usually, IS organizations purchase hardware components, software solutions, personnel, and other technological resources. These resources are used in the production phase and are transformed to marketable IS products.

The *make* process comprises all tasks for the management of IS product- and service production. Based on an industrial management procedure, the make process is divided into portfolio management, development management, and production management. The focus is therefore on the efficient planning, development, and production of IS components.

The *delivery* process is responsible for the customer relationships management and depicts classical sales. The main objective is to transform customer demands into internal requirement specifications for IS production. Otherwise, it communicates internal capabilities and basic conditions to the customer. Hence, the delivery process has a mediator function between the internal *make* and the customer's *source* process.

Based on the original SCOR model, we include a *return* process into the supply chain operations. The *return* phase depicts the processes of recycling, preserving and reusing tangible and/or intangible resources, clarifying that possessed resources or means of production used or produced in the value chain are recyclable, and fundamental information (e.g., customer requirements) has to be documented and preserved for internal analysis and future strategic directions of the company. Moreover, it ensures a life cycle oriented view on IS products and services, including a waste management and reutilization of products in the value chain.

In addition, stakeholders' interests are taken into account. The reason for doing so is that the diversity of stakeholders, such as shareholders, policy-makers, suppliers, labor unions, customers and others can have a major impact on corporate - in this case IS management - performance. In summary, the model cuts the value chain into four core processes that have to be considered simultaneously to implement sustainability in IS management.

2.2.2 Understanding the Concept of Sustainability

Sustainability has been extensively discussed within corporate management[7] under the synonyms of corporate social responsibility (CSR), greening the business, eco-efficiency, and eco-advantage. Although many studies concerning sustainable management have been introduced, sustainability in IS has not been evaluated until now. Global development and challenges (see Section B.2.1), as well as the general need to align IS strategy to corporate strategy, form the need for an integrated concept of sustainability in IS.

The word "sustain" derives from the Latin "sustenere" (Hülsmann & Grapp, 2005). In its primary sense, it can be described as survival assurance, meaning that an economical, ecological or social system should be preserved for future generations and, thus, necessary resources should only be exploited to a degree to which it is possible to restore them within a regeneration cycle. The most common definition, from the Brundtland Commission, defines sustainability as a "development that meets the needs of the present without compromising the ability of future generations to meet their own needs" (World Commission on Environment and Development, 1987). All definitions of sustainability have the preservation of the economical, ecological and social system for the benefit of future generations in common. These dimensions represent the three main pillars of sustainability and are known as the triple bottom line concept (Elkington, 1997). The triple bottom line concept provides a framework for companies to measure and report their performance and organizational success in relation to these pillars.

Especially at the business level, sustainability is mainly equated with economical or financial sustainability (Dyllick & Hockerts, 2002). However, integrated corporate sustainability is achieved

---

[7] For some works on the topic, see (Epstein, 2008; Esty & Winston, 2006; Porter & van der Linde, 1995; Schaltegger & Wagner, 2006; Smith, 1992).

by recognizing the interdependence of the three dimensions over time and keeping an optimal balance between them (Marcus, 2005).

2.2.3 Sustainability within the Resources of IS

Owing to the importance of resources in sustainable management, we apply the resource-based view of the firm. This view argues that a firm's competitive advantage depends upon its ability to accumulate, generate, deploy and secure unique and valuable resources (Barney, 1991; Grant, 1991). Following the RBV, a sustainable competitive advantage evolves if the resources are also not easily duplicated by competitors (Barney, 1991; Hart, 1995). This indicates a highly economically oriented understanding of sustainability. Competitors are not the only determinant of a sustainable competitive advantage. Resources face various influences by stakeholder groups, thereby determining the sustainability of a competitive advantage or its loss, for example, through governmental regulation.

Categories of resources include core resources that lead to a competitive advantage over competitors; threshold resources that are essential for competing in a market; and unnecessary resources that can be neglected by the firm (Johnson & Scholes, 2006). Focusing on resources allows us to explain differences in profitability and strategy among firms in terms of resource differences (Clemons & Row, 1991).

A challenge is to define what is meant by a resource. Researchers and practitioners have used a variety of different terms to talk about a firm's resources (Amit & Schoemaker, 1993; Grant, 1991; Johnson & Scholes, 2006). Hart (1995) defines resources as the basic units of analysis and includes physical and financial assets, as well as employees' skills and organizational processes.

In this paper, we follow the definition of Wade and Hulland (2004). They define resources "...as assets and capabilities that are available and useful in detecting and responding to market opportunities or threats". Assets and capabilities therefore define the firm's resources[8]. Assets are either tangible or intangible and are used in the firm's processes to create, produce and/or deliver its goods and/or services to a market (Sanchez et al., 1996). Assets can serve as inputs to a process, or as the outputs of a process (Srivastava et al., 1998). From an IS point of view, tangible assets are, for example, information systems hardware, network infrastructure or server buildings, while intangible assets are, for instance, software patents or stored information (Itami & Roehl, 1991; Srivastava et al., 1998). Capabilities transform inputs into outputs of higher value (Amit &

---

[8] Note: Following Wade and Hulland (2004) we view the terms capabilities, competencies, and core competencies as essentially synonymous.

Schoemaker, 1993; Sanchez et al., 1996). Capabilities include, for example, skills, managerial abilities, and processes (Wade & Hulland, 2004).

Sustainability in IS can have two meanings: On the one hand, sustainability can be seen as a capability that a company can accumulate and possess (Hart, 1995). On the other hand, sustainability can be seen as a cross-sectional objective that applies to all IS resources, to improve their accumulation, generation, deployment, and securing, thereby generating competitive advantages. In this paper, we focus on the latter perspective.

2.3 Theoretical Foundation of Sustainable IS Management

Since we follow the IS value chain (Section B.2.2.1), we assign three different theories to justify sustainable management in each of the phases: Transaction cost theory (TCT) can be applied to *source*, production theory (PT) to *make* and stakeholder theory (ST) to *govern* and *deliver*.

Resources are either produced internally from other resources or acquired from the firm's environment (Clemons & Row, 1991). TCT investigates the coordination of transactions, which can be defined as the transfer of a resource's property rights between two contracting parties (Coase, 1937; Williamson, 1985).

The specificity and uncertainty connected to this transaction determines the transaction costs for different types of coordination possibilities. These possibilities range from in-house production (make) over long-term contracts (hybrid) to spontaneous market acquisitions (buy) (Picot et al., 2003). TCT claims that the higher the specificity and uncertainty of the transaction are, the more efficient a sustainable solution becomes, in the form of long-term contracts and eventually in in-house coordination because of transaction costs. Sustainable management of the resource strengthens the ties between the contracting parties beyond the economical level within the sourcing process, thereby intensifying and securing their long-term relationships. Especially for resource transactions with high specificity and uncertainty, this would lead to lower transaction costs in comparison to other coordination mechanisms. That is the reason why some companies that have employees as their core resources offer additional social incentives to intensify and secure this relationship.

PT deals with the efficient input-output relations. Nowadays, many resources, especially those with high ecological and social impact, are connected with economic incentives imposed by stakeholders. These incentives might, for instance, derive from government regulations to secure more efficient technologies for lower energy consumption, green investments, or they could be immaterial, for example an award acknowledging the company's sustainable behavior. It is obvious that these ecological and social incentives need to be recognized to determinate an optimal input-output relationship for IS product and service production. Schaltegger and Synnestvedt (2002) point out that a limited amount of ecological and social activities[9] lead to an increase in economic success up to a point; thereafter, the costs of these activities exceed the benefits, leading to decreasing economic success. The managerial challenge as Schaltegger and Synnestvedt (2002) state is to choose the optimal level of ecological and social activities to achieve the highest economic success and to obtain this level at the lowest possible costs.

Stakeholder theory is a normative theory of corporate social responsibility. It states that the manager's duty is to balance the shareholders' financial interests against the interests of other stakeholders such as employees, customers and the local community, even if it reduces the shareholder returns. The managers' objective within the stakeholder theory is to balance profit maximization with the long-term ability to do business. Stakeholders are voluntarily or involuntarily connected to the companies' resources, making them potential risk bearers for the companies' fortune (Smith, 2003). A possible classification distinguishes between five typical groups of stakeholders: investors and risk assessors, rulemakers and watchdogs, idea generators and opinion leaders, business partners and competitors, and consumers and the community (Porter & van der Linde, 1995).

The sustainable management of resources, within the economical, ecological and social dimensions, seems to provide orientation on how to balance profit maximization and stakeholders' interests. An increasing extent of sustainability activities leads to higher costs but also to lower calculated expenditures due to declining stakeholder risks (Figure B.3).

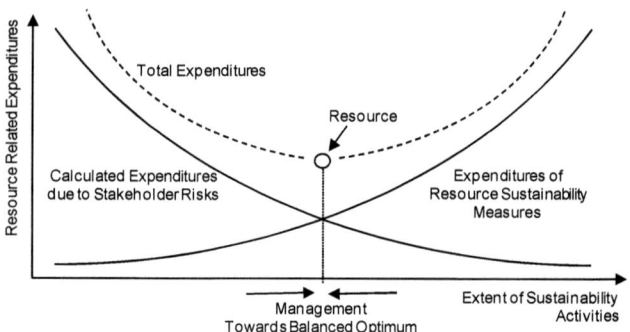

Figure B.3: The Connection Between Sustainability and Stakeholder Risks

---

[9] Note: Schaltegger and Synnestvedt (2002) use the term "Environmental activities". In this paper we see "Environmental activities" as a generic term for ecological and social activities.

The objective of sustainable management is therefore to identify and obtain a balanced optimum by keeping the resource related expenditures at a minimum. Notable is the fact that over time the calculated expenditures due to stakeholder risks, such as new regulations or customer expectations, might shift, thereby creating a demand for active management.

2.4 Implementing Sustainability in IS – A Procedural Model

In Section B.2.2 and Section B.2.3 we showed the relevance of sustainable IS management from a theoretical perspective. This creates the need for a model or framework that supports a practical implementation and leads us back to the initial question: How can sustainability be efficiently implemented in IS management?

In this section, we propose a procedural model for the implementation of sustainable IS management that is applied over the entire value-chain of IS (Figure B.4). The starting point is IS resources. They are evaluated with regard to their impact on the economic success, the ecology and their social relevance. Thereafter, the measures need to be prioritized before they finally get implemented. Continuous controlling will ensure balance of the sustainability objectives.

2.4.1 Resource Identification

There are many approaches for identifying IS resources: McKeen and Smith (2003) divide IS resources into technology, people and processes, which are needed to meet the challenges of the firm. Bharadwaj et al. (1999) suggest six dimensions: IT/business partnerships, external IT linkages, business IT strategic thinking, IT business process integration, IT management, and IT infrastructure. Wade and Hulland (2004)[10], analyze a broad variety of IS studies, dealing with the resource-based view and extracted eight key IS resources: external relationship management, market responsiveness, IS business partnerships, IS planning and change management, IS infrastructure, IS technical skills, IS development, and cost effective operations.

---

[10] Note: For a more comprehensive overview see (Wade & Hulland, 2004)

Figure B.4: Procedural Model for Sustainable Information Systems Management

Practitioners from the Office of Government Commerce (OGC) (Rudd & Lloyd, 2007) distinguish between capabilities such as management, organization, processes, knowledge, and assets such as information, applications, infrastructure, and financial capital, which are combined to create goods or services of value. In general, it can be said that resources of IS infrastructure include tangibles, such as buildings, machinery, IS hardware, electrical equipment, and any kind of office installations, as well as intangibles that enable their usage, such as electricity, water, paper or location. Knowledge resources can be seen as capabilities that include the insights, understanding, and practical know-how of employees (Galliers & Leidner, 2003). This knowledge can be classified into tacit and explicit knowledge (Nonaka, 1994). Tacit knowledge is connected to people and is deeply rooted in action, commitment, and involvement in a specific context, which makes it hard to externalize (e.g., skills, talents, way of thinking, attitude, manners, and cultural competence). Explicit knowledge is transmittable in formal, systematic language and is generated by combination or externalization (e.g., applications, manuals, and reference models) (Nonaka, 1994). IS governance is defined by Weill and Ross (2004) as "specifying the decision rights and accountability framework to encourage desirable behavior in the use of IT." Resource of IS governance therefore subsume capabilities dealing with management, organization or processes.

Certain resources are interconnected, as Hart (1995) states, meaning the accumulation, generation, deployment and securing of certain resources might depend upon other resources being developed first.

2.4.2 Assessment of IS Resources

The first step in the assessment is the characterization of each IS resource as core, threshold, or unnecessary (see Section B.2.2.3). Core resources have to be preserved in order to remain competitive in the present and future. Threshold resources might not lead to a competitive advantage, but there might be no possibility to get rid of them either (e.g., electricity, local authorities). Unnecessary resources are not inevitably useless to IS; they might even generate some benefits, but they are not essential for survival and can be sold, outsourced, or just neglected in the future. Helpful questions to determine the type of resource are provided by Weill and Ross (2004): "What is the unique and valuable position targeted by the firm?" and "What core processes embody the organization's unique market position?"

In the next step, the ecological and social impact, which determines the amount of externalities, has to be evaluated. A high amount of externalities, by a resource increases the potential risk from stakeholders. This offers ways to differentiate from competitors and makes external incentives more likely. A low amount of externalities makes sustainable management less advisable. Generally, portfolio planning models represent a two-dimensional, matrix-based framework that can be used to evaluate business unit performance, to formulate business unit strategies, and to set performance targets (Grant, 2005).

The significance of the IS resource and its externalities can be positioned in a portfolio to generate strategic orientation of the degree to which sustainable measures should be taken or not (Figure B.5).

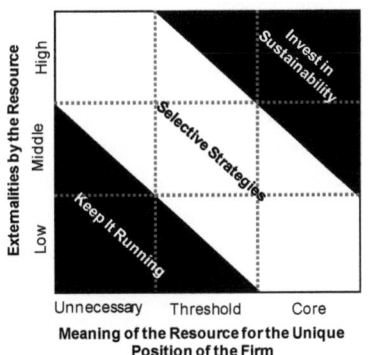

Figure B.5: Assessment of Resources

As shown in the portfolio, three strategic directions can be derived: "Keep it running", "Selective strategies", and "Invest in sustainability". While "Keep it running" matches a lower importance of the resource with a low externality, the strategy "Invest in sustainability" represents a major impact on the performance by the resource and high externalities as well. Resources categorized in this quadrant can be defined as core resources that need to be managed sustainably.

2.4.3 Identification of Measures

The next step is to identify measures that support the ecological and social dimensions of a resource in order to control or minimize its externalities. Applying sustainability to IS management requires an integrated view of the entire value chain of IS organizations. For each of the phases of IS organizations that provide hardware, software or services, we open up an initial continuum of appropriate measures. Table B.7 gives an exploratory overview, and depicts some already existing concepts that are currently under discussion. Grid computing, for instance, is a concept that describes the collaboration of computers to perform very large computing tasks together. Its objective is to provide the maximum service output with a minimum of computing power input, which leads to lower energy consumption in total. Therefore, we positioned grid computing in the *make* phase of IS services. In the deliver phase, standardized reporting is recommended. An example of this is the EU Code of Conduct for Data Centers to which the organization could refer in order to underline its commitment towards stakeholders.

2.4.4 Prioritization and Implementation

In the next step, the selected measures assigned have to be prioritized with respect to feasibility, importance, and cost-effectiveness. The decision to pursue specific measures within certain resources can be based on costs, values and risks that result from those measures. Many techniques are already present for prioritizing projects that can also be used in this case: Some well known methods are the cost-benefit or value benefit analysis, the portfolio analysis, the analytic hierarchy process or the prioritization via specific criteria in a checklist. Regardless of the method of choice, it is essential to take a top-down approach. The prioritization process should be aligned to the actual business strategy (e.g., revenue increase, expense reduction, and efficiency gains). In addition, the firm's strategic position affects the decision: A first mover or an innovator, for instance, will have different preferences to a fast follower. Furthermore, the dependencies between several resources should be considered, so that the sustainable measures of one resource can have a positive or negative impact on others. The value benefit analysis provides a solution and is similar to the analytic hierarchy process (Jiang & Klein, 1999). In this case, certain criteria have to be identified and selected. Such criteria can be the minimization of risk or the economic impact of the resource. The decision-makers have to assess each chosen criteria for its contribution to the firm's performance and strategic direction, based on these criteria. This is a critical step because improper selection of weights can influence the decision.

The next step is to score each resource across all defined parameters in order to determine the overall resource score. The resources should be scored by executives for their degree of agreement on a specific scale. As those priorities change because of the altered strategic relevance of IS to an organization, the weights can be adjusted correspondingly, so that the score for each resource is always in line with the business strategy. When all selected resources are scored, they can be ranked to determine the highest score. Finally, the number of resources that will be selected can be based on total investments available or on other constraints under which the firm operates. Once the measures are prioritized, they can be implemented.

Value Chain	General Objectives	Types of ICT Products		
		Hardware	Software	Services
Source	- Demand transparency - Demand compliance to standards - Create lasting incentive systems	- Check for fair labor conditions - Secure natural resources - Check for ISO 9001, 14001	- Recruiting - Comply with social standards	- Check for eco-labels (e.g., Energy Star) - Negotiate lasting service level agreements (SLAs) - Check for certified suppliers (e.g., ITIL)
Make	- Minimize input - Maximize output - Control risks - Comply to standards	- Reduce emission and waste - Efficient production technologies - Minimize hazardous substances (e.g., RoHS, WEEE)	- Knowledge management - Knowledge management tools - Efficient coding - Use of lasting standards - Development of environmental software	- Virtualization - Grid computing - Cloud computing - Green IT hardware - Thin clients - Cooling and auxiliary
Deliver	- Underline commitment - Use standardized reporting - Cooperate with stakeholder groups	- Environmental marketing - Comply to transparency guidelines (e.g., GRI) - Customer relationship management - Comply with stakeholder standards (e.g., Greenpeace)	- Documentation - Comply to transparency guidelines - Training - Customer relationship management	- Environmental marketing - Comply with transparency guidelines (e.g., EU Code of Conduct for Data Centers) - Customer relationship management (e.g., ITIL)
Return	- Reuse all possible resources - Secure and manage remaining resources - Evaluate and improve	- Recycling of components - Use customer input - Safe disposal of waste	- Reuse of modules - Reuse of knowledge - Validate knowledge - Use customer input	- Reuse of infrastructure - Use of lost heat - Use customer input

Table B.7: Objectives and Exemplary ICT Sustainability Measures

2.4.5 Monitor and Evaluate

In this step, the applied sustainability actions have to be measured and evaluated with appropriate indicators. This approach can help business managers to continuously monitor the efforts towards sustainable IS management. Indeed, the reporting is an essential part of corporate sustainability. While it highlights inefficiencies in operations to managers, it can also be used for showcasing the sustainability efforts that have been undertaken by the company to reduce risks and to seize opportunities for improving competitive advantages. This increase of transparency can improve the company's attractiveness to investors and customers.

The reporting guidelines published by the Global Reporting Initiative (GRI) provide the most widely used sustainability reporting framework, as well as principles and indicators that can be used by organizations to measure and report their economic, environmental, and social performance (Global Reporting Initiative, 2006). These standardized guidelines make it possible to benchmark organizational performance with respect to regulators such as lawmakers or industry oversight committees. Moreover, it forms the basis for communicating organizational commitment to sustainable development and to satisfy the information needs of internal and external stakeholders.

In order to define appropriate metrics, the sustainability measures identified in Table B.7 have to be translated into measurable goals (Epstein & Roy, 2001). The goals have to be in accord with the corporate strategy as well as with the basic conditions within each value chain phase (e.g., sourcing strategy). An example for such metrics within the *source* process could be the number of ISO 14001 certified suppliers, or the percentage of suppliers with green or eco-labeled products such as the TCO label for IT equipment or the energy star label, which defines certain energy efficiency criteria for each product (Proto et al., 2007).

For translating sustainability strategy into specific performance indicators, existing management systems such as the balanced scorecard by Kaplan and Norton can be widened with a sustainability perspective (Figge et al., 2002).

Another possibility for reporting the effectiveness of sustainable IS management is to create a sustainability maturity model. Based on the capability maturity model (CMM) that was designed by the Software Engineering Institute of the Carnegie Mellon University as a process improvement approach, a sustainability maturity model can be defined to guide the organization towards sustainable IS management via specific goals and management ratios. The organization's structuring into certain maturity levels will show opportunities to improve its performance in order to get into the next higher level. In addition, the maturity level of the IS organization can be used as a performance indicator to customers and other stakeholders.

2.4.6 Case of an IS Service Provider

To illustrate the procedural model of sustainable IS management, we apply it to an IS service provider (ISP). The ISP mainly works for the airline and aviation industry. It has more than 3,000 employees in offices in 16 countries. Its consulting portfolio addresses all airline business processes. As a system integrator, it also runs a sophisticated data center and covers the entire spectrum of IS services, including consulting, application development and implementation, and reliable 24-hour operation.

According to the procedural model (Figure B.4), the first step is to identify all resources, capabilities and assets of the ISP and group them into the categories of core, threshold, and unnecessary. Besides others, the data center can be considered a core resource. The next step is to assess the data center along the IS value chain, to evaluate its externalities (see Table B.7, column "Services"). During the *source* process, it needs the constant availability of electricity and data lines from external suppliers. The *make* process consumes high amounts of electricity to create services. In the *deliver* process, the data center might provide services that are vital to other organizations. This leads to many externalities. From the portfolio analysis, a recommendation for an investment in sustainable measures is derived. These measures need to be identified. Concerning energy consumption, concepts such as server virtualization or efficient cooling equipment can provide energy reduction methods. Limitations of any kind, such as financial constraints, demand a prioritization of available measures that would lead to potential projects and an implementation. After the implementation, the economical, ecological, and social effectiveness have to be monitored and evaluated before the process of sustainable IS management restarts.

2.5 Conclusion and Future Research

In this paper, we have shown that sustainability is relevant in IS management. While sustainability has been successfully adopted in several sectors, the ICT industry is challenged to develop its own view on the topic. We provided a theoretical foundation for the topic and suggested a procedural model for implementing sustainability in IS management, using the resource-based view. This approach can be adopted by IS managers and CIOs for applying the concept into their daily business.

To refine the suggested model, our future research will follow the next steps:

1. further rounds of case studies and expert interviews, using the Delphi method;
2. integrated implementation of a sustainability strategy by adding sustainability into approved management systems such as IT balanced scorecard;
3. development of a sustainability maturity model (Section B.2.4.5) with certain management ratios to monitor and evaluate the progress of IS organizations towards sustainable IS management; and
4. exemplary benchmarking of IS organizations on the basis of the maturity model.

IS organizations must know how important sustainable measures are to remain competitive in the future. In addition to the enhanced efficiency through operations via product or service innovations, sustainability in IS management can improve the corporate reputation, the firm's competitive advantage, and its attractiveness to investors and customers. Given the rising prices of energy and other resources, the relevance of sustainability will gain even more importance in the future.

Hence, sustainability has an increased relevance for policy-makers, practitioners, and researchers. As a result, we reason that sustainability is applicable in IS business and can have a positive impact on IS business performance.

3 Influence of Green IT on Consumers' Buying Behavior of Personal Computers: Implications from a Conjoint Analysis

Title of Article	Influence of Green IT on Consumers' Buying Behavior of Personal Computers: Implications from a Conjoint Analysis
Authors	Nils-Holger Schmidt* nschmid@uni-goettingen.de Timo Schmidtchen* info@timo-schmidtchen.de Koray Erek✝ koray.erek@tu-berlin.de Lutz M. Kolbe* lkolbe@uni-goettingen.de Rüdiger Zarnekow✝ ruediger.zarnekow@tu-berlin.de *Georg-August-Universität Göttingen Chair of Information Management Platz der Göttinger Sieben 5 37073 Göttingen ✝Berlin Institute of Technology (TU Berlin) Chair of Information and Communication Management Strasse des 17. Juni 135 10623 Berlin
Published	Proceedings of the 18th European Conference on Information System (ECIS 2010) (Schmidt et al., 2010d)
Abstract	The increasing focus on information technology's (IT) environmental impact demands reorientation from IT hardware and service organizations. Consumers are more sensitive than ever before about the environmental impact of the products and services they buy. Environmental attributes therefore play an important role in the buying process. While the concept of Green IT has been primarily researched from the corporate perspective, the consumer perspective has widely been neglected. The purpose of this paper is to evaluate the influence of Green IT attributes of PCs (Personal Computers) on consumers' buying behavior. As a contribution to the ongoing discussion about Green IT, we provide marketing data gathered from 500 participants on the importance of Green IT, using conjoint and cluster analysis. It is shown that the market share for Green IT PCs could be as large as 26.6%. Especially female customers value environmentally friendly attributes. We make recommendations regarding the marketing mix of IT hardware and service organizations. The results should provide researchers and practitioners with new insights and measures about Green IT's relevance and its application in the scope of PCs.

Table B.8: Fact Sheet of Publication No. 3

3.1 Introduction

Due to the growing global impact of information technology (IT) on the economy, ecology and society, management in IT hardware manufacturers and IT service organizations is increasingly being challenged to take sustainability and Green IT into account for their products and services. A 2005 study on the global power consumption of servers revealed that worldwide, including related cooling and auxiliary infrastructure, servers used 123,000 GWh (Giga Watt hours) of electricity, an amount comparable to the power consumption of a country such as Poland (Koomey, 2007; Schmidt et al., 2009a). IT accounts for two percent or 820 million tons of CO_2 emissions per year (Heng, 2009). Waste of electronic products (e-waste) is increasing three to five percent each year, making it the fastest growing waste stream in the industrialized world (United Nations Environment Programme, 2007). At least five million tons per year of information and communication technology (ICT) related waste is being produced, which is comparable to the weight of almost 9,000 fully loaded Airbus A380 passenger planes containing dangerous metals, such as lead, mercury, and cadmium. These environmental impacts of IT have recently been discussed under the heading of "Green IT" (Schmidt et al., 2009a).

Scientific literature on Green IT primarily looks at the topic from a corporate perspective (Erek et al., 2009; Mines & Davis, 2007; Molla, 2008; Velte et al., 2008). To determine the general relevance of Green IT, this one-sided perspective is insufficient. It is necessary to ask if Green IT attributes actually influence the consumers' buying behavior of a product or service. The hardware manufacturer Apple, for example, follows a Green IT product strategy for its notebooks with its MacBook Pro (Apple Inc., 2009).

Consequently, the question is asked regarding Green IT attributes ability to influence consumers' behavior when they buy PCs. Marketing research on green purchasing behavior for other product types indicate that consumers appraise environmentally friendly product attributes, and that women value them more than men (Chitra, 2007; Lee, 2009).

In the setting of this study, we presented twelve different product concepts of PCs to 500 participants, asking them to order them according to their own preferences. Using conjoint analysis, we were then able to calculate partial utility estimates for each of the Green IT attributes. Through cluster analysis, implications for the marketing mix of IT hardware and service organizations were derived. Through this research, these organizations are able to efficiently address the environmental demands of their customers in the scope of PCs.

3.2 Theoretical Background and Research Questions

The term "Green IT" comprises a very large domain of many different measures and perspectives, making its underlying concept diffuse and ambiguous. In practice, no common definition has been found for Green IT, which hampers a clear view on the topic. One widespread definition is provided by the Green IT Observatory of the RMIT University (Royal Melbourne Institute of Technology University), which defined Green IT as follows:

"Green IT addresses a broad range of business sustainability and corporate social responsibility concerns. This includes the efficient design of data centers and IT architecture to reduce both energy consumption and cost, as well as IT's adoption of environmentally friendly technologies and environmentally preferable IT management practices" (RMIT University, 2009).

This broad definition, from a business perspective, refers to the general strategic, organizational and technical aspects of Green IT. For this research, a more technical and consumer oriented definition is needed, from which Green IT attributes for PCs can be derived. The definition followed in the paper is provided by Elliot and Binney (2008), who refer to Green IT as "the design, production, operation and disposal of ICT and ICT-enabled products and services in a manner that is not harmful and may be positively beneficial to the environment during the course of its whole-of-life". PCs belong to ICT. From the customers' perspective, the energy consumption during operation and disposal of a PC at the end of its life cycle can be considered as Green IT attributes.

Initial studies in Germany demonstrated that Green IT attributes, operationalized through energy consumption and disposal specifications, potentially have an influence on the buying behavior of ICT, e.g., notebooks, mobile phones, and PCs (BITKOM, 2008). Specifically with regard to PCs, this leads to the first question to be answered in this research.

Question 1: What impact do PCs' Green IT attributes have on consumers' buying behavior?

From the operationalization of Green IT attributes into energy consumption and disposal specifications, two subordinated questions are derived.

Question 2: What impact do PCs' energy attributes have on consumers' buying behavior?

Question 3: What impact do PCs' disposal attributes have on consumers' buying behavior?

Consequently, the question arises regarding the size of the potential market share for PCs with Green IT attributes. Hints are provided by the consumer group LOHAS. LOHAS stands for "lifestyle of health and sustainability" and describes a "movement with strong influence on consumption and values" (Ray & Anderson, 2001; Wenzel et al., 2007) within society. This lifestyle does not portray an exclusive target group but a "new social majority" (Wenzel et al.,

2007). The trend can be observed in the food industry with the increasing prominence of organic food. It is likely to disseminate into other industries (Ray & Anderson, 2001).

The expanding share of LOHAS on the German market was estimated to be one-third in 2007 (Wenzel et al., 2007). Applying these findings to the PC market leads to the expectation that one-third of PC consumers would potentially prefer a PC with Green IT attributes, rather than an ordinary PC. Therefore, the fourth question to be answered is:

Question 4: How big would the potential market for a PC with Green IT attributes be?

After estimating the potential market size, the possible measures to market a Green IT PC need to be developed.

Question 5: Which measures should be applied to successfully market a Green IT PC?

The marketing planning measures will be structured according to the different dimensions of the marketing mix. In this four-element framework, marketers have to decide on the product, the price, the promotion, and the place (McCarthy, 1960). The theoretical marketing mix is widely accepted by researchers and practitioners (Constantinides, 2006). Regarding the product, decisions have to be made about the product program, as well as the development and improvement of existing products. The price of a product or service has to be set in terms of the target group and the given market situation. Promotion covers all aspects of communication that aim to influence the knowledge, attitude and behavior of market participants. The place relates to all decisions that deal with the distribution way of the product to the end consumer (McCarthy, 1960).

3.3 Methodology

The conjoint analysis is used for the development of new products and services. It is a statistical technique used in marketing research to determine how people value different attributes of an individual product or service. With the traditional conjoint analysis, market shares with a deviation of 5.1% can be predicted (Heidbrink, 2006). This analysis belongs to the category of multivariate statistics of interdependence analysis. The conjoint analysis is a widely used and scientifically approved approach to marketing research (Dellaert et al., 1996; Hair et al., 2009; Luce & Tukey, 1964; Wittink et al., 1994). It enables testing of different product concepts for a market, using a simulation (Wyner, 1992). Thereby, the respondents must order a representative sample of product concepts according to their preferences. On the basis of the overall assessment, comparative importance and utility estimates of attribute specifications can be calculated. Compared to the self-explicated approach, the conjoint analysis tends to deliver more precise results regarding the consumers' buying behavior (Agarwal & Green, 1991; Backhaus et al., 2008; Hair et al., 2009).

For data collection, an online survey is recommended. This allows a fast and economic investigation of a bigger sample size.

For the survey, an online questionnaire with twelve different PC product concepts was developed. Three of these product concepts served as test cases to determine the validity of the results. To achieve feasibility for the conjoint analysis, the attributes of a product concept for a PC were limited to four, namely price, performance, energy, and disposal. Pre-tests indicated that consumers perceive price and performance as the two most important attributes of a PC. The attributes of energy efficiency and disposal were derived from Elliot and Binney's (2008) Green IT definition and proved to be relevant to consumers during the pre-test. For each of these four attributes, three different specifications were given, according to characteristics of real PC offers. Attributes used in a conjoint analysis are regarded as being discrete (Albers, 1984). Therefore, the assumption was made that all attribute specifications for price, performance, energy and disposal are discrete.

The survey was advertised by pop-up ads on approximately 30,000 German language web pages. From 16 May 2009 until 11 July 2009, the survey was completed by 556 participants. Because of obviously false and non-coherent data, the sample was revised, producing 500 analyzable data sets. Besides the preferences regarding certain PC product concepts, questions of socio-demographic characteristics and general data concerning PC utilization were asked. The collected sample consists of 80.2% male and 19.8% female participants. The average age is 26.6 years.

3.4 Findings

The preference order illustrates the PCs that were respondents' first choice (Table B.9). The performance attributes do not strictly refer to real processors but to processors with multiple cores.

Rank	Specifications	First Choice of the Respondents
1.	Performance: 4 processors with 3 GHz Price: 400 Euro Energy: Energy consumption of 100 watt Disposal: No information about recycling	n = 228 45.6%
2.	Performance: 4 processors with 3 GHz Price: 400 Euro Energy: Energy consumption of 175 watt Disposal: PC can completely be recycled	n = 125 25.0%
3.	Performance: 2 processors with 3 GHz Price: 500 Euro Energy: Energy consumption of 100 watt Disposal: PC can completely be recycled	n = 50 10.0%
...		
12.	Performance: 1 processors with 3 GHz Price: 500 Euro Energy: Energy consumption of 175 watt Disposal: No information about recycling	n = 3 0.6%

Total: n = 500

Table B.9: Preference Order of the First Choice PC Concepts for the Respondents

The conjoint analysis was applied to the respondents' preference orders to evaluate the partial utility estimates for each of the attribute specifications (Table B.10). The partial utility estimates are absolute values. A positive value indicates a utility increase. A negative value implies a utility decrease by the attribute specification. Under the assumption of an additive model, the partial utility estimates for the attribute specification and the general utility, which in this case is 5.000 for all respondents, added up to the total utility of a PC concept. The highest utility increase is achieved by the processor with the highest performance. This specification takes the first place. The second highest utility increase is achieved by the ability to recycle the PC entirely.

To evaluate the quality of the conjoint analysis, the correlations between observed and estimated preferences are calculated. The correlations of Pearson, as well as the rank correlation of Kendall's tau have a value of 1.000 with a significance of 0.000. Kendall's tau for the three test cases (concept to verify the results validity) results in a value of 1.000, with a significance of 0.059. This indicates that the results of the conjoint analysis reflect the collected data very well.

Attribute	Attribute Specifications	Utility Estimate	Rank
+ Performance	1 processor with 3 GHz	-1.414	12.
	2 processors with 3 GHz	-.004	7.
	4 processors with 3 GHz	1.418	1.
+ Price	400 Euro	.587	4.
	500 Euro	.005	6.
	600 Euro	-.592	9.
+ Energy	Energy consumption of 100 watt	.614	3.
	Energy consumption of 175 watt	.023	5.
	Energy consumption of 250 watt	-.637	11.
+ Disposal	PC cannot be recycled	-.619	10.
	No information about recycling	-.098	8.
	PC can completely be recycled	.717	2.
= Total Utility			

Table B.10: Partial Utility Estimates for Each of the PC Specifications from the Consumers' Perspective

Backhaus et al. (2008) recommend classifying the conjoint analysis results. It can be assumed that the answers are seldom homogenous. To classify the data, we executed a cluster analysis, using the Ward method. To determine the distance, the squared Euclidean distance was applied (Backhaus et al., 2008; Hair et al., 2009).

For a cluster analysis, the optimal quantity of clusters has to be assigned. The computation should be based on statistical criteria and not on a plain logical interrelation like the division into LOHAS and non-LOHAS (Backhaus et al., 2008). Therefore, the sum of squared errors of the distances between respondents was calculated. The "elbow method" is used to calculate the optimal quantity of clusters, which in this case is four.

The analysis shows that for each cluster, one of the attributes is especially important. Owing to this, the clusters are labeled "performance oriented", "price oriented", "energy oriented" and "disposal oriented" (Figure B.6). The performance oriented respondents represented the largest fraction with

B.3 Influence of Green IT on Consumers' Buying Behavior of Personal Computers

45.6%, followed by the price oriented respondents with 27.8%. For up to 26.6% of the participants, one of the Green IT characteristics is an important issue during PC purchase. From these, 62% are disposal oriented while 38% are more energy oriented. It is surprising that more consumers are concerned about disposal than about energy, since energy contributes to life cycle costs, while disposal generally doesn't. An explanation could be that consumers perceive a stronger relationship between disposal and waste management to environmental protection than between electrical energy consumption and environmental protection, which only accounts for indirect CO_2 emissions. Also, the recent public focus on IT hardware manufacturers regarding hazardous substances, take back policies, and general environmental behavior might provide an explanation for the results (Greenpeace International, 2009; van Huikstee & de Haan, 2009).

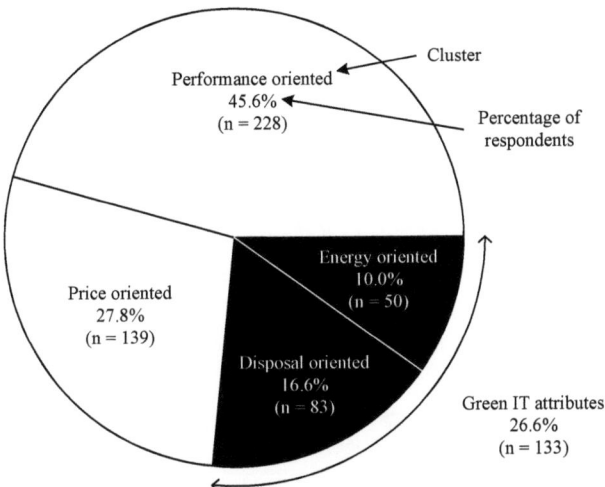

Figure B.6: Clusters of Respondents According to Their Preferred Attribute

To quantify the attributes' importance, the relative importance is calculated. For that purpose, as shown in Table B.11, the spread of the partial utility estimates of an attribute is placed in relation to the sum of all spreads. The higher the importance of an attribute is, the larger the impact on the potential purchase decision of a consumer is. The sum of the relative importance adds up to 100%. The importance of the energy consumption results in 19.2%. The disposal attributes account for 21.2%, following closely behind the price, with 21.6%. The performance attributes are most important, reflected by 37.9%. In summary, the cumulative importance of Green IT attributes amounts to 40.4%, which is below the expected average of 50% for two of four attributes. Therefore, it can be noted that Green IT attributes possess a below average importance for consumers.

Cluster		Total	Performance Oriented	Price Oriented	Energy Oriented	Disposal Oriented
Attribute	Amount	n = 500 100%	n = 228 45.6%	n = 139 27.8%	n = 50 10.0%	n = 83 16.6%
Performance	Importance SD	37.9% 22.8	59.6% 12.1	22.2% 9.9	20.2% 10.3	15.4% 9.7
Price	Importance SD	21.6% 17.0	13.8% 8.0	42.2% 17.1	14.5% 7.4	12.8% 7.4
Energy	Importance SD	19.2% 14.1	14.4% 9.0	17.2% 10.2	49.5% 11.9	17.3% 10.0
Disposal	Importance SD	21.2% 18.1	12.1% 9.2	18.4% 10.9	15.7% 7.0	54.5% 11.8

Table B.11: Relative Importance of PC Attributes for the Clusters

In the next step, the groups that were formed as a result of cluster analysis take on more distinguishing characteristics. To this end, a discriminant analysis with the cluster affiliation and nine variables that were surveyed in the questionnaire was conducted. Table B.12 shows the five variables with the highest discriminatory relevance for the clusters. The discriminatory relevance ranges from 0 to 1. The higher the values, the better the characteristic separates the cluster. The level by which others, including family, friends and acquaintances are advised before they purchase a new PC separates the clusters effectively. This question was answered on a scale ranging from 1 for "very seldom" to 5 for "very often". Especially the performance oriented give advice to others above average. A striking fact is that the share of women within the disposal oriented cluster is significantly higher than in the other clusters. Energy oriented people possess a higher level of education and are slightly older than the average. Overall Green IT attributes are preferred by older respondents. However, this interrelation is not significant (0.156) and might have originated randomly.

Cluster	Characteristics	Advise Others (scale: 1 to 5)	Gender Female / Male	Education (Ratio of Graduates)	Average Age (in Years)	New PC within the Next Year
Total		3.2	19.8% / 80.2%	15.2%	26.6	32.2%
Performance Oriented		3.5	15.8% / 84.2%	14.9%	25.7	36.1%
Price Oriented		2.8	18.0% / 82.0%	10.8%	26.6	31.4%
Energy Oriented		3.1	20.0% / 80.0%	30.0%	29.3	28.0%
Disposal Oriented		2.9	33.7% / 66.3%	14.5%	27.2	25.4%
Discriminatory Relevance		.537	.296	.286	.233	.233
Significance for Tests of Equality of Group Means		.000	.005	.046	.156	.000

Table B.12: Characteristics of the Clusters

For PC sales, the likelihood of a purchase by the respondents within the next twelve months is crucial. Here the Green IT attributes perform below average. Therefore, it can be concluded that the market is driven by the performance and price oriented consumers.

The results show that the ability to recycle a PC entirely, as well as low energy consumption, creates a high positive utility for the respondents. For 16.6% of the respondents, the disposal of a

PC is the most important decision criteria. For 10% of the respondents, the energy consumption is pivotal for the selection of a PC. Therefore, it can be concluded that Green IT has a positive impact on the customers' buying behavior. However, the importance for the purchase decision amounts to only 40.4% and is thereby denoted as below average.

As indicated in Section B.3.2, the potential market for Green IT PCs was assumed to be comparable to the portion of LOHAS in Germany. By calculating the amount of energy and disposal oriented consumers, an estimated market share of 26.6% can be estimated. This value is slightly below the LOHAS amount. Therefore, it can be concluded that the trend towards environmentally oriented products has not yet fully reached the market for IT hardware in the same way as it has reached, for example, the food industry.

The results provide a better understanding of the potential consumers of PCs and offer the opportunity to develop concrete measures to market Green IT PCs.

3.5 Implications

From these results, implications for the marketing mix of IT hardware manufacturers and IT service organizations can be derived. The measures to market a Green IT PC are structured according to the four instruments of the marketing mix, namely product, price, place and promotion (McCarthy, 1960).

Product: The results prove that Green IT attributes have a positive influence on consumer choices. Low energy consumption and a disposal concept that includes recycling are important requirements for the consumers. PC developments and improvements should focus on the disposal attribute, which is of higher importance (62%) than the energy attribute (38%). The extension of the product line with a limited number of Green IT PCs is recommended to satisfy the demands of the energy and disposal oriented consumers.

Price: Especially for Green IT PCs, the price can be seen as a quality indicator. The study revealed a willingness to pay higher prices for PCs with Green IT attributes. The price should be set for the target group of graduates and older persons, who tend to have an above average income and are less price oriented. From this derives the recommendation to place a PC with Green IT attributes in the upper price segment. This also makes it possible to cover the extra costs as a result of necessary developments and recycling.

Promotion: The promotion should use communication channels and advertisements to reach graduates and older consumers. Special attention should be paid to female consumers, since they tend to be more interested in Green IT than men. Owing to Green IT oriented consumers advising others less than the average, it can be concluded that this group demands extra arguments for their purchase. Therefore, it is recommended to clearly outline the environmental attributes of the PC in commercials and product descriptions.

Place: The distribution of Green IT PCs should differ from the distribution of ordinary PCs. Since the consumers value environmental aspects, this should be considered in the supply chain, the presentation of the product and the salesroom. Personal support and sound additional information is needed to fully explain the complexity and the background of the Green IT PC.

With these measures, a market segment of up to 26.6% for Green IT PCs could be served. This offers the opportunity of attracting new customers and of gaining extra revenues.

These results also lead to implications for IT service organizations within companies that provide PCs for the office environment and pay attention to customer orientation. It can be assumed that employees value Green IT PCs as much as ordinary end consumers. The consideration of these demands potentially increases the satisfaction of the business with its IT service organization. Therefore, IT service organizations should include Green IT PCs in their service portfolio and communicate the benefits of this to general management, as well as to an environmental or sustainability responsible person.

3.6 Conclusion and Future Research

In this paper, we have shown that Green IT attributes are relevant during consumers' purchase of PCs. The conjoint analysis with 500 participants outlined that Green IT attributes concretized by energy and disposal attributes play a role when people buy PCs. Still, performance remains the dominant criteria. It was revealed that the market share for Green IT PCs could be as much as 26.6%. Especially female customers value environmentally friendly attributes.

Owing to the chosen method of data collection, the illustrated results are limited to German-speaking online users. The self-selection of the participants was unavoidable. Therefore, it is possible that people who are more interested in PCs than the average consumer participated in the survey. The conclusions drawn from this study are limited to the attributes and specifications used in the survey. Other PC attributes such as computer brand, which might have played an important role, were not further investigated due to the feasibility limitations of conjoint analysis.

The derived implications offer IT hardware manufacturers and CIOs the possibility to market Green IT in a way that can generate extra profits and increase corporate reputation. Given the rising prices for energy and increasing focus on environmental issues, the relevance of Green IT for PCs is destined to gain greater importance in future.

In future, research will have to further validate the achieved results by conducting comparable studies. It can be expected that the attitude towards Green IT on the German market deviates from other regions. Since most IT hardware manufacturers distribute their products globally, it is necessary to also collect data from other markets. Future studies should also investigate whether a PC that is manufactured in a way that reduces the environmental impact has an effect on purchasing behavior. Furthermore, the question arises regarding the extent to which the results are transferable to internal markets in corporations. For this, a survey with employees who receive their PCs from an internal IT service organization is scheduled. Finally, the impact of Green IT attributes on IT services needs to be investigated further.

4 Search Engines and Social Business – Implications from the Case of Ecosia

Title of Article	Search Engines and Social Business – Implications from the Case of Ecosia
Author	Nils-Holger Schmidt nschmid@uni-goettingen.de Georg-August-Universität Göttingen Chair of Information Management Platz der Göttinger Sieben 5 37073 Göttingen
Published	Proceedings of the 4th International Conference - Information Systems & Economic Intelligence (SIIE 2010) (Best paper award) (Schmidt, 2011)
Abstract	The environmental impact of search engines has been getting much public attention in the context of Green IS and Green IT. The search engine Ecosia takes advantage of this situation by pursuing a social business model that distinguishes itself from other major search engines in the market. Enterprises that follow this concept aim to make positive social or environmental contributions to society. They do not aim to maximize profit. Ecosia contributes to society by spending most of its revenues on environmental matters: At least 80% of its revenues are donated to the World Wildlife Fund (WWF). Regarding this, the question arises regarding social business models. Do they possess the potential for success in the search engine market? This is related to the question regarding users' perception of this kind of sustainable behavior and whether this has an impact on the utilization of search services. To investigate these questions, we do case study research to generate an initial hypothesis and insights. The findings highlight the implications on the relevance and impact of social businesses in the scope of web services and information systems (IS) research. It also generates insights on the overall significance of sustainability in web services. This paper provides a starting point for further research on social businesses and IT-based green business models in IS. It contributes to the emerging research on sustainable IS, which investigates social and environmental aspects in the scope of IS research.

Table B.13: Fact Sheet of Publication No. 4

4.1 Introduction

The increasing dissemination and utilization of Information Technology (IT) into all areas of life lead to rising energy consumption and growing environmental problems. IT accounts for two percent or 820 million tons of the global CO_2 emissions each year (Buhl & Laartz, 2008).

In information systems (IS), the environmental impact of IT and related measures for its reduction and management are being discussed under the headings "Green IS" and "Green IT" (Kuo & Dick, 2010; Schmidt et al., 2009a; Watson et al., 2010; Yi & Thomas, 2007).

Within the scope of this discussion, the environmental impact of search engines and their enormous data centers face increasing public attention. The market leader Google, for example, operates approximately 450,000 servers, consuming about 800 Giga Watt hours (GWh) of electricity per year (Chou, 2008). Thereby, Google is indirectly responsible for enormous amounts of CO_2 emissions, because electricity is most often generated by coal or gas combustion, which creates CO_2 emissions.

Estimations of the level of CO_2 emissions caused by a Google search request vary between 1g to 10g and are discussed controversially (Glass, 2009; Leake & Woods, 2009). Thus, regardless of the financial success, Google has come under environmental criticism.

The search engine Ecosia takes advantage of this situation by pursuing an IT-based green business model that distinguishes itself from the main search engines in the market. Ecosia does not aim to maximize profit. Instead, it follows the emerging concept of social business as the context within which it makes a positive environmental contribution to society (Yunus, 2008a).

To achieve its objectives, Ecosia cooperates with nonprofit organizations (NGOs) and established search engine providers Bing and Yahoo.

Research in other domains illustrates that sustainable products and services can positively influence consumer behavior (Du et al., 2007; Lichtenstein et al., 2004; Luo & Bhattacharya, 2006). This trend can be especially observed in the food industry with the increasing prominence of organic food. It is likely to disseminate into other industries (Ray & Anderson, 2001).

Regarding the social business model of Ecosia, the following research questions arise:

1. Do social business models possess the potential for success in the search engine market?
2. How big could the potential market share of a social business enterprise be in the search engine market?
3. How can social businesses influence competition in the search engine market?

These three questions are answered by an explorative case study of the search engine Ecosia and a thorough literature review. The aim of this paper is to develop first hypotheses regarding social business in the scope of web services and IS research.

In IS research, the emerging topic of social business still lacks theoretical foundation and demands further scientific investigation. This paper aims to show professionals and researchers new opportunities as a result of social business models. It is a starting point for future business start-ups and further research.

This paper belongs to the emerging research branch of sustainable IS, which investigates social and environmental questions and aspects in the scope of IS (Schmidt et al., 2009b; Watson et al., 2010).

4.2 Related Research

4.2.1 Traditional Business Models

A good business model is essential to every successful enterprise or organization (Magretta, 2002). It should describe a path from basic human needs to continuous financial success (Magretta, 2002). For this, the business model substantiates all essential elements. According to Teece (2010), the essence of a business model is "... in defining the manner by which the enterprise delivers value to customers, entices customers to pay for value, and converts those payments to profit. It thus reflects management's hypothesis about what customers want, how they want it, and how the enterprise can organize to best meet those needs, get paid for doing so, and make a profit."

This customer and profit focused definition neglects the fact that other business actors and organizations can also play an important role in a business model. Furthermore, the objectives of these actors can be monetary or nonmonetary. Especially companies that do social business (see Section B.4.2.2) pursue nonmonetary objectives.

Timmers (1998) offers a broader definition that also mentions other business actors and general benefits. From his point of view, a business model is defined as "... an architecture for the products, services and information flows, including a description of various business actors and their roles, a description of the potential benefits for the various business actors, and a description of the sources of revenues."

In a business model, involved parties are not all necessarily business actors. Governmental and nongovernmental organizations can also play a substantial role. They are generally referred to as "stakeholders" (Freeman, 1984). Therefore, Timmer's (1998) definition has to be expanded to include social business models.

Hence, a business model describes the architecture of the products, services and information flows, including a description of relevant economic and noneconomic stakeholders and their roles, a description of the potential economic, social and environmental benefits for the various business stakeholders, and a description of the sources of revenues.

4.2.2 Characteristics of Social Businesses

Social business can be interpreted as a form of business model that primarily pursues social and environmental objectives under the constraint of cost-coverage. It reverses the profit maximization principle by a benefit maximization principle (Yunus, 2006). For this reason, it distinguishes itself clearly from traditional business models. The two models are compared in Table B.14.

Social business has grown from the work of the Nobel Peace Prize recipient Muhammad Yunus (Yunus, 2008a). According to Yunus, companies that align their business model according to the social business model measure their success by the impact on people or the environment, rather than on the amount of profit made in a given period (Yunus, 2008b). Their value creation is done by satisfying basic human needs for a more peaceful, righteous and preserved world.

Attribute	Traditional Business Model	Social Business Model
Objective	Profit maximization	Maximization of social and/or environmental benefits
Side condition	Socially and environmentally reconcilable	Full cost recovery
Main target group	Shareholders	Society
Appropriation of profits	Dividends to shareholders, reinvestment	Reinvestment, extension of activities, payback of investors
Objectives of investors	Added value (one-dimensional)	Contribution to society, conservation of value (multi-dimensional)

Table B.14: Comparison of Traditional and Social Business Models

From a financial perspective, social business enterprises can be classified into four categories (Yunus, 2006), namely:

1. no cost recovery;
2. some cost recovery;
3. full cost recovery; and
4. more than full cost recovery.

The side condition of a social business enterprise is to operate at or beyond the cost recovery point (Yunus, 2008a). Therefore, donations can play a significant role as a source of revenue.

The investors of social business models generally do not receive any dividends or speculative profits. This is expressed by Yunus (2008a):

"Thus, a Social-Business might be defined as a non-loss, non-dividend business."

Instead, profits are passed on to the target group or are used to increase social and environmental activities. Investors seek a double bottom line profit – financial value conservation as well as positive social and environmental impact.

A related economic concept is the "bottom of the pyramid". The expression describes the poorest socio-economic group of the global population. The concept illustrates opportunities for companies to approach this neglected customer segment and to obtain a market position (Olsen & Boxenbaum, 2009).

We define a social business model that is primarily based on IT and that pursues environmental objectives as an IT-based green business model.

4.3 Methodology

The questions in this paper are answered by applying case study research. Case study research is a widely acknowledged and used methodology in IS research (Dubé & Paré, 2003).

Case study research can serve multiple purposes: to describe phenomena, to test theories or to develop new theories and hypotheses (Benbasat et al., 1987; Eisenhardt, 1989a). This corresponds with the paper's intention to derive a hypothesis regarding social business enterprises in the search engine market.

The paper generates insights by examining a phenomenon in its natural setting (Benbasat et al., 1987; Yin, 2002). Case study research is suitable for exploration of new topic areas that lack empirical validation (Crane, 1999; Eisenhardt, 1989a; Robertson, 1993). This applies to the given situation of social business models in the search engine market; therefore, the application of case study research is appropriate.

Social business models in the search engine market are rare. Most of them do not provide sufficient information for any kind of analysis, but exceptions are Forestle, Znout and Ecosia, which were all founded by Christian Kroll (Kroll, 2010). Due to unresolved legal issues, Forestle and Znout have ceased development (Kroll, 2010). Therefore, this paper is based on the search engine Ecosia, which provides substantial and verifiable data on its own activities.

Case study research employs various data collection methods, such as document and literature analysis, interviews, observations, and questionnaires (Eisenhardt, 1989a). Our investigation is based on:

- multiple interviews with the founder and CEO of Ecosia, Christian Kroll;
- an in depth analysis of all information provided by Ecosia;
- comprehensive market and media research; and
- extensive literature research.

Owing to the limitations of case study research, our findings demand further validation through quantitative and qualitative research regarding social business in IS.

4.4 Ecosia's Social Business Model

4.4.1 Company Overview

Ecosia is an independent, non-profit internet search engine that defines itself as a social business enterprise (Yunus, 2008a). Ecosia donates at least 80% of its revenues to a rainforest protection program run by the WWF. Therefore, each web search saves up to 2 m² of rainforest. Thereby, over 202 million m² of rainforest, equal to more than 28,000 football pitches, have been protected (see Figure B.7).

Figure B.7: Web Interface of Ecosia's Search Service

The project donates the money specifically for the sustainable protection of rainforests in the Brazilian Juruena National Park (Ecosia, 2010a; WWF, 2009). This distinguishes the search engine from others in the market.

Ecosia is an example of a social business model in the search engine market (see Table B.15).

Ecosia	
Foundation	2009
Headquarter	Wittenberg / Germany
Industry	Internet, social business
Products and services	Internet search services
Short description	Ecosia is an independent, non-profit website. At least 80% of its search income goes to a rainforest protection program run by the WWF. Bing and Yahoo provide search results and sponsored links to generate advertising revenue
Partners	Yahoo, Bing, WWF
URL	http://www.ecosia.org
Revenue (estimated 2010)	approx. Euro 140,000
Donations to WWF (estimated 2010)	approx. Euro 112,000
Employees	3 core employees, 10 to 15 supporters
IT infrastructure	1 server, use of the external infrastructure from Yahoo and Bing

Table B.15: Overview of Ecosia

4.4.2 Mechanics of the Social Business Model

Bing and Yahoo provide Ecosia with search results and sponsored links (see Figure B.8). Ecosia does not run its own search index because of financial restrictions. Its revenues are generated by user clicks on sponsored links. A small portion of these revenues goes to technology partners. Ecosia receives an average of €0.13 per click on a sponsored link. At least 80% of this amount is donated to WWF. The remaining 20% are used for salaries, servers, domains, marketing, and alliances with other enterprises. In doing so, the CEO pays himself a salary of less than 1,000 Euro per month (Vensky, 2010).

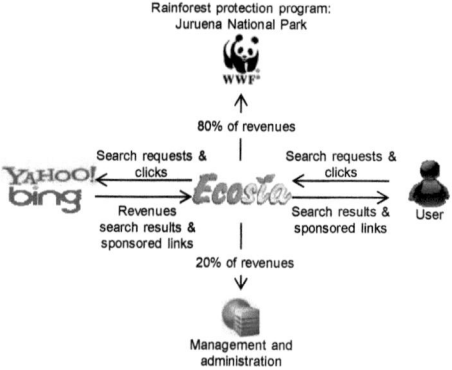

Figure B.8: Social Business Model of Ecosia

Ecosia therefore operates just at full cost recovery and can be classified as a class 3 social business enterprise (see Section B.4.2.2).

Since the foundation of Ecosia in 2009, the number of search requests has steadily grown. In April 2010, Ecosia generated over €11,000 of revenues, with around 9 million search requests, producing a market share of approximately 0.2% among the German search engines (comScore, 2010; Ecosia, 2010b). Most of Ecosia's search requests originated in Germany (55%), Switzerland (13%) and France (10%) (Ecosia, 2010c).

The social business model imposes a narrow financial scope for Ecosia. It depends on marketing tools such as word-of-mouth advertising, press releases, and media interviews. This marketing strategy has been successful in Germany and is confirmed by numerous publications (FOCUS Online, 2009; Otten, 2010; Vensky, 2010).

In the long run, Ecosia aims to gain a global market share of one percent. According to its own account, the company is confronted with the following strategic challenges to achieve this goal (Kroll, 2010):

- self-financing by increased revenues;
- relationship management of existing partnerships;
- obtaining Google as an additional partner;
- internationalization of user groups, especially in the US; and
- development of university and school partnerships.

Managing the existing relationships is of vital importance to Ecosia, because the company does not operate its own search index and is therefore dependent on the search technology provided by Bing and Yahoo to provide competitive search services.

Obtaining the market leader Google as an additional partner would enhance Ecosia's search services significantly. Users would then be able to select one of the three search engines. This could potentially lead to more users and higher revenues, which would enable Ecosia to donate more money for rainforest protection.

To reach a global share of one percent in the search engine market, Ecosia needs to internationalize its user groups and grow beyond the German and European market.

Young and better educated people tend to be more interested in environmental issues. For this reason, Ecosia is developing university and school partnerships to get in contact with this target group.

4.5 Findings

4.5.1 Market Potential

The case study shows a steadily increasing number of Ecosia users (see Section B.4.4). According to Facebook.com, Ecosia's growing popularity is illustrated by over 150,000 people who "like" the search engine (Facebook - Ecosia, 2010).

From this derives the question about the potential market share of a social business model in the search engine market. In this section, we will answer the first research question (see Section B.4.1).

In the case of Ecosia, the user acquisition is not done by a typical product or service differentiation. Instead, the environmental focus of the business model is advertised and communicated with the users. Therefore, users who are receptive to environmental topics belong to Ecosia's target group.

Hints regarding the market potential are provided by the consumer group LOHAS. LOHAS stands for "lifestyle of health and sustainability" and describes a "movement with strong influence on consumption and values" within society (Ray & Anderson, 2001; Wenzel et al., 2007). This lifestyle does not portray an exclusive target group but a "new social majority" (Wenzel et al., 2007). This trend can be observed in the food industry with the increasing prominence of organic food. It is likely to disseminate into other industries (Ray & Anderson, 2001).

The expanding share of LOHAS in the German market was estimated to be one-third in 2007 (Wenzel et al., 2007). If these findings are transferred to search engine users, it can be assumed that one-third of all users would prefer a search engine with a social business model than a traditional search engine.

Research on the marketing of Green IT PCs shows similar findings. Results from a conjoint-analysis of 500 internet users estimate a potential market share for PCs with environmental friendly product attributes of as much as 26.6% (Schmidt et al., 2010d). For this target group, environmental attributes are relatively more important than price and performance. The members of this target group are significantly older, better educated and mainly female (Schmidt et al., 2010d). Other research confirms that women value environmentally friendly products and services more than men (Lee, 2009).

These findings lead to the hypothesis that at least one quarter of all users could be enticed to use a social business search engine, such as Ecosia. It can be assumed that the relevant target group is likely to be older, better educated, and female.

4.5.2 Competitive Potential

Bing and Yahoo provide Ecosia's technical support. Ecosia would like to establish a partnership with Google (see Section B.4.4) but the internet giant seems hesitant. This leads to the question regarding how a social business model can be a strategic instrument and influence competition in the search engine market. In this section, we will answer the second research question (see Section B.4.1).

First, an analysis of the competitive environment must be done. With a market share of 89.6%, Google dominates the German search engine market (WebHits, 2010). Bing and Yahoo merely possess a market share of respectively 2.2% and 2.6% (WebHits, 2010). The German search engine market (4%) is smaller than the US market's 17% share of all global search requests (comScore, 2010). Internationally, Google is unchallenged, although not as explicitly as in Germany. In the US, the three major search engines, Google (65.1%), Yahoo (13.8%), and Bing (13.0%), share about 92% of the market (Nielsen Wire, 2010).

Besides Ecosia, there are other providers in the search engine market that claim to do social business (see Table B.16).

It is hard to verify these providers' statements impartially; therefore, we treat them with caution. An exception is Ecosia, which provides detailed information concerning users, revenues and donations, proved by transfer forms.

Except for GoodSearch, all above mentioned companies were founded in the past two years. This illustrates the growing importance of social business models for web services. The overview (see Table B.16) shows that every major search engine provider cooperates in some form with social businesses; Yahoo being more actively involved than Bing and Google.

Bing and Yahoo are motivated to cooperate with Ecosia because every new Ecosia user is likely to have used Google before (Kroll, 2010). Therefore, Bing and Yahoo view Ecosia as a strategic instrument to take market share away from Google and to exert pressure on Google in the scope of environmental issues.

As a profit maximizing company, it does not seem reasonable for Google to cooperate with Ecosia, because a growing user number of Ecosia would mean decreasing profits for Google. Nevertheless, switching costs for search engine users are very low. Therefore, this development exerts pressure on the market leader Google, demanding a reaction. Especially if the number of Ecosia users keeps growing, public attention increases, and Bing and Yahoo stay committed to their partnership with Ecosia. This could finally lead Google to also cooperate with Ecosia, or to initiate its own projects in this topic area.

Name	URL	Launched	Partners	Commitment
Benefind (2010)	benefind.de	2009	Yahoo, Bing	Donation of 0.5 Euro Cent per search query to charitable purposes
Blackle (2010)	blackle.com	2010	Google	Energy saving internet search by black background
Ecocho (2010)	ecocho.eu	2008	Yahoo	Purchase of CO_2 certificates
Ecosia (2010a)	ecosia.org	2009	Yahoo, Bing, WWF	Donation of 80% of all revenues to the WWF
Forestle (2010)	forestle.de	2008	Yahoo, The Nature Conservancy	Donation of 90% of all revenues to The Nature Conservancy
GoodSearch (2010)	goodsearch.com	2005	Yahoo	Donation of 50% of its profit for charitable purposes
TREEHOO! (2010)	treehoo.com	2008	Yahoo, Trees for the Future	Donation of 50% of its profit to „Trees for the Future" to plant trees
Znout (2010)	znout.org	2008	Google	Purchase of CO_2 certificates

Table B.16: Selection of Social Business Web Search Services

If Ecosia succeeds in skimming the market potential (see Section B.4.5.1), a race to the top can be expected (Hahn, 2009). In this situation, the three major search engines will start to compete over their social and environmental contribution to serve the people and the planet better (Yunus, 2006). The environmental contribution of the whole search engine market to society would therefore grow.

4.6 Business and Research Implications

Finally, we discuss the implications for business and research, derived from our findings.

First, there are clear implications for Ecosia. The analysis of the market potential (see Section B.4.5.1) backs Ecosia's business model. Ecosia should direct its communication towards older, better educated, and female users. This also needs to be considered when selecting appropriate marketing tools and channels. Ecosia furthermore has to develop the overall sustainability of its social business model. The vital dependence on the strong personal commitment of the founder imposes a risk. Therefore, Ecosia should be supported by multiple actors. This would allow a continuous transformation process without putting the search engine at risk.

Second, there are implications for business. Ecosia illustrates that an internet based social business model with strong personal commitment can be successful and creates positive benefits for society (see Section B.4.4). The potential market share of a social business search engine should be around one-quarter. Furthermore, the case study illustrates that Ecosia's business model offers the possibility to acquire a market niche, even in a quasi monopolistic market such as the global search engines market. The commitment of one company can cause other companies to follow – leading to a competition over social and environmental contributions: a race to the top. This effect can indirectly cause achievement of the objectives of a social business (see Section B.4.5.2).

Furthermore, the value of a service is not only determined by its performance, quality or price; the business model also influences the users' perceptions. Therefore, including social and environmental aspects into a traditional business model leads to an emergence of new business models. This leads to a multiplicity of opportunities beyond the search engine market. Markets in which social and environmental issues have been neglected and the target group of environmentally oriented consumers has not been addressed seem especially suitable (see Section B.4.5.1). A possible example of this would be the idea of an eco-Ebay.com or a socially oriented Amazon.com, which would donate a certain percentage of their revenues to an environmental cause. By doing so, it should be possible to quickly obtain a significant number of customers or users.

Third, there are implications for research. This paper represents an initial attempt at grasping the relevance of social business in IS research. The dynamic of the IS field makes it highly relevant for this concept. Nevertheless, the topic lacks a theoretical foundation and demands further scientific investigation. Applicable theories and concepts are needed to further elaborate on this idea. Investigating the race to the top effect in IS or estimating the relevance of environmental protection in IS services should be the next steps of research.

Further research should also focus on the idea of IT-based green business models, of which Ecosia is an example. An analysis of present examples and the development of new IT-based green companies should contribute to the research on Green IS.

4.7 Conclusion and Discussion

The case study illustrates how a market niche in a quasi monopolistic market, such as search engines, can be conquered by a social business model. In this situation, the support by other market actors seems likely. For them, it provides a strategic instrument to tackle the market leader (see Section B.4.5.2).

The development can lead companies to a competition over social and environmental contributions, called a "race to the top".

Owing to the application of single case study research, there are a number of clear limitations. These findings demand further validation. Future research will follow the next steps:

- surveys with the users of Ecosia and other search engines should provide additional data on the market potential of social business search engines;
- multiple case studies with other internet based social business enterprises are recommended (Yin, 2002); this should provide findings on the market relevance and future significance of these types of business models; and
- implementation of an experimental, student-run social business.

Giving the growing dissemination and application of IT, and the societal shift, the relevance of social and environmental topics is destined to gain even more importance in the future. In this context, social business enterprises within the scope of IS are a new development that demands further investigation. Therefore, this paper contributes a first concept and initial hypotheses by analyzing the social business phenomenon in the search engine market.

5 Ökobilanzierung in der Informationstechnik – Zwei Distributionsformen der Musikindustrie im Vergleich

Title of Article	Ökobilanzierung in der Informationstechnik – Zwei Distributionsformen der Musikindustrie im Vergleich[11]
Authors	Nils-Holger Schmidt* nschmid@uni-goettingen.de Meike Schmehl† mschmeh@uni-goettingen.de Florian Thies* florian.thies@gmx.de Jutta Geldermann† geldermann@wiwi.uni-goettingen.de Lutz M. Kolbe* lkolbe@uni-goettingen.de Georg-August-Universität Göttingen *Chair of Information Management Platz der Göttinger Sieben 5 37073 Göttingen †Chair of Production and Logistics Platz der Göttinger Sieben 3 37073 Göttingen
Published	HMD - Praxis der Wirtschaftsinformatik (Schmidt et al., 2010c)
Abstract	Life cycle assessment (LCA) provides a proven method to demonstrate the environmental impact of products and services. It helps decision-makers to develop and improve products and services, supports political decision processes, and provides additional arguments for marketing. The presented example illustrates the approach of LCA by comparing two forms of music distribution. It is shown that the distribution of music via the internet possesses an environmental advantage, which is, however, small because of the high energy consumption of data centers.

Table B.17: Fact Sheet of Publication No. 5

---

[11] © 2010 HMD - Praxis der Wirtschaftsinformatik. Reprinted, with permission.

5.1 Ökobilanzierung und Informationstechnik

Im Rahmen einer zunehmenden Ökologieorientierung der Gesellschaft beeinflussen ökologische Aspekte von Produkten oder Dienstleistungen vermehrt die Kaufentscheidung von Kunden. Aus Unternehmenssicht sind umweltschonende Technologien und Prozesse jedoch nicht nur für das Marketing interessant. Vielfach bieten sie Ansätze effizienter und kostengünstiger Leistungen am Markt anbieten zu können. Dennoch fehlt den Unternehmen in der Regel ein tiefergehendes ökologisches Verständnis ihrer eigenen Produkte und Dienstleistungen.

Eine bewährte Methode zur Darstellung von Umwelteinflüssen durch Produkte und Dienstleistungen bietet das Instrument der Ökobilanzierung. In jüngster Zeit hat sich diese Methode im Gebiet der Informationstechnik (IT) etabliert (Tabelle B.18). IT-Lösungen besitzen gegenüber traditionellen Lösungen häufig einen ökologischen Vorteil.

Untersuchtes Produkt bzw. Dienstleistung	Quelle
Mobilfunknetz UMTS	Frischknecht, R.; Faist Emmenegger, M.: Ökobilanz Mobilfunknetz UMTS deckt Optimierungspotenzial auf. ETH Zürich, 2003.
Netbooks	Grießhammer, R.; Quack, D.; Brommer, E.; Lüders, B.: PROSA-Kurzstudie: Tragbare Klein-Computer (Netbooks) - Umweltzeichen für klimarelevante Produkte und Dienstleistungen. Öko-Institut e. V., Freiburg, 2009.
Fast Ethernet und WLAN	Hottenroth, H.: Vergleich der signifikanten potenziellen Umweltbelastungen von Netzwerkinfrastrukturen - Eine Gegenüberstellung von Fast Ethernet und WLAN für die Anwendung im Local Area Networking. Öko-Institut e. V., Freiburg, 2004.
E-Paper	Kamburow, C.: E-Paper - Erste Abschätzungen der Umweltauswirkungen - Eine ökobilanzielle Betrachtung am Beispiel des Nachrichtenmedium Zeitung. Institut für Zukunftsstudien und Technologiebewertung, Berlin, 2004.
PC und Thin Client Arbeitsplatzgeräten	Knermann, C.; Hiebel, M.; Pflaum, H.; Rettweiler, M.; Schröder, A.: Ökologischer Vergleich der Klimarelevanz von PC und Thin Client Arbeitsplatzgeräten. Fraunhofer Institut, Oberhausen, 2008.
Master-Slave-Steckdosenleiste	Prakash, S.; Brommer, E.; Gießhammer, R.; Lüders, B.: PROSA Master-Slave-Steckdosenleiste - Kriterien für das Umweltzeichen für klimarelevante Produkte und Dienstleistungen. Öko-Institut e. V., Freiburg, 2009.
Virtueller Anrufbeantworter	Quack, D.; Gießhammer, R.: PROSA T-NetBox: Produkt-Nachhaltigkeits-Analyse eines virtuellen Anrufbeantworters. Öko-Institut e. V., Freiburg, 2005.
Online-Rechnung	Quack, D.; Möller, M.: Ökobilanzielle Analyse von Rechnung Online im Vergleich zu Rechnung per Brief. Öko-Institut e. V., Freiburg, 2005.

Tabelle B.18: Auswahl durchgeführter Ökobilanzen im Bereich der Informationstechnik

Ziel dieses Artikels ist es, das Vorgehen der Ökobilanzierung am Beispiel der Distribution eines Musikalbums per MP3 und traditioneller CD zu veranschaulichen. Damit sollen Praktiker die Möglichkeiten und Grenzen dieses Instruments kennenlernen und ein Beitrag zur Forschung im Bereich der Green IT erfolgen.

5.2 Grundlagen der Ökobilanzierung

Die Ökobilanzierung ist für Entscheidungsträger eine bewährte Methode, um Umweltauswirkungen von Produkten und Dienstleistungen zu analysieren. Sie dient damit insbesondere der Entwicklung und Verbesserung von Produkten und Dienstleistungen, der Unterstützung von politischen Entscheidungsprozessen und der Argumentationsunterstützung in Marketing und Vertrieb (Abbildung B.9) (Deutsches Institut für Normung e.V., 2009).

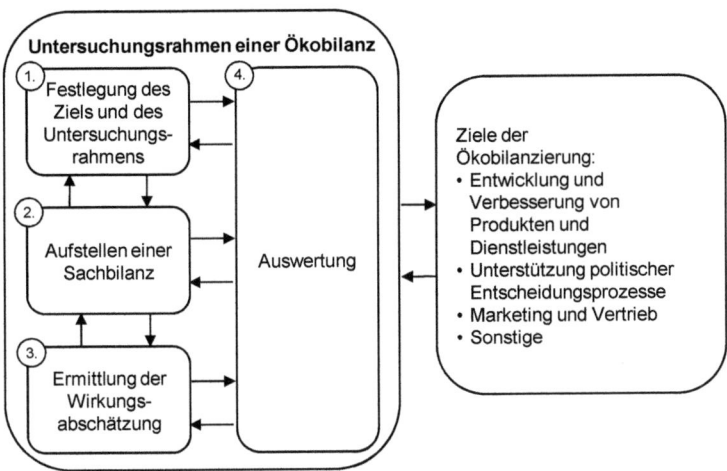

Abbildung B.9: Vorgehen der Ökobilanzierung, in Anlehnung an: (Deutsches Institut für Normung e.V., 2009)

Seit 1997 wird die Vorgehensweise der Ökobilanzierung in der Normreihe DIN EN ISO 14040 publiziert. Mit der Neuauflage der Normreihe im Jahr 2006 erfolgten eine komplette Überarbeitung und eine Aufteilung in zwei statt vier Normen (Deutsches Institut für Normung e.V., 2009).

Die Ökobilanzierung wird in vier Phasen durchgeführt (Abbildung B.9).

In Phase 1 werden das Ziel und der Untersuchungsrahmen einer Ökobilanz definiert. Dadurch wird insbesondere die Tiefe und Breite einer Ökobilanz bestimmt. Da die Erarbeitung einer Ökobilanz einem iterativen Prozess unterliegt, kann es dazu kommen, dass der anfänglich definierten Untersuchungsrahmen weiter ergänzt wird.

In Phase 2 wird die Sachbilanz aufgestellt. Sie beinhaltet Input- und Outputflüsse auf Grundlage der Leistungsmerkmale eines Produktes oder einer Dienstleistung. Bei Inputflüssen handelt es sich beispielsweise um energetische Ressourcen, die der Umwelt entnommen wurden. Emissionen in die Luft sind ein Beispiel für Outputflüsse.

In Phase 3 erfolgt die Wirkungsabschätzung der potentiellen Umweltauswirkungen der Input- und Outputflüsse.

In Phase 4 werden abschließend die Ergebnisse der Wirkungsabschätzung ausgewertet und beurteilt (Deutsches Institut für Normung e.V., 2009). Hieraus lassen sich Handlungsempfehlungen in Bezug auf das untersuchte Produkt oder Dienstleistung ableiten.

Das Aufstellen einer Ökobilanz kann durch entsprechende Software unterstützt werden, beispielsweise durch das Programm Umberto vom Institut für Umweltinformatik Hamburg und dem Institut für Energie- und Umweltforschung Heidelberg. Diese Software setzt auf Petri-Netze zur Abbildung des Stoffstromsystems, welches mit Hilfe von Transitionen (zur Darstellung von Umwandlungsprozessen), Stellen (zur Modellierung von Lagern, Inputs und Outputs) und Verbindungen (zur Abbildung von Stoffflüssen) modelliert wird (Schmidt & Häuslein, 1996).

5.3 Zwei Distributionsformen der Musikindustrie im ökobilanziellen Vergleich

Auf dem deutschen Musikmarkt wurden 2008 insgesamt 149 Millionen Musik-Alben verkauft. Davon wurden 2,6% als sogenannte „Bundles" online heruntergeladen und 97,4% als physische CD vertrieben. Während der Vertrieb von CDs seit 2003 stagniert, wuchs die Anzahl der online verkauften Alben im Vergleich zu 2007 um 50% (Bundesverband Musikindustrie e. V., 2009). MP3- und CD-Alben bedienen einen ähnlichen Kundenbedarf nach Musik. Trotz der im Detail unterschiedlichen Vor- und Nachteile werden beide Distributionsformen im Rahmen dieser Studie bezüglich ihres Nutzens als vergleichbar betrachtet und sind somit für eine Ökobilanzierung geeignet.

5.3.1 Zielsetzung

Das Potential der Ökobilanzierung soll anhand eines Vergleichs von zwei Distributionsformen der Musikindustrie, MP3-Album per Internet gegenüber traditionellem CD-Album, illustriert werden. Zur Vereinfachung wird hierbei nur auf das umweltschädliche Treibhausgas Kohlendioxid (CO_2) eingegangen. Andere Treibhausgase und Schadstoffe werden nicht betrachtet.

Unter der Distribution in der Musikindustrie werden hier die Prozesse von der Herstellung des Tonmediums, sofern dies erforderlich ist, bis hin zum Endkunden verstanden. Die zu analysierende funktionelle Einheit der zu vergleichenden Distributionsformen umfasst ein Musik-Album mit einer durchschnittlichen Gesamtspiellänge von rund 54 Minuten und durchschnittlich 14 Liedern pro Album. Für ein MP3-Album mit einer angenommen MP3-Kodierungsrate von 320Kbit/s (Kilobits pro Sekunde) beträgt das Datenvolumen somit ca. 127MB (Megabyte).

B.5 Ökobilanzierung in der Informationstechnik

Für beide Distributionsformen wird festgelegt, dass ein vervielfältigungs- und distributionsreifes Musik-Album, inklusive Musikaufnahme, Cover, Booklet und Inlay vorliegt. Es wird angenommen, dass sowohl das Abspielen der CD als auch die Wiedergabe der MP3-Dateien mittels Laptop erfolgt und hierfür nahezu der gleiche Energiebedarf benötigt wird. Die Nutzungsphase ist somit aus ökobilanzieller Sicht für beide Distributionsformen identisch und wird im Vergleich nicht weiter berücksichtigt. Die Entsorgungsphase wird nicht näher betrachtet.

5.3.2 Untersuchungsrahmen: CD-Album

Die ersten Prozessschritte für das CD-Album umfasst die Herstellung der einzelnen Bestandteile des CD-Musik-Albums (CD, CD-Hülle, Cover/Booklet und Inlay). Anschließend wird das Album konfektioniert, ggf. beim Hersteller zwischengelagert und an die Händler ausgeliefert. Es wird angenommen, dass ein CD-Album beim Händler direkt in den Verkaufsbereich gelangt und durchschnittlich nach zwei Wochen von einem Kunden erworben wird.

Abbildung B.10 zeigt den Untersuchungsrahmen für den Distributionsprozess eines Musik-Albums als CD.

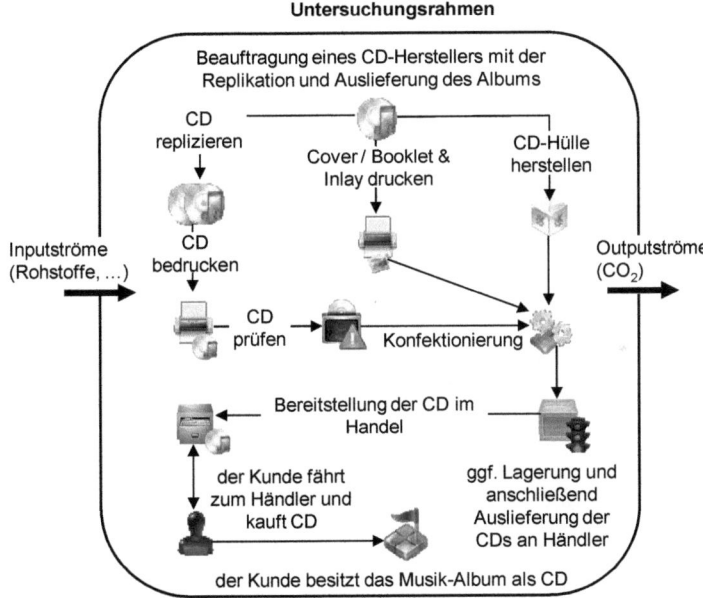

Abbildung B.10: Untersuchungsrahmen der CD-Distribution

5.3.3 Sachbilanz: CD-Album

In dieser Sachbilanz werden die CO_2 Stoffströme der einzelnen Prozessschritte fokussiert. Die Daten der CD-Distribution beruhen auf Aussagen verschiedener CD-Hersteller, Musiklabels und CD-Fachhändler, die im Rahmen dieser Studien interviewt wurden sowie auf der Datenbank ecoinvent v2.1.

Eine CD besteht im Wesentlichen aus 15g Polykarbonat. Gemäß den Emissionsfaktoren nach (Hischier, 2007) ergibt sich für eine CD eine CO_2-Emission von 90g. Eine CD-Hülle wird aus 68g Polystyrol gefertigt. Damit sind Emissionen von 184,3g CO_2 verbunden (Hischier, 2007). Das Booklet sowie das Inlay bestehen aus ca. 13g hochwertigem holzfreiem Papier, das eine CO_2-Emission von 23,5g verursacht (Hischier, 2007). Insgesamt können den Materialen eines CD-Albums damit 297,8g CO_2 zugewiesen werden.

Der Stromverbrauch für die Herstellung, die interne Logistik und Lagerhaltung für ein Musik-CD-Album beträgt nach Expertenschätzung etwa 0,12kWh. Dies entspricht gemäß dem Strommix Deutschland 2007 etwa 74,9g CO_2 (Umweltbundesamt, 2009).

Das CD-Album wird vom Hersteller direkt zu den Händlern im In- und Ausland ausgeliefert. Die Auslieferung erfolgt vorwiegend mittels kleiner LKW (3,5t bis 7,5t). Die durchschnittliche Auslieferungsdistanz beträgt nach Expertenangaben ca. 500km. Ein LKW der Euro-Norm 5 verursacht 604,6g CO_2 pro Tonnenkilometer (tkm) (Spielmann et al., 2007). Ein Tonnenkilometer entspricht dabei dem Transport einer Tonne über die Distanz von einem km. Ein CD-Album wiegt durchschnittlich 98,8g. Der direkte Transport einer CD vom Hersteller zum Händler verursacht damit 29,9g CO_2.

Ein Quadratmeter beheizte Fläche im „Non-Food-Bereich" des Einzelhandels verbraucht pro Jahr durchschnittlich 464kWh Energie (Schlomann et al., 2004). Um in einem Geschäft die Produkte den Kunden zugänglich zu machen, besteht ein wesentlicher Teil der Verkaufsfläche zusätzlich aus Gängen, dem Kassenbereich und weiteren Nebenflächen. Aus diesem Grund wird der Energieverbrauch mit dem Faktor 1,5 multipliziert. Damit werden 696kWh pro Quadratmeter angesetzt. Schätzungen bei CD-Fachhändlern ergaben, dass ca. 320 CDs pro m²-Verkaufsfläche angeboten werden. Bezogen auf zwei Wochen und auf die Anzahl der CDs pro m² ergibt sich der Energieverbrauch von 0,084kWh für die Bereitstellung einer CD. Dies entspricht gemäß dem Strommix Deutschland für 2007 ca. 52,42g CO_2.

Ein durchschnittlicher Einkaufsweg des Konsumenten beträgt pro Strecke 6,4km (Verron et al., 2005). Für diese Studie wird angenommen, dass der Kunde die Gesamtstrecke von 12,8km mit einem PKW zurücklegt. Ein Einkauf wird in der Regel nicht nur wegen eines Musik-Albums getätigt. Auf Grund fehlender statistischer Daten wird angenommen, dass ein Kunde

B.5 Ökobilanzierung in der Informationstechnik

durchschnittlich sechs Artikel pro Einkauf erwirbt, die vereinfacht gleichermaßen an der CO_2-Emission des Transportwegs beteiligt sind. Es wird ein Emissionsfaktor von 191g CO_2/km für einen PKW mit einem Mix aus Diesel und Benzin Motor zugrunde gelegt (Spielmann et al., 2007). Damit verursacht der Transport einer CD vom Händler zum Kunden insgesamt 407,5g CO_2.

5.3.4 Untersuchungsrahmen: MP3-Album

Der Distributionsweg eines MP3-Albums gliedert sich in die Bereitstellung auf dem Server im Rechenzentrum sowie die Datenübertragung (Download) mittels Internet-Breitbandanschluss. Während der Übertragung eines Musik-Albums (127MB) vom Server der Download-Plattform zum Endgerät des Kunden durchlaufen die Daten mehrere Router und können dabei unterschiedliche Routing-Wege durch das Internet zurücklegen. Es wird angenommen, dass der Kunde in Besitz eines Laptops ist und diesen für den Download des Albums verwendet. Außerdem wird vorausgesetzt, dass der Kunde für den Zugang zum Internet einen multifunktionalen DSL-Router benutzt, der sowohl DSL-Modem, Router/ Switch und Wireless-Lan-Accesspoint und weitere Funktionalitäten vereint.

Für die Distribution von MP3-Alben wurden führende Musiklabels, Betreiber von Musik-Download-Plattformen, Rechenzentren sowie Netzwerkbetreiber befragt.

5.3.5 Sachbilanz: MP3-Album

Die Anbieter stellen MP3-Alben in der Regel mittels Servern und notwendiger Infrastruktur in Rechenzentren bereit. Die Höhe des Stromverbrauchs eines Rechenzentrums kann je nach Hardware, Kühlung, Stromversorgung und baulicher Eigenschaften stark variieren. Schätzungen ergeben, dass die Bereitstellung von 1MB Daten im Durchschnitt 0,007kWh Elektrizität verbraucht (Weber et al., 2009a). Daraus ergibt sich für ein MP3-Album mit 127MB ein Stromverbrauch von 0,889kWh. Dies entspricht gemäß dem Emissionsfaktor von 624g CO_2/ kWh einer Emission von 554,7g CO_2.

Die durchschnittliche Downloadgeschwindigkeit über das Internet beträgt für Deutschland 3,59Mbit/s (Akamai Technologies Inc., 2009). Der eigentliche Download eines Albums mit 127MB dauert somit 4 Minuten und 43 Sekunden. Hinzu kommen nach eigenen Messungen ca. acht Minuten, die auf die Prozesse von der Erstellung eines Benutzerkontos über die Auswahl des Zahlungsmittels bis hin zum Start des Downloads entfallen. Die Verbindung zum Server besteht damit für 12 Minuten und 43 Sekunden. Experimente mit 15 Internetnutzern und dem Diagnose-Werkzeuges „Traceroute" ergaben, dass durchschnittlich neun öffentliche Router bei der Datenübertragung vom Server zum Laptop des Kunden (Client) durchlaufen werden. Internetknoten im Bereich des „öffentlichen" Internets haben nach Aussagen des German Internet Exchange DE-SIX im Durchschnitt eine Leistungsaufnahme von ca. 5000Watt und einen

Gesamtdatendurchsatz von 1Gbit/s. Bei einer Downloadgeschwindigkeit von 3,59Mbit/s wird jeder Router zu 0,29% belegt. Dies entspricht einer anteiligen Leistungsaufnahme von 14,65Watt. Über neun Router und den Zeitraum von 12 Minuten 43 Sekunden ergibt sich damit ein Stromverbrauch von 0,028kWh. Dies entspricht gemäß dem Emissionsfaktor für Deutschland einer Emission von 17,4g CO_2.

Zu den durchlaufenen Internet-Routern ist zusätzlich der DSL-Router im privaten Haushalt zu berücksichtigen. Der Stromverbrauch eines solchen DSL-Routers, der eine Internetverbindung ermöglicht, beträgt für unterschiedliche Geräte im Betrieb durchschnittlich 6,45Watt (Stiftung Warentest, 2009a). Die Benutzung über 12 Minuten 43 Sekunden verbraucht 0,0013kWh und hat CO_2-Emissionen in Höhe von 0,9g zur Folge.

Der Stromverbrauch eines Laptops, der zum Download eines Albums eingesetzt wird, basiert auf Messungen sieben getesteter Laptops von 15,6 bis 16 Zoll. Durchschnittlich liegt der Stromverbrauch bei 37,5Watt im Betrieb (Stiftung Warentest, 2009b). Tests an 25 unterschiedlichen Laptops ergaben, dass für das Hoch- und Runterfahren im durschnitt 129 Sekunden benötigt werden. Inklusive der Zeit für das Herunterladen des MP3-Albums wird der Laptop somit 14 Minuten 52 Sekunden. Der Stromverbrauch durch den Laptop liegt damit bei 0,0093kWh verbunden mit CO_2-Emissionen in Höhe von 5,8g.

Anhand des analysierten Szenarios mit den Werten aus der Praxis und den getroffenen Annahmen hat der Download eines MP3-Albums einen Energieverbrauch von 0,928kWh und verursacht 578,8g CO_2-Emissionen.

5.4 Wirkungsabschätzung und Auswertung

Für eine vollständige Wirkungsabschätzung ist die Berücksichtigung aller Treibhausgase, wie Kohlenstoffdioxid, Methan, Distickstoffmonoxid, Fluorkohlenwasserstoffe und Schwefelhexafluorid notwendig. Zur Vereinfachung wird hier nur auf CO_2 eigegangen, dass als klimaschädliches Treibhausgas, maßgeblich für den Klimawandel verantwortlich gemacht wird.

In Summe ergeben sich für die Distribution eines CD-Albums CO_2-Emissionen von 862,5g. Die Distribution eines MP3-Albums verursacht 578,8g CO_2. Abbildung 3 stellt die CO_2-Quellen der beiden Distributionsformen kumuliert dar, sodass ersichtlich wird, welche Prozesse bzw. Komponenten relativ hohe CO_2-Emissionen zur Folge haben.

B.5 Ökobilanzierung in der Informationstechnik

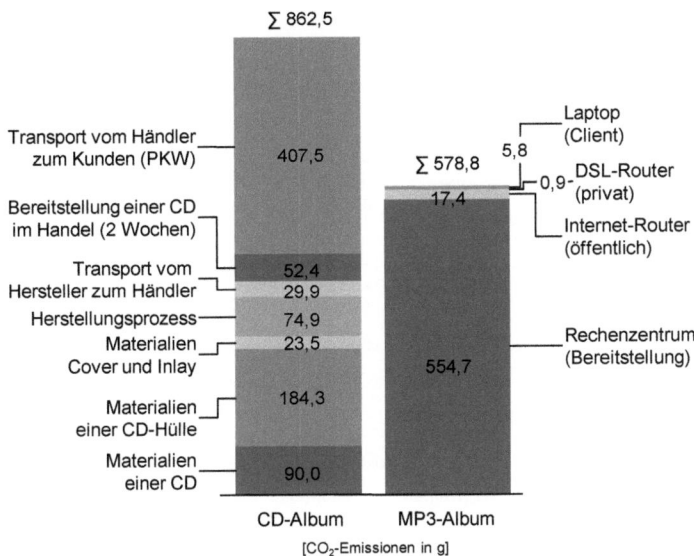

Abbildung B.11: CO_2-Emissionen der Distributionswege im Vergleich

Die Ergebnisse zeigen, dass die Distribution eines CD-Albums über den traditionellen Einzelhandel im Vergleich zur Distribution eines MP3-Albums über das Internet um ca. 33% schädlicher in Bezug auf die Freisetzung von CO_2 ist.

Bei der Distribution eines CD-Albums hat der Transport vom Händler zum Kunden mit ca. 47% den höchsten Anteil der gesamten CO_2-Emission, so dass dieser Prozessschritt ein großes Optimierungspotenzial aufweist. Wenn der Kunde nicht mit dem PKW sondern mit dem Fahrrad fährt, ist diese Variante klimafreundlicher als die Distribution eines MP3-Albums per Internet.

Bei der Bereitstellung eines MP3-Albums über das Internet entfallen 96% der CO_2-Emissionen auf das Rechenzentrum, welches somit das größte Optimierungspotenzial aufweist. Initiativen im Rahmen von Green IT, wie z.B. Server-Virtualisierung und -Konsolidierung, setzen an diesem Punkt an.

Der ökologische Vorteil einer Distribution per Internet ist insbesondere von der Datenmenge abhängig. Die Beanspruchung und damit auch die CO_2-Emissionen eines Rechenzentrums steigen mit zunehmendem Datenvolumen. Demgegenüber sind die CO_2-Emissionen der physischen Auslieferung von der Datenmenge unabhängig. Bestimmungsfaktoren sind hierbei insbesondere Gewicht, Volumen und Entfernung.

Werden die größten Optimierungspotenziale beider Distributionsformen betrachtet, der Transport vom Händler zum Kunden bzw. das Rechenzentrum, stellt sich die Frage, ob eine alternative Distributionsform diese Schwächen umgehen kann. Eine Lösung wäre eine Kombination aus Online- und Offlinedistribution, bei der die CD über das Internet bestellt und per Paketdienst zugestellt wird. In diesem Fall entstünden deutlich geringere Emissionen für den Datentransfer (ca. 22g CO_2) und die Auslieferung (47,2g CO_2). Diese mittlere Variante wäre mit 471,8 g CO_2 aus ökologischer Sicht die effizienteste.

Die Schwierigkeiten der Ökobilanzierung sind speziell in der Erhebung und Qualität der notwendigen Daten begründet. Aufgrund individueller Gegebenheiten können die Ergebnisse einer Ökobilanz für gleiche Produkte oder Dienstleistungen zwischen verschiedenen Anbietern stark variieren. Die Ergebnisse der Ökobilanzierung können daher nicht pauschal verallgemeinert werden, sie geben aber wichtige Hinweise.

Eine weitere Herausforderung stellt die hohe Anzahl der durchlaufenden Wertschöpfungsstufen dar, insbesondere bei der Distribution per Internet. Zusätzlich ist die Datenlage für den Energieverbrauch von Rechenzentren unzureichend. Genauere Messungen im Rechenzentrum sind notwendig, um möglichst nicht auf Schätzungen zurückgreifen zu müssen.

5.5 Handlungsempfehlungen und Ausblick

Das vorrangegangene Beispiel verdeutlicht die Bedeutung der Ökobilanzierung als wirkungsvolles Instrument zur strukturierten Analyse der eigenen Produkte und Dienstleistungen. Die Ergebnisse geben Hinweise auf Optimierungspotentiale. Dadurch können auch im IT-Bereich Innovations- und Verbesserungspotentiale aufgedeckt werden, die letztendlich zu Umsatzsteigerung oder Kosteneinsparungen führen. Im Rahmen eines ökologieorientierten Marketings bieten die Ergebnisse zusätzliche Argumente und Möglichkeiten der Differenzierung.

Eine Ökobilanzierung sollte kontinuierlich erfolgen, um Entwicklungen im Zeitverlauf aufzuzeigen und interne Zielvorgaben aufzustellen. Dabei gilt es die Ansprüche an eine Ökobilanz nach Vollständigkeit sowie Praktikabilität und Verständlichkeit im Ausgleich zu halten. Hierfür ist es notwendig interne Vorgaben zur Aufstellung von Ökobilanzen gemeinsam zu entwickeln und anzuwenden. Softwareanwendungen, wie z.B. Umberto und die Standards der ISO 14040 können diesen Prozess unterstützen.

Gerade IT-Leistungen besitzen gegenüber konventionellen Lösungen häufig einen ökologischen Vorteil. Vor dem Hintergrund der aktuellen Diskussion um Nachhaltigkeit und Green IT stellt die Ökobilanzierung eine geeignete und praktisch erprobte Methodik für Praktiker und Forscher dar, deren Potenzial noch nicht ausgeschöpft ist.

6 Sustainability in Information Systems: Assortment of Current Practices in IS Organizations

Title of Article	Sustainability in Information Systems: Assortment of Current Practices in IS Organizations
Authors	Koray Erek[+] koray.erek@tu-berlin.de Nils-Holger Schmidt* nschmid@uni-goettingen.de Rüdiger Zarnekow[+] ruediger.zarnekow@tu-berlin.de Lutz M. Kolbe* lkolbe@uni-goettingen.de [+]Berlin Institute of Technology (TU Berlin) Chair of Information and Communication Management Strasse des 17. Juni 135 10623 Berlin *Georg-August-Universität Göttingen Chair of Information Management Platz der Göttinger Sieben 5 37073 Göttingen
Published	Proceedings of the 15th Americas Conference on Information Systems (AMCIS 2009) (Erek et al., 2009)
Abstract	The increasing dissemination of information systems into all areas of business and personal life has drawn attention to its environmental effects. IS organizations are becoming aware that they have to take up their responsibility by thinking seriously about sustainability management for information systems. While measures for using computing resources efficiently have received considerable attention, the topic of sustainability in IS management still lacks a theoretical foundation. The purpose of this paper is to explore current environmental efforts in sustainable IS management. Based on fifteen expert interviews with CIOs, IS and environmental managers from IS organizations, the paper provides researchers and practitioners with an explorative study on the situation of sustainability in IS operations and, thus, makes a contribution to this emerging IS research topic.

Table B.19: Fact Sheet of Publication No. 6

6.1 Introduction

Sustainable management describes the long-term, simultaneous optimization of economical, ecological and social objectives to generate a lasting, superior financial performance for the business (Elkington, 1997; Epstein, 2008). Owing to the growing global impact of IS on the economy, ecology and society, firms are increasingly extending the scope of sustainable management to the domain of information systems. This is done in order to achieve benefits such as cost reduction, risk avoidance and improved reputation for IS management. Measures that aim to reduce the ecological impact of the IS have been discussed under the heading "Green IT". Even though Green IT has been used extensively by marketing departments to label their IT products and services as environmentally friendly, the term and its underlying measures have remained rather vague.

The necessity for sustainable IS management derives from ever-growing power demands, waste streams, data amounts and future performance expectations of IT. Google, for instance, operates about 450,000 servers, consuming nearly 800 million kWh a year (Chou, 2008). Now, Google uses customized evaporative cooling to significantly reduce its data centers' energy consumption (Kurp, 2008). However, the impact of IT on the environment is broader than just energy consumption and deduced CO_2 emissions. High technological intensity, rapid technological progress and short life time cycles of IT products contribute significantly to the waste stream of electronic products (e-waste). Information and communication equipment as well as monitors make up 25% of the approximately 20 to 50 million tons of e-waste generated each year (United Nations Environment Programme, 2007). This development brings legislation and other stakeholders on to the IS management scene. Regulative and reputational risks pose an additional threat to IS management, besides the problem of volatile and, in the long run, rising prices of natural resources. CIOs, IT managers and environmental experts are forced to rethink the way they manage their IS. The issue is no longer about whether an IS organization needs to care for environmental concerns but more about how to tackle them more efficiently, while connecting them with the general sustainability strategy of the firm. The research questions arising from this are:

- How can the scope of Green IT and its underlying measures be defined?
- Why are companies really doing Green IT?
- What is state of the art in the scope of Green IT?

For this purpose, interviews with subject matter experts (SMEs), such as CIOs, IS and environmental managers from fifteen different, cross-sectoral IS organizations, thereof three US and twelve European companies, have been carried out as an explorative study. The state of the art analysis will provide researchers and practitioners alike with a better understanding and a roadmap for this emerging field of research. This provides a theoretical foundation to the topic for further research. The first step of the paper is to create a clear view on the concept "sustainability and IS management". Derived from expert interviews, the most important measures for implementing sustainability along the value chain of IS management are displayed. Based on these results, an evaluation is done regarding the current situation of sustainable IS management; research gaps are identified; and recommendations are made for scientists and practitioners.

6.2   Related Research

6.2.1   The Principle of Corporate Sustainability

Sustainability has been discussed extensively within corporate management[12] under the synonyms of corporate social responsibility (CSR), greening the business, eco-efficiency or eco-advantage. Although many studies concerning sustainable management have been introduced, sustainability in IS has not been evaluated until now. Global development and challenges (see Section B.6.1), as well as the general need to align IS strategy to corporate strategy, form the need for an integrated concept of sustainability in IS. In its primary sense, sustainability can be described as survival assurance, meaning that an economical, ecological or social system should be preserved for future generations and, thus, necessary resources should only be exploited to a degree at which it is possible to restore them within a regeneration cycle. The most common definition from the Brundtland Commission defines sustainability as a "development that meets the needs of the present without compromising the ability of future generations to meet their own needs" (World Commission on Environment and Development, 1987). All definitions of sustainability have the preservation of the economical, ecological and social system for the benefit of future generations in common. These dimensions represent the three main pillars of sustainability and are known as the triple bottom line concept (Elkington, 1997). The triple bottom line concept provides a framework to companies to measure and report their performance and organizational success in relation to these pillars. Thus, the primary objective of a corporate sustainability program is to account for the triple bottom line. Corporate sustainability is about minimizing a business' negative impacts on people, societies and the environment, while maintaining or enhancing value for customers, business partners and shareholders. Especially at the business level, sustainability is mainly equated with the economical or financial sustainability (Dyllick & Hockerts, 2002). However, integrated

---

[12] For some works on the topic see (Epstein, 2008; Esty & Winston, 2006).

corporate sustainability is achieved by recognizing the interdependence of the three dimensions over time and keeping an optimal balance between them.

6.2.2 The Value Chain of IS Management

In order to define the field of research, it is necessary to identify the relevant scope of IS management and to outline the key activities of IS service provisioning. The IS business consists of internal (in-house) and external organizations that provide products and services, such as hardware, software and services that can be assigned to IS organizations. These types of organizations generally follow the processes *source, make, deliver,* and *return* through which the value creation takes place. The management of these processes defines the scope of IS management. The foundation for this process oriented concept originated from the supply chain operations reference (SCOR) model (Supply-Chain Council Inc., 2006), a well-known value chain concept in industrial management, which makes it applicable for IS hardware providers. Zarnekow et al. (2006) transferred the SCOR model to IS software and IS service providers by developing the integrated information management (IIM) model. The IIM model focuses on the whole IS value chain, including customer and supplier relationship, while traditional IS management concepts focus on the management of applications (Hochstein et al., 2006). Figure B.12 illustrates the value chain of IS business, including a return process and the stakeholders' interests:

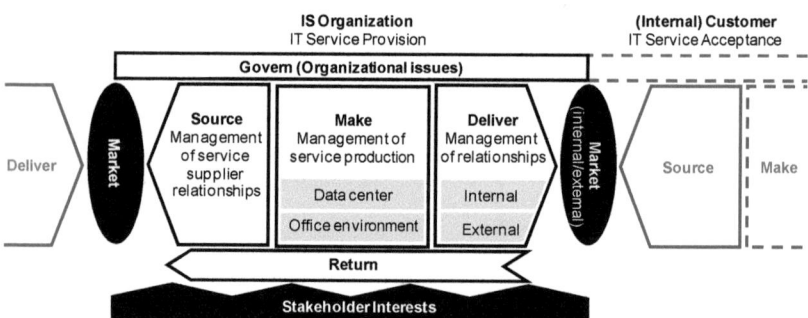

Figure B.12: Value Chain of IS Management (Following Zarnekow et al. (2006))

The *govern* function encompasses strategic procedures and measures, which ensure that allocated IS products and services contribute to the business objectives. In particular, IS governance determines the supervisory functions, organizational structures, and processes.

The *source* process covers all tasks within the supplier relationship management. Usually, IS organizations purchase hardware components, software solutions, personnel or other technological resources. These resources are used in the production phase and are transformed to marketable IS services.

The *make* process comprises all tasks for the management of IS service production. In this paper, focus is put on the two main places of IS service production: the data center and the office environment. Attention is therefore drawn to the efficient planning, development and production of IS services in these two areas.

The *delivery* process is responsible for the management of internal and external relationships. The main objective is to meet all types of internal and external demands in an adequate manner. This does not only comprise IS services but also demands for compliance and transparency. The delivery process can be seen as a mediating function between the internal *make* and the resulting *source* process.

Based on the original SCOR model, we included a *return* process in the IS value chain. The return phase depicts the processes of recycling, preserving and reusing tangible and/or intangible resources. It ensures a life cycle oriented view on IS services, including a waste management and reutilization of products in the value chain.

To frame the value chain of IS management, *stakeholders' interests* are taken into account. The reason for doing so is that the diversity of stakeholders, such as shareholders, policy-makers, suppliers, labor unions, customers, and others can have a major impact on corporate - in this case IS management - performance. Summing up, the model cuts the value chain into four core processes that have to be considered simultaneously when implementing sustainability in IS management.

6.3 Expected Outcomes and Data Collection

6.3.1 Expected Connections Between Sustainability Objectives, Green Measures and Their Benefits

For each phase of the value chain of IS management, a continuum of green measures is applicable. Building on the work of Schmidt et al. (2009a), this section provides an overview of proposed connections between the main objectives of sustainable IS management, possible measures to achieve those, and expected benefits. The objectives and measures do not claim to be complete, but show that sustainable IS management should look beyond data centers to broader issues, such as resource consumption, transparency, and marketing. Table B.20 gives an exploratory overview of the expected connections. These causal relationships were tested using data from the collected interviews.

	Source	Make	Deliver	Return
Objectives of sustainable IS management	Achieve transparency of suppliers, its products and services	Minimize the consumption of resources while maximizing the output	Meeting internal and external demands	Recycle and reuse of resources
Green IT Measures	• Audits of suppliers • Demanding certifications • Life cycle considerations for products and services	• New technologies and concepts for increased efficiency in data centers and the office environment	• Communication of all applied efforts • Dialogs with stakeholders • Benchmarking of performance	• Environmentally sensitive disposal • Disassembly of parts and products • Reusing of parts
Associated Benefits	• Risk avoidance • Better quality of products and services	• Cost reduction • Higher flexibility	• Risk reduction • Reputational improvement	• Risk reduction • Cost reduction

Table B.20: Expected Connections in the Scope of Sustainable IS Management

The procuring IS organization is connected to the risks associated with the suppliers' reputation, its products, and services. Therefore, transparency of these aspects is the main objective during the *source* process. A supplier's unethically or environmentally unfriendly behavior can easily be carried on the downstream supply chain, leading to uncontrollable problems. Besides that, the performance of products and services within their life cycle predetermines the capabilities of all resultant processes, influencing costs, flexibility, and reputation. Hence, sustainable IS management requires measures to achieve transparency. Supplier audits, certain certifications, such as ISO 14001, or special labels for products and services (e.g., Energy Star for desktop computers) can reduce asymmetric information and behavioral uncertainty. Organizations might also install a more sophisticated, centralized sourcing management by committing themselves to general sustainable sourcing principles to purchase products and services in a way that takes into account the long-term impact on people (social perspective), profits (economic view) and the environment (ecological view). Two well known examples for eco-labels are TCO and Energy Star. The TCO certification program ensures that CRT-based computer displays have a low electro-magnetic discharge and include criteria on energy consumption, ergonomics, and the use of hazardous materials in construction (Proto et al., 2007). The Energy Star label is designed to promote and recognize energy efficiency in monitors, climate control equipment, and other technologies (Environmental Protection Agency, 2009).

In the *make* process, IS service provision should be achieved by minimizing the consumption of resources while maximizing the service output. This objective is directly connected to the benefits of cost reduction. However, consuming and using less resources, especially physical ones, also increases the flexibility of the IS organization to deal with change and transition processes. Sustainable IS management therefore looks for new technologies and concepts to increase efficiency in data centers and the office environment. Despite some already existing concepts, such as server virtualization, new possible measures such as grid computing evolve. Grid computing is a collaboration concept that describes performing very large computing tasks together, by connected IT infrastructure. Another example is cloud computing, which is an internet-based architecture through which real-time scalable resources are provided as a service over the internet. An often-quoted example is Google Apps, which provides common business applications online that are accessed from a web browser, while the software and data are stored on Google servers (Thomas, 2008). Good power management can reduce the electricity consumption significantly in the data center and the office environment by installing software that automatically shuts down unused systems or by instructing users to turn off idle machines. An effective power management strategy can save a significant sum of money, as well as lower environmental pollution through reduced energy consumption.

In the *deliver* process, the objective of the IS organization is to meet the internal and external demands of all stakeholders. By integrating the *deliver* process with all other processes of the IS value chain, additional benefits, such as the reduction of external risks and reputational improvement, can be achieved. Employees like to work for a responsible sustainable organization and are highly motivated to contribute to this objective. Other stakeholders differ greatly in their information interests. Therefore, sustainable IS management has to identify measures to complement their services with appropriate communication strategies. A tool that serves this goal is a standardized reporting guideline. The reporting guideline published by the Global Reporting Initiative (GRI) is a widely used sustainability reporting framework and provides principles and indicators that can be used by organizations to measure and report on their economic, environmental, and social performance. These standardized guidelines make it possible to benchmark organizational performance with respect to regulators such as lawmakers or industry oversight committees. Moreover, it forms the basis for communicating organizational commitment to sustainable development and for satisfying the information needs of internal and external stakeholders. Special consortiums, such as the green grid or uptime institute, are working on specific topics of IS and formulating new standards that could potentially become mandatory for the industry.

The *return* process aims to recycle and reuse as many resources as possible. It comprises all measures and methods for recycling, preserving and reusing tangible and/or intangible resources. Thus, concepts regarding waste treatment and securing of natural resources have to be defined and applied.

6.4 Data Collection and Assessment of Current Measures

Between October 2008 and January 2009, interviews with SMEs from fifteen different IS organizations of large-scale international enterprises were carried out, using a structured interview guideline. The sample selection was based on company size and industry, ensuring a cross-sectoral analysis. The questions of the interview guideline were structured around the underlying concept of the value chain of IS management (see previous section):

1. Introduction: Position, responsibilities and experiences of the SME
2. Green IT: Personal opinion on the relevance and future development
3. Sustainability: Perspective on sustainability by the company and the IS organization
4. Stakeholders: Important stakeholders and their demands on the IS organization
5. Source: Measures implemented and achieved benefits
6. Make: Measures implemented and achieved benefits
7. Deliver: Measures implemented and achieved benefits
8. Return: Measures implemented and achieved benefits
9. Closing: Open questions and further suggestions

The structure and questions were developed from literature research. To ensure that no important issues were neglected, open interview questions were asked. Interview partners were CIOs, IS and environmental managers. The fifteen companies came from the following industries: 5 IT service providers, 3 hardware and software providers, 2 telecommunication providers, 2 financial services providers, 1 internet provider, 1 semiconductors provider, 1 pharmaceuticals and chemicals provider. All interviews were recorded and transcribed. The transcription was sent back to the interview partner for final confirmation. Due to the open response options and the cross sectional character of the interviews, not all questions could be answered completely. Because of the small sample, conclusions are limited to the interviewed IS organizations. Nevertheless, the results indicate possible relationships and results for other IS organizations. From the interviews, all mentioned measures that are, from a SMEs perspective, connected to Green IT were collected and rated concerning their implementation status (see Table B.21).

Status	Value	Description
Implemented	+	Measure has been generally implemented
Partially implemented	0	Measure has been partially implemented. Ongoing considerations and planning
Not implemented	-	Measure has not been implemented into daily operations
No known actions		No information concerning the current status of the measure available

Table B.21: Implementation Scale of Green IT Measures

The results are shown in Table B.22. For each measure, the minimum of total implementation is calculated to highlight its significance and dissemination within the interviewed IS organizations.

Domain and Measures	SME1	SME2	SME3	SME4	SME5	SME6	SME7	SME8	SME9	SME10	SME11	SME12	SME13	SME14	SME15	Total implementations
Industry	Semiconductors	Hardware, Software	Hardware, Software	Hardware, Software, IT services	IT services	IT services	IT services	IT services	IT services	Telecommunications	Telecommunications	Internet	Financial services	Financial services	Pharmaceuticals, chemicals	
1. Organizational issues																
Elaborated environmental management system	+	+	+	+	+	+	+		-	+	+	+	+	+	+	13
Environmental officer responsible for IT	+	+	+	+	+	+	+	-		+	+	+	-	+	+	12
CO2 targets as business objectives		+	0	+	+	+	-		-	+	+	+	+	-	+	10
Internal environmental auditing of IT	+	+	-	+	+	+	+	-	-		+	+	-	+	-	9
Environmental target agreements for IT	+	+	+		+	+	+	-		+	+	+	+	+		9
CO2 targets and measuring for IT operations	+	-		+	+	+	-		-	+	+	0	+			7
Certified after ISO 14001	+	0	0	+	+	+	-	-	-		-	-	+	+		6
External environmental auditing of IT	-	-		+	+	-	+	-	-		-	-	-	+	-	4
Cost allocation of electricity		0	0		0	0		0	-		0		0	0	0	0
2. Source																
Consider energy consumption in the RFPs	+	+	+	+	+	+	+	+	+	0	+			+		12
WEEE)	+	+		+	+	+	+		-	+	+	-	+	+	+	11
Life cycle considerations for IT	+	+	+	+	+	+	+	-	-	+	-	+		+		10
Checking for eco labels (e.g., Energy Star)	+	+		+	+	+	+		-				+	+	+	9
Centralized sourcing	+	+			+	+							+	+	+	7
Own certification program for products		+		+	+			-	-		+		+	+	-	6
Checking for subsidies			+				+	-		+		+				4
Sourcing of standardized systems						+		+	-					+		3
Use of regenerative energies		0	0	+	0	+	-	-	-		-	-				2
3. Make																
Data center																
Server virtualization	+	+	+	+	+	+	+	+	+		+	+	+	+	+	14
Cooling optimization	+	+	+	+	+	+	+	+	+	+	-		+	+	0	13
Storage virtualization	+	+	+	+	+		+	+	+	+	+		+	+	0	12
Network and auxiliary optimization		+	+	+	+	+	+	+	+	-		+		+	-	11
Monitoring of electricity consumption	+	+		+	+	+		+	0	+	0	+		+	+	10
Power down of systems		+		+	+	+		+			0	+				6
Use of external consulting	-	-	-	+	+	+	+	-	0			+		+	-	5
Grid computing							-	+	+		-					2
Utilization of fuel cell	-	-			+	-			-		-	-	-	-	-	1
Cloud computing	0	-				-	-	-						-		0
Office environment																
Video conferencing	+		+	+	+		+	-	-		+	-	+	+	-	9
Training and informing of employees	0		0	+	0	0	+	-	-		+	+	+	+	0	7
Printing optimization								+				+	+	+		4
Desktop virtualization	+		-	+	+	0	0	0	0					0	0	3
Wake on LAN (Remote shut down of desktops)													+	+		2
Primarily utilization of notebooks	-		+			-	-	-				-				1
Shared desk		-		+			-	-	-							1
4. Deliver																
Internal Communication																
Internal marketing of Green IT activities	-	+	+	+	0	0	+	0	+	-	-	+	+	+	-	8
Surveys with internal stakeholders	-	+		+			+	-	-		+	+				5
External Communication																
Dialog with stakeholders (e.g., WWF, green grid)	+	+	+	+	+	+	+	0	-	+	+	+	+	+	+	13
External environmental reporting	+	+	+	+	+	+	+	-		+	+	-	+	+	+	12
Compliance to reporting guidelines (e.g., GRI)	+	+	-	+	+	+	-	+	-	-			+	+	+	10
Listed in indices for sustainability		+		+	+	-	-	-	-		+	-	+	+	+	7
Surveys with external stakeholders		+		+	-		+	-	-		+	+		+	+	7
Using Green IT activities for marketing	+	+	-	+	+	0	-	-	-	+	+	0	-	-	-	6
Sharing best practices		+	+	+		-	-	-		-						4
5. Return																
Elaborated recycling concept existent	+	+		+	+	+	+	-	-		+	-				7
Recycling infrastructure	+	+		+	+	+	-	-	-			-				5

Table B.22: Scope of Green IT Measures and Their Implementation

6.5 Analysis: Insights from IS Organizations

The insights from the interviews will be summarized to emphasize the status and associated benefits of each measure. Special focus is put on the most important findings from the processes of the IS value chain.

6.5.1 CO_2 Targets are Gaining Ground but Electricity Consumption of IT is Hard to Measure

Many large-scale enterprises have set up defined targets to reduce their overall emissions of greenhouse gases, including CO_2. These targets primarily aim to reduce the costs of resource consumption, build up a positive image of the enterprise, set incentives to optimize processes and prevent further regulation by legislation. Especially in the United States, experts consider the possibility of an upcoming carbon tax that could be applied first to utility companies and later on to other industries. To measure their emissions, the enterprises mainly follow the greenhouse gas protocol guidelines from the World Business Council for Sustainable Development (WBCSD), and the World Resources Institute (WRI). The guidelines distinguish between direct emissions, for example from business travel; and indirect emissions, for example from purchased electricity. As a large consumer of electricity, the IT infrastructure in data centers and the office environment contributes to the indirect greenhouse gas emissions of the company. Therefore, CO_2 reduction targets in the form of electricity savings are partially passed down to IT operations. A challenge lies in the exact measurement of electricity consumption of IT. Many times, data centers are located in a building with other offices, making it hard to separate individual consumptions. Even harder is measuring within the office environment: Until now, the exact energy consumption of desktops, monitors, notebooks, networks, printers, and communication equipment were only estimated. Therefore, cost allocation of electricity consumption is, in some cases, done only for servers in the data center but never for all IT equipment. Reportedly, some companies have switched their accounting from floor space utilization in the data center (e.g., rack space), to energy used by devices. This new cost accounting approach forces business units to think seriously about the energy efficiency in their IT supported processes. Nevertheless, new technical solutions to measure the exact consumption of electricity by IT, as well as an accounting by the costs-by-cause principle are needed. This would create stronger incentives to manage IS in a sustainable manner.

6.5.2 The Main Area of Interest: The Data Center

Of all interviewed SMEs, data centers get the most attention. This is indicated by the overall number of mentioned measures, as well as their high implementation rate. Especially popular are server and storage virtualization and optimizations regarding the cooling of the data center, the network and additional auxiliary equipment. Server virtualization, for instance, can be used to consolidate the operations of many disposed servers onto fewer physical machines. Storage virtualization helps to perform the tasks of backup and archiving by abstracting logical storage from physical storage; thereby disguising the actual complexity of the storage area network. There are several reasons for focusing on the data center:

1. The data center consumes high amounts of electricity, leading to large expenditures.
2. Servers and equipment in the data center are expensive; space is limited. Optimizing their utilization can result in longer life cycles, performance gains or less equipment binding financial capital.
3. Building new data centers is very expensive. To handle future performance demands, they need to be oversized. New technological concepts such as cloud computing or grid computing pose a threat to the future importance of data centers.
4. The data center with its applications is the heart of all business operations, making it an indispensable resource from the business perspective.
5. The data center is in under the sole responsibility of the CIO. This makes it easier to apply measures and concepts aimed at resource reduction.

Most IS organizations have a high level of maturity in the scope of data centers. This finding is supported by the low implementation level of external consulting. Still, the future relevance of data centers has not been determined. Further optimization potentials lie in the inter-corporate trading of computing capacities as it is already applied for electricity at utility companies. This could eventually lead to an external sourcing of data center services and the disappearance of company owned and operated data centers.

6.5.3 Behavioral Challenges in the Office Environment

In contrast to the data center, the office environment provides no clear picture of preferred measures implemented by IS organizations. Besides video conferencing, it seems that initiatives are rare and scattered. Nevertheless, noticeable resource savings can be achieved. Experts stated, for example, that printers that request a personal pin to start the print job can reduce the paper consumption by up to 40%. Similar results can be expected from reorganization, by abandoning personal printers and putting them in the hallway or in a printing room. In many companies, a considerable amount of electricity is wasted when employees do not switch off their desktop computers after work because they want to start up more quickly the next day. This could be reduced or avoided by using "Wake on Lan" functions to shut off computers remotely at a special hour or by intensified environmental training and employee education. Both measures are applied seldom. Another measure is desktop virtualization, which decouples the user's physical machine from the desktop by emulating his or her desktop hardware environment and running a virtual machine alongside the existing operating system. The operating system can be located on the local machine or can be delivered to a thin client from a data center server (Gibbs, 2008). By simplifying the load on a much smaller, cheaper, and less power consuming thin client, additional cost savings can be achieved. As the cost of hardware plunges while the cost of energy and disposing of waste rises, advantages of thin clients grow. Despite reachable cost savings at the desktop level, evaluations from the interviewed companies indicate that tremendous amounts of servers have to be added to run thin clients, making it tough to calculate business cases. Overall, the office environment shows an inconsistent and underdeveloped situation. The reason for this lies in the challenge to change end users' behavior. Expected inconveniences in an environment in which IT and business responsibilities overlap demand proactive communication to overcome resistance to resource saving projects.

6.5.4 Stakeholder Dialogs and Green IT

The interviews indicate that almost all IS organizations are in some kind of dialog with stakeholders about Green IT. Missing standards, little scientific research and the fear of missing out on something important might explain this high engagement. Although Green IT is frequently prejudiced as a hype theme, it remains a hot topic for IS organizations. More and more environmental reports feature Green IT-related aspects to communicate the organizations' activities to stakeholders. In addition, some companies use their Green IT activities for marketing purposes.

Most interviews with SMEs verified that the telecommunication industry is very active in the scope of Green IT. This high level of Green IT activities forces other companies to follow. However, the results also show that very few companies are convinced about the potential benefits of Green IT-related marketing, focusing on environmental aspects.

6.6 Conclusion and Further Research

Green IT comprises a very large area with many measures and perspectives. In practice, no common definition has been found for Green IT. This hampers a clear view on the topic. Misleadingly, many organizations focus on the issue of energy consumption, neglecting the significance of materials and behavioral aspects in IT. Green IT covers the environmental aspect of sustainable IS management. It comprises all kinds of strategic, process oriented and technical measures applied in the governing, sourcing, making, delivery and returning processes of an IS organization to increase resource efficiency and to decrease environment-related risks.

This research is an initial attempt at describing the current environmental aspects of sustainability in IS. Through fifteen interviews with subject matter experts, the scope of Green IT and its underlying measures are outlined. Based on these results, scientists should be encouraged to do further research regarding single aspects of this study. CIOs, IT and environmental managers can compare their own achievements with the results from this study to evaluate their capabilities. Furthermore, the elaborated structure of Green IT provides a common basis for communication and future projects in this field.

Given the rising prices of energy and other resources, the relevance of sustainability in IS is destined to gain more importance in the future. IS organizations must be aware that sustainable measures are no longer a question of choice; it is a necessity if they want to remain competitive in the future. The potential business benefits of sustainable IS management can be seen in terms of reduced costs, streamlined processes, and more efficient collaboration with suppliers and customers. In addition to the enhanced efficiency through operations, sustainability in IS management can improve the corporate reputation, the competitive advantage, and the attractiveness to investors and customers by demonstrating a corporate commitment to environmental awareness.

Building on this research, the next step will be a large-scale survey with a representative sample of CIOs and IT managers to prove or disprove gained hypotheses. In particular, the expected causal relationships in the scope of sustainable IS management (Table B.20), which have primarily been derived theoretically will be validated, using a representative sample. Further rounds of case studies and expert interviews will follow. The objective is to add sustainability to approved management systems, such as an IT balanced scorecard. Also, the development of a sustainability maturity model for IS organizations is intended. This would enable a benchmarking of different IS organizations. Therefore, existing standards for sustainable IS management can be evaluated and new ones can be developed.

7 Examining the Contribution of Green IT to the Objectives of IT Departments: Empirical Evidence from German Enterprises

Title of Article	Examining the Contribution of Green IT to the Objectives of IT Departments: Empirical Evidence from German Enterprises
Authors	Nils-Holger Schmidt* nschmid@uni-goettingen.de Koray Erek† koray.erek@tu-berlin.de Lutz M. Kolbe* lkolbe@uni-goettingen.de Rüdiger Zarnekow† ruediger.zarnekow@tu-berlin.de *Georg-August-Universität Göttingen Chair of Information Management Platz der Göttinger Sieben 5 37073 Göttingen †Berlin Institute of Technology (TU Berlin) Chair of Information and Communication Management Strasse des 17. Juni 135 10623 Berlin
Published	Australasian Journal of Information Systems (Schmidt et al., 2010a)
Abstract	The article examines Green IT activities' contribution to IT department objectives by analyzing empirical data from 116 companies, using exploratory factor analysis. The outcomes indicate that Green IT contributes to the objectives of efficient internal operations, reputational management, and market competitiveness. In particular, reputational management plays a major role in Green IT engagement. These findings provide CIOs, IT managers, and environmental officers with new insights, and enable a more systematic application of Green IT measures.

Table B.23: Fact Sheet of Publication No. 7

7.1 Introduction

Enterprises are increasingly being challenged by the changing demands of their stakeholders in the scope of eco-awareness and social consciousness (Hewlett et al., 2009). Dealing proactively with social and environmental issues is much more than just a cost-driven exercise; it can be a source of opportunity, innovation, and competitive advantage (Porter & Kramer, 2006).

This general movement has reached information technology (IT) departments in which the environmental impact of IT is being discussed under the term "Green IT". Green IT has been driven primarily by business, and is seen as one of the major concerns of chief information officers (CIOs) (Kurp, 2008; Molla et al., 2008).

Scientific research and industry literature outline the importance of Green IT by referring to its multifaceted benefits (Erek et al., 2009; Fujitsu Australia, 2009; Gadatsch & Juszczak, 2009; Mines & Davis, 2007; Molla, 2008). Kuo and Dick assume that Green IT implementation is a response to pressures from competition, legitimation, and social responsibility (Kuo & Dick, 2010). In this research, we consider Green IT as an IT department instrument to pursue certain objectives. To explore these objectives, we investigate the underlying factors of Green IT benefits. Describing this interdependency will provide researchers and practitioners alike with a better understanding of the topic. The article aims to answer the following three research questions.

- What do IT departments want to achieve with Green IT?
- How do the objectives relate to the domains and processes of IT departments?
- Which recommendations can be derived for researchers, CIOs, IT managers, and environmental officers?

In the next step, the research questions will be answered, using the results of a large cross-sectoral survey of 116 German companies. We apply factor and correlation analysis to discover the underlying objectives. These findings contribute to the existing knowledge on Green IT and provide practical recommendations for CIOs, IT managers, and environmental officers, as well as new opportunities for further research in this field.

7.2 Theoretical Background

7.2.1 The Principle of Corporate Sustainability

Sustainability has been extensively discussed within corporate management under the synonyms of corporate social responsibility (CSR), greening the business, eco-efficiency and eco-advantage. Although many studies concerning sustainable management have been introduced, sustainability in information systems (IS) research has not been evaluated until now. Global development and challenges, as well as the general need to align IS strategy to corporate strategy, form the need for an integrated concept of sustainability in IS. In its primary sense, sustainability can be described as survival assurance, meaning that an economical, environmental or social system should be preserved for future generations, and that necessary resources should only be exploited to a degree at which it is possible to restore them within a regeneration cycle. The most common definition, from the Brundtland Commission, defines sustainability as a "development that meets the needs of the present without compromising the ability of future generations to meet their own needs" (World Commission on Environment and Development, 1987). All definitions of sustainability have the preservation of the economical, environmental and social system for the benefit of future generations in common. These dimensions represent the three main pillars of sustainability and are known as the triple bottom line concept (Elkington, 1997). The triple bottom line concept provides a framework for companies to measure and report their performance and organizational success in relation to these pillars. Thus, the primary objective of a corporate sustainability program is to account for the triple bottom line. Corporate sustainability is about minimizing the negative impacts of a business on people, societies and the environment, while maintaining or enhancing value for customers, business partners, and shareholders. Especially at the business level, sustainability is mainly equated with economical or financial sustainability (Dyllick & Hockerts, 2002). However, integrated corporate sustainability is achieved by recognizing the interdependence of the three dimensions over time, and keeping an optimal balance between them.

7.2.2 The Value Chain of IT Departments

In order to define the field of research, it is necessary to identify the relevant scope of IS management, and to outline the key activities of IT departments. The IT business consists of internal (in-house) and external organizations that provide products and services, such as hardware, software, and services that can be assigned to IT departments. These types of departments generally follow the processes *source, make, deliver,* and *return* through which the value creation takes place. The management of these processes defines the scope of IT management. The foundation for this process-oriented concept originated from the supply chain operations reference (SCOR) model (Supply-Chain Council Inc., 2006), a well known value chain concept in industrial management, which makes it applicable for IT hardware providers. Zarnekow et al. (2006) transferred the SCOR model to IT software and IT service providers by developing the integrated information management (IIM) model. The IIM model focuses on the whole IT value chain, including customer and supplier relationships, while traditional IT management concepts focus on the management of applications (Hochstein et al., 2006). Figure B.13 illustrates the value chain of IT business, including a return process and the stakeholders' interests.

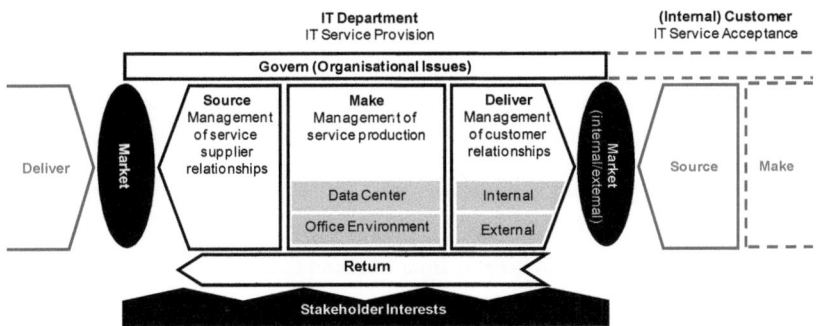

Figure B.13: Value Chain of the IT Department (Source: Erek et al. 2009)

The *govern* function encompasses strategic procedures and measures that ensure that allocated IT products and services contribute to the business objectives. In particular, IT governance determines the supervisory functions, organizational structures, and processes.

The *source* process covers all tasks within the supplier relationships management. Usually, IT departments purchase hardware components, software solutions, personnel, and other technological resources. These resources are used in the production phase and are transformed to marketable IT services.

The *make* process comprises all tasks for the management of IT service production. This paper focuses on the two main locations of IT service production: the data center and the office environment. Attention is therefore drawn to the efficient planning, development and production of IT services in these two areas.

The *delivery* process is responsible for the management of internal and external relationships. The main objective is to meet all types of internal and external demands in an adequate manner. This not only comprises IT services, but also demands for compliance or transparency. The delivery process can be seen as a mediator function between the internal *make* and the customers' *source* process.

Based on the original SCOR model we included a *return* process into the IT value chain. The return phase depicts the processes of recycling, preserving and reusing tangible and/or intangible resources. It ensures a life cycle oriented view on IT services, including waste management and reutilization of products in the value chain.

To frame the value chain of IT departments, *stakeholders' interests* are taken into account. The reason for doing so is that the diversity of stakeholders, like shareholders, policy-makers, suppliers, labor unions, customers, and others can have a major impact on corporate - in this case IT management - performance. In summary, the model cuts the value chain into four core processes, which have to be considered simultaneously when implementing sustainability in IT management.

Green IT measures can be structured according to the strategic, operational and technical levels of an IT department (Schmidt et al. 2009). They can also be assigned to the value chain of IT management; more specifically to the *source, make, deliver* and return processes (Molla 2008; Schmidt et al. 2009).

7.2.3 Comparison of benefits from CSR and Green IT

For our Green IT survey, we draw on research from the scope of CSR. A literature review shows a broad variety of potential benefits from CSR for the corporate level (Table B.24). Wagner (2007) categorizes these benefits in an empirical investigation into the three categories of objectives: internal operations, market competitiveness and reputation management. Literature review on Green IT reveals benefits that are comparable to those of CSR. Due to the similarity of the benefits, we assume that Wagner's (2007) categories also apply to Green IT.

		Corporate Social Responsibility	Green IT
		Benefits on the Corporate Level	Benefits on the IT Department Level
Categories of Main Objectives (Wagner, 2007)	Internal Operations	• Asset utilization (Figge, 2005) • Optimized production processes (Schaltegger & Synnestvedt, 2002) • Cost savings (Schaltegger & Synnestvedt, 2002)	• Cost efficiency (Erek et al., 2009; Gadatsch & Juszczak, 2009; Mines & Davis, 2007) • Increased flexibility (Erek et al., 2009) • Energy efficiency (Fujitsu Australia, 2009; Gadatsch & Juszczak, 2009) • Improved business efficiency (Molla, 2008) • Reduced carbon emissions (Molla, 2008)
	Market Competitiveness	• Customer satisfaction (Luo & Bhattacharya, 2006) • Buying intention (Klein & Dawar, 2004; Sen & Bhattacharya, 2001) • Attitude towards products and services (Berens et al., 2005)	• Influence the mindset of customers (Molla, 2008) • Better quality of products and services (Erek et al., 2009) • Strategic differentiator and competitive advantage (Fujitsu Australia, 2009; Molla, 2008) • Facilitating innovations (Gadatsch & Juszczak, 2009) • Enabler of other green initiatives (Molla et al., 2008) • Increased customers (Fujitsu Australia, 2009)
	Reputation Management	• Corporate image (Yoon et al., 2006) • Attractiveness for investors and business partners (Tsoutsoura, 2004) • Workplace attractiveness (Turban & Greening, 1997) • Reputational improvement (Fombrun, 2005; Schwaiger, 2004; Tsoutsoura, 2004; Verschoor & Murphy, 2002) • Stronger brand (Brown & Dacin, 1997; Sen & Bhattacharya, 2001)	• Risk reduction (Erek et al., 2009) • Influence mindset of investors (Molla, 2008) • Reputational improvement (Erek et al., 2009) • Increased staff morale (Fujitsu Australia, 2009) • Positive brand image (Fujitsu Australia, 2009; Gadatsch & Juszczak, 2009; Molla, 2008) • Regulatory compliance (Fujitsu Australia, 2009; Mines & Davis, 2007; Molla, 2008)

Table B.24: Comparison of CSR and Green IT Value Drivers and Their Possible Categorization

7.3 Methodology

7.3.1 Research Model

The proposed research model, as shown in Figure B.14, is based on the findings of the literature review. Green IT measures are implemented in one of the processes (govern, source, make, deliver, and return) of the value chain of IT departments. These measures generate certain benefits for the IT department or the entire enterprise.

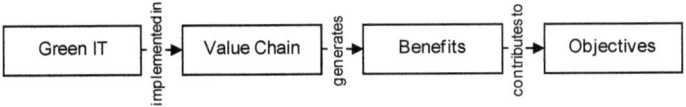

Figure B.14: The Connection Between Green IT, Value Chain, Benefits, and Objectives

All benefits relate to some type of overall objective. Through these mediators, Green IT contributes to the strategic objectives of the IT department. Understanding the relationships helps to select adequate Green IT measures that also align with the IT department's objectives.

7.3.2 Questionnaire and Statistical Analysis

A cross-sectional survey was conducted to evaluate the proposed research model. A paper-based questionnaire was posted in September 2009. Each letter included a covering letter, a self-addressed envelope and the basic definition of Green IT. The addressees were CIOs, IT managers, environmental managers and staff responsible for Green IT from 619 major companies listed in German stock indexes. To increase the response rate, respondents were offered a report of the results. Over three weeks, we received 116 anonymous replies, amounting to a response rate of 18.7%. This response rate is consistent with rates in similar surveys in IS research (Mani et al., 2010; Poppo & Zenger, 2002).

The questionnaire was based on a previous survey within the scope of CSR (Wagner, 2007). Additional questions were developed regarding the findings of fifteen case studies conducted on Green IT (Erek et al., 2009). Further questions were added from the survey results of Fujitsu Australia (2009). General questions about the enterprise and the perception of Green IT were integrated. A panel of five academic experts reviewed the questions to confirm that the constructs were adequately described by the item wording. The statistical analysis was done using the software SPSS Statistics 17.0. All questions for the factor analysis had a 5-point Likert scale, ranging from "Agree strongly" to "Disagree strongly" (Hague, 2002). For the survey, a practical definition of Green IT was provided to the participants, which comprised the above-mentioned aspects under the given limitations of space and perceivability.

We defined Green IT as follows:

"Green IT comprises the management of all activities and measures of the IT department, which are aimed to reduce the resource consumption by IT, e.g. in terms of energy, material or paper. Furthermore, it includes instruments to control, steer, and communicate the success".

This is a broad view of Green IT, which also includes management aspects. The environmental impact, for example in the form of carbon dioxide emissions, was not pointed out explicitly, since we see this as the consequence of reduced resource consumption. We apply exploratory factor analysis, which can be used to reveal underlying variables (Field, 2009). Exploratory factor analysis is a widely used and broadly applied statistical method in the social sciences to discover structures in large variable sets (Costello & Osborne, 2005). Factor analysis aims to reduce complexity by looking at the variables that seem to cluster together in a meaningful way (Field, 2009). All correlation coefficients are calculated using Spearman's rho (r_s) for non-parametric data.

7.3.3 Sample Profile

All findings are based on the sample profile shown in Table B.25. The participating enterprises belong to a variety of industries, such as manufacturing (35%), trade and commerce (19%), information and communication technologies (16%), and others (30%), which are representative of Germany.

Annual Turnover 2008 in Million of Euros			Employees of the Enterprise			Employees of the IT Department		
	Percent	Frequency		Percent	Frequency		Percent	Frequency
1-4	6%	7	1-99	9%	10	1-4	10%	12
5-9	3%	4	100-499	16%	19	5-9	8%	9
10-49	5%	6	500-999	9%	11	10-49	29%	34
50-499	25%	29	1,000-4,999	30%	35	50-499	18%	21
500+	53%	62	5,000+	35%	41	500+	35%	40
Missing values	7%	8		N=116			N=116	
		N=116						

Table B.25: Turnover and Employees of the Responding Companies

The annual turnover and the number of employees indicate that large enterprises dominate the sample. The total number of employees significantly corresponds to the number of employees in the IT department, $r_s = .74$, $p < .001$.

Following Zarnekow et al. (2006), the participants were asked about their IT department's target market. The results in Table B.26 show that the internal market is most relevant to the respondents' IT departments.

B.7 Examining the Contribution of Green IT to the Objectives of IT Departments

Employees in the IT Department			Target Market of the IT Department		
	Percent	Frequency		Percent	Frequency
1 - 4	10%	12	Internal market	76%	88
5 - 9	8%	9	Internal and external market	16%	19
10 - 49	29%	34	External market	3%	3
50 - 499	18%	21	Missing values	5%	6
500 +	34%	40		N = 116	
		N = 116			

Table B.26: Size and Target Markets of the IT Departments

7.4 Results from the Empirical Analysis

7.4.1 Importance and Implementation

For 56% of all participants, Green IT is an important or very important topic. The importance of Green IT significantly relates to the overall environmental engagement of the company, $r_s = 0.542$, p (one-tailed) < 0.001. This illustrates that Green IT is seen in the environmental context of the enterprise. Green IT also correlates significantly with the number of employees in the enterprise, $r_s = 0.245$, p (one-tailed) < 0.001, and the number of employees in the IT department, $r_s = 0.374$, p (one-tailed) < 0.001. This indicates that larger companies tend to be more active in Green IT. Green IT is primarily implemented in the *make* process of the IT value chain in which the data center is the most considered domain for Green IT (Table B.27).

In which domains did you implement Green IT? (multiple answers allowed)				
# Item	Value Chain	Domain	Percent	Frequency
Q10.2	Govern	In-house training	14%	16
Q10.4		Remuneration of employees	2%	2
Q10.9	Source	Procurement	46%	53
Q10.6	Make	Data center	82%	95
Q10.3		Office environment	48%	56
Q10.5	Deliver	Internal and external communication	32%	37
Q10.1		Distribution	13%	15
Q10.7		Marketing	12%	14
Q10.8	Return	Disposal	53%	61
			N = 116	

Table B.27: Implementation and Domains of Green IT

7.4.2 Benefits and Objectives

To determine Green IT's contribution to the objectives of IT departments, an exploratory factor analysis was conducted. For the factor analysis, questions evaluating the benefits related to Green IT were included. The distributions of measured variables should be examined prior to conducting factor analysis (Fabrigar et al., 1999). Therefore, the distributions of these items were tested to see whether they deviated from a normal distribution. For the test of normality, the Kolomogorov-Smirnov test and Shapiro-Wilk test were applied (Field, 2009). With $p < 0.001$ for both tests, the distributions of measured variables were significantly non-normal.

If the assumption of normality is violated, the principal factor analysis method or principal axis factoring (PAF) (in SPSS) is recommended (Costello & Osborne, 2005).

All variables were examined regarding their usability for factor analysis. The reliability of factor analysis and individual variables can be determined using the Kaiser-Meyer-Olkin measure of sampling adequacy (KMO) (Kaiser, 1970). KMO values larger than 0.5 are barely acceptable (Kaiser, 1974). KMO values between 0.5 and 0.7 are mediocre, values between 0.7 and 0.8 are good, values between 0.8 and 0.9 are great and values above 0.9 are superb (Field, 2009). The anti-image correlation matrix provided Kaiser-Meyer-Olkin values for each individual variable. Scores below 0.5 are unacceptable and should be removed from the factor analysis (Hutcheson & Sofroniou, 1999). Therefore, one item with KMO = 0.484 was excluded.

A debate exists over the criterion used to decide whether a factor should be retained for analysis (Field, 2009). Kaiser recommends retaining all factors with eigenvalues greater than 1 (Kaiser, 1960). The scree plot graphs each eigenvalue (Y-axis) against the factor with which it is associated (X-axis). The cut-off point for selecting factors should be at the point of inflexion of this curve. Only factors left of the point of inflexion should be retained (Cattell, 1966).

An initial analysis was run to determine eigenvalues for each factor in the sample. Four factors had eigenvalues over Kaiser's criterion of 1, with the fourth factor being just above it, with an eigenvalue of 1.033. The scree plot was ambiguous and showed inflexions that would justify retaining three factors. The best choice for researchers to determine the number of factors is the scree test (Costello & Osborne, 2005). Furthermore, three factors were proposed in the research model of Section B.7.3.1. Therefore, the three factors, efficient internal operations, market competitiveness and reputation management were retained in the final analysis. The rerun of the examination with three factors showed an equally low crossloading of one item on two factors. Hence, it was dropped from the analysis, as suggested (Costello & Osborne, 2005).

A principal factors analysis (PAF) was conducted on the remaining 18 items with orthogonal rotation of varimax (Table B.28). The Kaiser-Meyer-Olkin measure verified the sampling adequacy for the analysis with KMO = 0.828 as 'great'. All KMO values for individual items were > 0.71, which is above the acceptable limit of 0.5 (Field, 2009). Bartlett's test of sphericity should be significant (p < .001) (Field, 2009). Bartlett's test of sphericity χ^2 (153) = 989.295, p < 0.001, indicated that correlations between items were sufficiently large for PAF. In the preliminary analysis, the sample was checked for multicollinearity (Field, 2009). The Pearson correlation coefficient matrix reported a determinant of 0.0000306, which is slightly larger than the necessary value of 0.00001, indicating that multicollinearity was not a problem.

The three factors explain 52.93% of the variance. Table B.28 shows the factor loadings after rotation. The items that cluster around the same factors suggest that factor 1 represents the objective of efficient internal operations, factor 2 represents the objective of market competitiveness and factor 3 represents the objective of reputation management. All factors have more than three strong loading items with 0.50 or better. Therefore, all factors are considered to be solid (Costello & Osborne, 2005).

#Item	Benefit	Objectives of Green IT		
		Factor 1 Internal Operations	Factor 2 Market Competitiveness	Factor 3 Reputation Management
Q32	Postpone investments	**.742**	.031	.050
Q34	Predict future investments	**.720**	.195	.109
Q33	Extend life-span of equipment	**.715**	-.003	.067
Q23	Shorter processes	**.669**	.313	.183
Q30	Better forecast of costs	**.630**	.246	.314
Q21	Lower capital investments	**.625**	.108	.098
Q22	Better utilization of equipment	**.593**	.015	.201
Q29	Improved process quality	**.582**	.246	.292
Q24	Reduced share of fixed costs	**.540**	.209	.172
Q28	Lower process costs	**.520**	.258	.267
Q16	Above average prices for current IT products /services	.083	**.865**	.155
Q18	More sales of current IT products/services	.118	**.747**	.318
Q17	Above average prices for future IT products/ services	.192	**.722**	.253
Q20	Gaining competitive advantage	.368	**.522**	.153
Q27	Decision criterion for the buyer of IT products/services	.178	.337	**.718**
Q26	Quality indicator for selecting contract partners	.214	.210	**.687**
Q25	Competence signal of the IT department	.212	.148	**.665**
Q36	Improved reputation of the IT department	.115	.136	**.651**
	Eigenvalues	4.400	2.677	2.453
	% of variance	24.426	14.874	13.635
	Cronbach's α	.889	.847	.816
	Most important factor for respondents in % (N = 103)	27.2	35.0	37.9

Note: Factor loadings over .40 appear in bold

Table B.28: Benefits of Green IT and Related Objectives

When using factor analysis, the consistency of the questionnaire should be checked using Cronbach's α, which should be around 0.8 (Field, 2009). The factors representing efficient internal operation, market competitiveness, and reputation management have high reliabilities with Cronbach's α = 0.889 / 0.847 / 0.816.

The objective of efficient internal operations is achieved by the following Green IT benefits: to postpone investments, to plan future investments and costs better, to extend life-spans of IT equipment, to shorten processes, to implement better utilization, to improve quality, and to lower process costs (Table B.28).

Market competitiveness is achieved by asking higher prices and selling more products or services (Table B.28). Green IT also serves as a quality indicator and a competence signal that increases the reputation of the IT department (Table B.28).

Even though the factor of efficient internal operation explains the greatest variance (24.4%), the majority of respondents (37.9%) perceive the contribution of Green IT to the objective of reputation management as most important, followed by market competitiveness (35.0%) and efficient internal operation (27.2%).

7.4.3 Domains and Objectives

Table B.29 highlights the correlations of the revealed objectives with the domains in which Green IT is applied. Each objective is significantly positively correlated with a compatible domain. Efficient internal operation is related to Green IT in the data center, $r_s = 0.276$, p (one-tailed) < 0.001, but not to the office environment. On the other hand, reputation management is linked to the office environment, $r_s = 0.250$, p (one-tailed) < 0.01. Reputation management is also correlated to communication, $r_s = 0.321$, p (one-tailed) < 0.001, as well as the overall number of domains in which Green IT is applied, $r_s = 0.310$, p (one-tailed) < 0.01. Market competitiveness shows a significant link to the domain of distribution, $r_s = 0.241$, p (one-tailed) < 0.01.

# Item	Value Chain	Domain	Factor 1 Internal Operations	Factor 2 Market Competitiveness	Factor 3 Reputation Management
Q10.2	Govern	In-house training	.084	-.002	.15
Q10.4		Remuneration of employees	-.021	.213*	-.066
Q10.9	Source	Procurement	.030	.098	.165*
Q10.6	Make	Data center	.276**	-.031	.212*
Q10.3		Office environment	.000	.226*	.250**
Q10.5	Deliver	Internal and external communication	.191*	.188*	.321***
Q10.1		Distribution	.000	.241**	.119
Q10.7		Marketing	.172*	.132	.082
Q10.8	Return	Disposal	-.067	-006	.029
		Number of Green IT domains	.136	.175*	.310**

Note: Spearman's correlation coefficients. Significance of correlation coefficients, * $p < .05$ (1-tailed), ** $p < .01$ (1-tailed), *** $p < .001$ (1-tailed)

Table B.29: Correlations Between Green IT Domains and Objectives of the IT Department

7.5 Implications

From these results in Section B.7.4.2, it can be concluded, with certain limitations, that Green IT measures and activities contribute to the objectives of an IT department, which are efficient internal operations, market competitiveness, and reputation management.

From the revealed objectives in Section B.7.4.2, reputational management (37.9%) is the most important, followed by market competitiveness (35.0%), and efficient internal operations (27.2%). As these outcomes indicate, doing Green IT is not just aimed at achieving efficient internal operations for reducing costs or emissions. Rather, Green IT is a tool used by a company to signal its own competence, quality and reputation to important relationship collaborates, such as suppliers and employees. Considering the factor of market competitiveness, it also aims at increasing the sales and prices of products or services.

The objectives are all correlated to the application of Green IT in specific domains (Section B.7.4.3). Efficient internal operations relate to Green IT in the data center but not to the office environment. This could be the result of benefits being easier to realize with greater impact in the data center. On the other hand, reputational management is linked to the office environment, communication, and the overall number of domains in which Green IT is applied. An explanation for this might be that Green IT measures in the office environment are aimed at creating involvement, positively influencing the employees' opinion of environmental protection, and at demonstrating own competence. Market competitiveness correlates with Green IT in the domain of distribution, which seems useful when products or services are advertised.

The results provide CIOs, IT managers, and environmental officers with recommendations for efficiently implementing Green IT into an IT strategy and an overall business strategy. Considering the business and IT strategy, CIOs and IT managers should decide which of the objectives - efficient internal operations, reputation management, and/or market competitiveness - are most relevant for doing business. Based on this analysis, they should implement Green IT in the relevant domains of the IT department value chain.

7.6 Limitations and Conclusion

There are a number of clear limitations in these preliminary findings. Foremost is the exploratory nature of the research and small sample size, which limits generalizability of these findings. The sample selection and the applied statistical methods impose specific limitations on the results. Due to the sample selection, the results of this study are only representative of German IT departments. The perception of Green IT might vary from region to region (Molla et al., 2008). Limitations also derive from the application of principal factor analysis. Conclusions are restricted to the sample collected and generalizations of the results can be achieved only if analysis using a different sample reveals the same factor structure (Field, 2009). Furthermore, correlations do not imply causality between two variables, because there could be other measured or unmeasured variables that affect the results (Field, 2009). To test for non-response bias, the responses were split into two groups, based on their chronological return. There is a difference between early and late respondents when cross-tabulated with "extent of Green IT planning and implementation": 61% of the early respondents had "planned" or "implemented and planned" Green IT, but this proportion decreased to 29% in the late respondent group. The chi-square statistic was significant at $p < .05$. An explanation for this could be that respondents who are currently planning Green IT activities are more likely to answer the questionnaire. It can be assumed that non-response bias has not caused any significant problems with the study.

Despite the given limitations, these results provide insights and guidelines for CIOs, IT managers, and environmental officers for applying Green IT in their daily business.

In this paper, we showed the contribution of Green IT to the objectives of IT departments. We provided a theoretical foundation to the topic and suggested practical recommendations for implementing Green IT along the value chain of IT departments. This enables CIOs, IT managers, and environmental officers to get further insights into Green IT and to take the appropriate actions to link Green IT with the IT and business strategy.

The results need further investigation and validation. Therefore, future research should replicate the survey in other countries to determine if the results are transferable. The outcomes should be discussed by conducting case studies and expert interviews.

Green IT can contribute to the IT strategy, as well as to the business strategy. The development of a procedural model, defining tasks, roles and responsibilities in the scope of Green IT for the entire enterprise seems useful.

IT departments have to be aware that environmental topics need to be addressed for the departments to remain competitive in the future. Given the rising prices of energy and other resources, and the increasing awareness of all stakeholders of environmental issues, the relevance of Green IT is destined to gain even more importance in the future. Hence, the concept of environmentally oriented IT has an increased relevance for policy-makers, practitioners, and researchers.

8 Predictors of Green IT Adoption: Implications from an Empirical Investigation

Title of Article	Predictors of Green IT Adoption: Implications from an Empirical Investigation
Authors	Nils-Holger Schmidt* nschmid@uni-goettingen.de Koray Erek[+] koray.erek@tu-berlin.de Lutz M. Kolbe* lkolbe@uni-goettingen.de Rüdiger Zarnekow[+] ruediger.zarnekow@tu-berlin.de *Georg-August-Universität Göttingen Chair of Information Management Platz der Göttinger Sieben 5 37073 Göttingen [+]Berlin Institute of Technology (TU Berlin) Chair of Information and Communication Management Strasse des 17. Juni 135 10623 Berlin
Published	Proceedings of the 16th Americas Conference on Information Systems (AMCIS 2010) (Schmidt et al., 2010b)
Abstract	The increasing focus on the environmental impact of IT (information technology) demands reorientation of IT departments. Research has outlined that the importance of Green IT is related to IT business alignment and environmental initiatives, while uncertainty potentially derives from a lack of standards, measurements, or internal support of Green IT. We assume that importance and uncertainty are the main determinants for Green IT adoption. However, these theoretical assumptions still lack empirical validation. As a contribution to the ongoing discussion of Green IT, we analyze data from 116 IT departments on the predictors of Green IT adoption, using multinomial logistic regression. It is shown that the outlined assumptions prove to be statistically significant. These findings contribute to existing knowledge on Green IT and provide practical recommendations for CIOs, IT managers, environmental and sustainability managers. They also highlight opportunities for further research in this field.

Table B.30: Fact Sheet of Publication No.8

8.1 Introduction

The movement of eco-awareness has reached IT (information technology) departments. The environmental impact of IT is being discussed under the term "Green IT". Green IT has been driven primarily by business, and is one of the major concerns of chief information officers (CIOs) (Kurp, 2008; Molla et al., 2008). Scientific research and practical literature outline the relevance of Green IT by referring to its multifaceted benefits (Erek et al., 2009; Mines & Davis, 2007; Molla, 2008).

The underlying hypothesis of this study is that the adoption of Green IT is dependent on its perceived importance and uncertainty. Literature indicates that the importance is related to IT business alignment initiatives in the scope of environmentally sustainable business strategies and practices (Elliot & Binney 2008; Molla 2009; Molla et al. 2008). Uncertainty might derive from a lack of standards, measurements, or internal support for Green IT (Elliot 2007; Erek et al. 2009; Molla 2009; Molla et al. 2008; Molla 2008; Schmidt et al. 2009). Despite growing research in this area, these theoretical assumptions still lack empirical validation.

We strive to contribute to the emerging field of research on Green IT by using empirical evidence to answer the following three research questions:

1. Which factors predict the importance of Green IT for IT departments?
2. Which factors predict the uncertainty about Green IT for IT departments?
3. How do importance and uncertainty predict the planning and implementation of Green IT?

In order to address these questions, we need to create a clear view of Green IT. Therefore, we develop an exploratory research model to illustrate the assumed connections between organizational factors, importance, uncertainty, and Green IT adoption. The research questions are answered using results from a large, cross-sectoral survey with 116 German enterprises. We apply multinomial logistic regression to evaluate the assumed relationships. Our findings contribute to existing knowledge of Green IT and provide practical recommendations for CIOs, IT managers, environmental and sustainability managers, as well as opportunities for further research in this field.

8.2 Theoretical Background of Green IT

Green IT represents an important topic for information systems (IS) research (Elliot, 2007). It is used as a generic term for measures and activities of an enterprises' IT department, aiming to contribute to the environmentally oriented objectives of corporate sustainability and corporate social responsibility (Chen et al. 2008; Schmidt et al. 2009). A comprehensive overview of current research on Green IT is provided by Molla (2009).

Even though Green IT has been extensively used by marketing departments to label their IT products and services as environmentally friendly, the term and its underlying measures have remained rather vague. Green IT can be seen as a holistic and systematic approach to address challenges of the IT infrastructure, the environmental impacts of business IT activities, IT's support for environmentally sustainable business practices, and IT's role in the low-carbon economy (Molla et al., 2008). This view does not solely comprise IT-focused issues but also business related topics in which IT is an enabler of corporate environmental improvements. This aspect has also been labeled "Green IS" (Boudreau et al., 2008).

For our survey, the participants were provided with a practical definition of Green IT, which comprised the above-mentioned aspects within the limitations of space and perceivability: "Green IT comprises the management of all activities and measures of the IT department, which are aimed to reduce the resource consumption by IT, e.g. in terms of energy, material or paper. Furthermore, it includes instruments to control, steer, and communicate the success." This is a broad view on Green IT and includes management aspects. The environmental impact, for example in the form of CO_2 emissions, was not pointed out explicitly since we see this as the consequence of reduced resource consumption.

8.3 Conceptual Framework

In this section, we develop a conceptual framework. This framework will be tested using empirical evidence (Figure B.15). We assume that the adoption of Green IT depends on its perceived importance and uncertainty. The adoption is formalized by the *extent of Green IT planning and implementation*, which refers to Green IT policies, practices, technologies, and systems, as mentioned by Molla (2009).

An *important* topic is recognized as substantial by people who are knowledgeable in the field. Furthermore, it has potential to positively contribute to the company or the IT department. The importance of a technology is also related to its usefulness, which, according to the TAM (Technology Acceptance Model), determines the intention to use it (Venkatesh & Davis, 2000). From this, we suggest that increased perception of the importance of Green IT increases the extent of Green IT planning and implementation.

Uncertainty describes a situation in which the outcome or success of an activity is not known (Hubbard, 2007). Research on online exchange relationships from a principal-agent perspective indicates that perceived uncertainty negatively influences a buyer's intentions to purchase products online (Pavlou et al., 2007). Uncertainty about the benefits of a new technology decreases the speed of diffusion (Hall & Khan, 2003). We therefore propose that uncertainty about Green IT leads to a lower extent of Green IT planning and implementation.

The *corporate management* and the overall *environmental strategy* of an enterprise are generally seen as major drivers of a Green IT strategy (Elliot & Binney, 2008; Molla, 2009; Molla et al., 2008). IT departments are urged to align their strategy with the business needs (Ward & Peppard, 2002). Therefore, we conclude that if the corporate management demands Green IT or if the enterprise is highly engaged in environmental activities, this should raise the importance of Green IT.

The effects of the *experience* curve can be a source of competitive advantage for enterprises (Ghemawat, 1985). Therefore, we assume that IT departments that are more experienced with Green IT are also more aware of benefits and best practices. They should also be less uncertain about the future relevance of Green IT.

Power emission and power utilization are important parameters that need to be measured to assess IT's environmental impact (Molla, 2009). Environmental strategies make it desirable to *measure* and monitor the entire life cycle costs of products and services (Elliot, 2007). Researchers have proposed implementing Green IT measures into management systems, such as the IT balanced scorecard (Schmidt et al., 2009a). Therefore, we assume that measurements of Green IT will decrease the uncertainty about Green IT.

Closely related to measurements are *standards* for Green IT. The absence of standards is often seen as an obstacle to Green IT implementation (Erek et al., 2009). Molla (2008) outlines the importance of developing Green IT standards across the enterprise. In our research framework, we assume that the existence of defined and accepted standards for Green IT decreases the uncertainty about Green IT.

Hypes are associated with overinflated expectations, resulting in potential disillusionment (Gartner Inc., 2009). Green IT is frequently prejudiced as a hyped topic (Erek et al., 2009). We therefore assume that considering it as a hyped topic increases the uncertainty about Green IT.

Researchers have indicated the importance of staff involvement to ensure the success of Green IT projects (Molla, 2008; Molla et al., 2008). We assume that there is less uncertainty if the IT staff initiates Green IT.

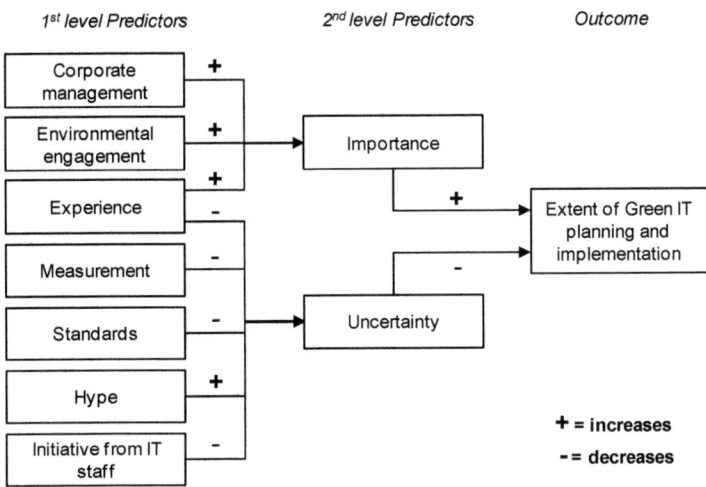

Figure B.15: Proposed Research Framework of Predictors for Green IT Adoption

The initial exploratory research framework is shown in Figure B.15. We assume that factors such as corporate management, environmental engagement, and experience with Green IT have a positive impact on its importance. Conversely, experience, measurements, standards, and IT staff initiative regarding Green IT are factors that potentially decrease uncertainty about it. The perception of Green IT being a hyped topic tends to increase uncertainty. As mentioned earlier, the final step tests whether importance and uncertainty are predictors for the planning and implementation of Green IT. Our framework does not claim to be complete. It has to be considered that other relevant predictors have not been included. Nevertheless, we consider it a starting point to be refined by future research.

8.4 Methodology

A cross-sectional survey was conducted to evaluate the proposed research model. A paper based questionnaire was posted in September 2009. Each letter included a covering letter, a self-addressed envelope and the basic definition of Green IT. The addressees were CIOs, IT managers, environmental managers and staff responsible for Green IT from 619 major companies listed in German stock indexes. To increase the response rate, respondents were offered a report of the results. Over three weeks, we received 116 anonymous replies, amounting to a response rate of 18.7%. This response rate is consistent with rates in similar IS research surveys (Mani et al., 2010; Poppo & Zenger, 2002).

The questionnaire was based on a previous survey within the scope of CSR (Corporate Social Responsibility) (Wagner, 2007). Additional questions were developed, based on findings from fifteen case studies conducted on Green IT (Erek et al., 2009), as well as from the survey results of Fujitsu Australia (2009). General questions about the enterprise and the perception of Green IT were integrated. A panel of five academic experts reviewed the questions to confirm that the constructs were adequately described by the item wording. The statistical analysis was done using the software SPSS Statistics 17.0. The relevant sample items for the exploratory research framework are shown in Table B.31.

Scale	Response Anchors	Sample Item
Corporate management	Likert 5-point scale, "strongly disagree/strongly agree"	The IT department is approached frequently by corporate management with the topic of Green IT.
Environmental engagement	Likert 5-point scale, "sufficiently engaged/highly engaged"	How would you rate the environmental engagement of your enterprise?
Experience	Likert 5-point scale, "strongly disagree/strongly agree"	Our enterprise possesses a lot of experience with Green IT.
Initiative from IT staff	Dichotomous, "yes/no"	Did IT staff instigate the Green IT initiative?
Measurement	Likert 5-point scale, "strongly disagree/strongly agree" (reversed)	The success of Green IT is difficult to measure. Reversed to: The success of Green IT is easy to measure.
Standards	Likert 5-point scale, "strongly disagree/strongly agree"	There are defined and generally accepted standards for Green IT.
Hype	Likert 5-point scale, "strongly disagree/strongly agree"	Green IT is a hyped topic and is overrated.
Importance	Likert 5-point scale, "very unimportant, very important", recoded to a 3-point scale, "unimportant, neutral, important"	How important is Green IT for the IT division of your enterprise?
Uncertainty	Likert 5-point scale, "strongly disagree, strongly agree", recoded to a 3-point scale, "high uncertainty, average uncertainty, little uncertainty"	The future significance of Green IT for our enterprise is uncertain.
Green IT planning and implementation	Likert 4-point scale, "not planned or implemented, planned, implemented, implemented and planned"	Green IT measures in our enterprise are...

Table B.31: Questionnaire Response Formats and Sample Items

To evaluate the proposed research framework, three multinomial logistic regressions are applied to the data. This type of logistic regression is used to predict membership of more than two categories (Field, 2009). In logistic regression linearity, no multicollinearity and independence of errors are assumed (Field, 2009). The correlation matrix indicates that no predictors correlate too highly with each other, $r > .9$ (Field, 2009). For all models, the VIF (Variance Inflation Factor) values confirm that multicollinearity is not a problem (Backhaus et al., 2008; Field, 2009). A visual inspection of the residuals shows no indication of heteroscedasticity or non-linearity. The histogram and normal probability plot test of the data prove the normality of residuals. The Durban-Watson values for all assumed models indicate little correlation between the residual terms, which is still acceptable

(Field, 2009). The recommended sample size for multinomial logistic regression should be 10 times the number of predictors, with a minimum sample size of 100 (Long, 1997). The maximum number of predictors used in the three regression models is five (uncertainty about Green IT). All three models have at least 111 valid samples. Therefore, the sample size is considered adequate for multinomial logistic regression.

The key terms of multinomial logistic regression can be explained as follows: The fit of the model is shown by the -2 log-likelihood statistic and its associated chi-square, which should be significant with $p < .05$ (Field, 2009). The Pearson and deviance statistics test whether the predicted values are significantly different from the observed values. For a good fit of the model, these measures should not be significant (Field, 2009). R and the corresponding R^2-value tell us how much of the variance in the outcome is accounted for by the regression model from the sample (Field, 2009). In logistic regression, Cox and Snell's R^2 and Nagelkerke's R^2 can be considered as being similar to R^2 from linear regression. The Wald statistic, which has a chi-square distribution, indicates whether the b coefficient for that predictor is significantly different from zero. If the coefficient is significantly different from zero, then it can be assumed that the predictor makes a significant contribution to the prediction of the outcome (Field, 2009). Most important for the interpretation of logistic regression is the value of the odds ratio, which is an indicator of the change in odds, resulting from a unit change in the predictor (Field, 2009). The odds ratio can be interpreted in terms of change in odds.

$$\text{odds ratio} = \Delta \text{odds} = \frac{\text{odds after a unit change in the predictor}}{\text{original odds}}$$

A value larger than 1 indicates that as the predictor increases, the odds of the outcome occurring increase. A value less than 1 indicates that as the predictor increases, the odds of the outcome occurring decrease.

8.5 Findings

All findings are based on the sample profile shown in Table B.32. The participating enterprises belong to a variety of industries, including manufacturing (35%), trade and commerce (19%), information and communication technologies (16%), and others (30%), which are representative of German industry.

Annual Turnover 2008 in Million of Euros			Employees of the Enterprise			Employees of the IT Department		
	Percent	Frequency		Percent	Frequency		Percent	Frequency
1-4	6%	7	1-99	9%	10	1-4	10%	12
5-9	3%	4	100-499	16%	19	5-9	8%	9
10-49	5%	6	500-999	9%	11	10-49	29%	34
50-499	25%	29	1,000-4,999	30%	35	50-499	18%	21
500+	53%	62	5,000+	35%	41	500+	35%	40
Missing values	7%	8			N=116			N=116
		N=116						

Table B.32: Turnover and Employees of the Enterprises

The annual turnover and the number of employees indicate that large enterprises dominate the sample. The total number of employees significantly corresponds to the number of employees in the IT department, $r_s = .74, p < .001$.

To test for non-response bias, the responses were split into two groups, based on their chronological return. There is a difference between early and late respondents when cross-tabulated with "extent of Green IT planning and implementation": 61% of the early respondents had "planned" or "implemented and planned" Green IT, but this proportion decreases to 29% in the late respondent group. The chi-square statistic was significant at $p < .05$. An explanation for this could be that respondents that are currently planning Green IT activities are more likely to answer the questionnaire. It can be assumed that non-response bias has not caused any significant problems in the study.

8.5.1 Importance of Green IT (Research question 1)

To increase the explanatory power of the model and to reduce the problem of large standard errors, the sample item for the importance of Green IT is recoded from a 5-point to a 3-point scale. The sample distribution regarding the three final categories is shown in Table B.33.

Categories: Importance of Green IT	N	Marginal Percentage
unimportant	21	18.4%
neutral	29	25.4%
important	64	56.1%
valid	114	100.0%
missing	2	

Table B.33: Importance of Green IT

The model for the importance of Green IT shows a significantly good fit of the data (-2 log-likelihood = 103.716, χ^2 = 70.303, p < .001). This is supported by the Pearson and deviance statistics (both p > .05), which are not significant. The model explains between 46% (Cox & Snell) and 53.5% (Nagelkerke) of the variance of Green IT importance. Therefore, the model has a good explanatory power of the importance of Green IT.

For simplification, we only compare the most converse Green IT categories: "Green IT is important" with "Green IT is unimportant". The category of average importance is not compared and investigated further. This leads to the following results (Table B.34).

Importance of Green IT		b	Std. Error	Sig.	Odds Ratio	95% Confidence Interval for odds ratio	
						Lower Bound	Upper Bound
important vs. unimportant	Intercept	-9.498	1.935	.000			
	Corporate management	1.168	.524	.026	3.216	1.152	8.982
	Environmental engagement	1.734	.424	.000	5.664	2.466	13.010
	Experience	1.140	.393	.004	3.128	1.448	6.758

Table B.34: Parameter Estimates for the Importance of Green IT

- *Corporate management:* The extent to which corporate management approaches the IT department with the topic of Green IT significantly predicts whether Green IT is considered important or unimportant, b = 1.168, Wald χ^2 = 4.969, p < .05. The odds ratio indicates that as this variable increases by one unit, the change in the odds of Green IT being important is 3.216. In short, Green IT is likely to be more important when the IT department is approached frequently by corporate management.

- *Environmental engagement:* The extent of the enterprise's environmental engagement significantly predicts whether Green IT is considered as important or unimportant, b = 1.734, Wald χ^2 = 16.707, p < .001. The odds ratio indicates that as this variable increases, the change in the odds of Green IT being important is 5.664. In other words, Green IT is likely to be more important when the enterprise engages in environmental protection.
- *Experience:* The experience with Green IT significantly predicts whether Green IT is considered important or unimportant, b = 1.140, Wald χ^2 = 8.420, p < .01. The odds ratio shows that as this variable increases, the change in the odds of Green IT being important is 3.128. In other words, it is more likely that Green IT is considered important, rather than unimportant, if a higher level of experience with Green IT exists.

The odds ratios show that corporate management, environmental engagement, and experience are predictors of the importance of Green IT. The strongest effect size comes from the environmental engagement of the enterprise. The effect size of the corporate management and the experience are comparable. Therefore, we assume that the overall attitude of the enterprise towards ecological issues has the highest impact on the importance of Green IT.

Regarding the first research question, it can be stated that corporate management, environmental engagement and experience are good predictors of Green IT importance.

8.5.2 Uncertainty about Green IT (Research question 2)

According to the previous model, the uncertainty about Green IT is recoded from a 5-point to a 3-point scale. The sample distribution regarding the three final categories is shown in Table B.35.

Categories: Uncertainty about Green IT	N	Marginal Percentage
little uncertainty	41	36.9%
average uncertainty	32	28.8%
high uncertainty	38	34.2%
valid	111	100.0%
missing	5	

Table B.35: Uncertainty about Green IT

The model for the uncertainty about Green IT has a significantly good fit of the data (-2 log-likelihood = 165.158, χ^2 = 73.442, p < .001). This is supported by the deviance statistics (p > .05), which is not significant. Pearson indicates that predicted values are significantly different from the observed values (p < .001). However, the dispersion parameters (Pearson = 1.38, Deviance = 0.83) are both close to the ideal value of 1 and therefore no cause for concern regarding overdispersion (Field, 2009). The model explains between 48.4% (Cox & Snell) and 54.5% (Nagelkerke) of the variance of the uncertainty about Green IT. Therefore, the model explains the uncertainty about Green IT well.

For simplification, we only compare the most converse Green IT categories: little uncertainty about Green IT with high uncertainty about Green IT. The category of average uncertainty is not further compared and investigated. Table B.36 illustrates the findings.

Uncertainty about Green IT		b	Std. Error	Sig.	Odds Ratio	95% Confidence Interval for odds ratio	
						Lower Bound	Upper Bound
little uncertainty vs. high uncertainty	Intercept	-3.659	1.746	.036			
	Experience	1.082	.355	.002	2.952	1.471	5.924
	Measurement	.838	.345	.015	2.312	1.175	4.549
	Standards	1.025	.411	.013	2.788	1.246	6.239
	Hype	-.948	.325	.003	.387	.205	.732
	Initiative from IT staff (no = 0)	-2.047	.688	.003	.129	.034	.498
	Initiative from IT staff (yes = 1)	0^a	.	.	.	.	.

a. This parameter is set to zero because it is redundant.

Table B.36: Parameter Estimates for the Uncertainty about Green IT

- *Experience:* The experience with Green IT significantly predicts whether the uncertainty about Green IT is little or high, b = 1.082, Wald χ^2 = 9.273, p < .01. The odds ratio shows that as this variable increases, the change in the odds of having little uncertainty about Green IT is 2.952. In other words, little uncertainty is more likely than high uncertainty if a higher level of experience with Green IT exists.
- *Measurement:* The extent to which the measurement of Green IT success is perceived as easy significantly predicts whether the uncertainty about Green IT is little or high, b = 0.838, Wald χ^2 = 5.888, p < .05. The odds ratio indicates that as this variable increases by one unit, the change in the odds of having little uncertainty about Green IT is 2.312. In short, when the measurement of Green IT success is perceived as easy, it is more likely that uncertainty about the topic will be reduced.
- *Standards:* The existence of defined and generally accepted standards for Green IT significantly predicts whether the uncertainty about Green IT is little or high, b = 1.025, Wald χ2 = 6.228, p < .05. The odds ratio indicates that as this variable increases by one unit, the change in the odds of having little uncertainty about Green IT is 2.788. This means known standards for Green IT reduce uncertainty.
- *Hype:* The perception of Green IT as an overrated and hyped topic significantly predicts whether the uncertainty about Green IT is little or high, b = -.948, Wald χ^2 = 8.533, p < .01.

The odds ratio indicates that as this variable increases by one unit, the change in the odds of having little uncertainty about Green IT decreases to .387. This means that perceiving Green IT as a hyped topic makes it more likely to increase uncertainty about Green IT.

- *Initiative from IT staff*: The origin of the Green IT initiative significantly predicts whether the uncertainty about Green IT is little or high, b = -2.047, Wald χ^2 = 8.849, p < .05.[13] The odds ratio indicates that as the initiative for Green IT changes from "no, not from IT staff" (0) to "yes, from IT staff" (1) the change in the odds of possessing little uncertainty compared to high uncertainty is .129. In other words, the odds of having little uncertainty about Green IT compared to high uncertainty is 1/0.129 = 7.752 times higher if the initiative for Green IT comes from the IT staff.

The odds ratios show that experience, measurement of Green IT success, Green IT standards and the initiative from the IT staff decrease the uncertainty about Green IT. Considering Green IT as hype increases the uncertainty. Experience with Green IT and Green IT standards have the strongest effect size but measuring Green IT success is also important.

Regarding the second research question, it can be stated that experience, measurement, standards, hype, and initiative from IT staff are good predictors of the uncertainty about Green IT.

8.5.3 Planning and Implementation of Green IT Measures (Research question 3)

The sample distribution regarding the categories of Green IT planning and implementation is shown in Table B.37.

Categories: Green IT planning and implementation	N	Marginal Percentage
not planned or implemented	23	19.8%
planned	32	27.6%
implemented	37	31.9%
implemented and planned	24	20.7%
valid	116	100.0%
missing	0	

Table B.37: Planning and Implementation of Green IT

The model for the planning and implementation of Green IT is a significantly good fit of the data (-2 log-likelihood = 69.252, χ^2 = 57,531, p < .001). This is supported by the Pearson and deviance statistics (both p > .05), which are not significant. The model explains between 39.1% (Cox &

---

[13] At this point, the values of the original publication are faulty and have been corrected. This change has no effect on implications or conclusions.

Snell) and 41.8% (Nagelkerke) of the variance of the planning and implementation status of Green IT. Therefore, the model has a good explanatory power. For simplification, we only compare the most converse Green IT categories: "implemented and planned", with "not planned or implemented". The other categories are not further compared and investigated. Table B.38 illustrates the results.

Green IT planning and implementation		b	Std. Error	Sig.	Odds Ratio	95% Confidence Interval for odds ratio	
						Lower Bound	Upper Bound
implemented and planned vs. not planned or implemented	Intercept	-2.119	1.987	.286			
	Importance	2.214	.610	.000	9.149	2.766	30.265
	Uncertainty	-1.195	.532	.025	.303	.107	.859

Table B.38: Parameter Estimates for Planning and Implementation of Green IT

- *Importance:* The importance of Green IT significantly predicts whether Green IT measures are implemented and planned, b = 2.214, Wald χ^2 = 13.153, p < .001. The odds ratio indicates that as the importance of Green IT increases by one unit, the change in the odds of Green IT measures being implemented and planned is 9.149. Therefore, it is more likely that Green IT measures will be implemented and planned than not if Green IT is considered to be an important topic.

- *Uncertainty:* The uncertainty about Green IT significantly predicts whether Green IT measures are implemented and planned, b = -1.195, Wald χ^2 = 5.047, p < .05. The odds ratio indicates that as the uncertainty about Green IT increases by one unit, the change in the odds of Green IT measures being implemented and planned (rather than not planned or implemented) is .303. In short, it is unlikely that Green IT measures will be implemented and planned if the uncertainty about Green IT is high.

Regarding the third research question, it can be stated that importance and uncertainty are good predictors for the planning and implementation of Green IT measures. The findings also show that explanatory power of importance and uncertainty increases along the four adoption levels of Green IT.

8.6 Implications and Limitations

The findings verify our proposed research framework. From this, we draw practical implications for CIOs and IT managers, as well as environmental and sustainability officers. The implications come with specific limitations, mentioned below.

CIOs and IT managers should be aware of the factors that influence the importance of and uncertainty about Green IT, thereby avoiding mistakes when dealing with it. The needs of corporate management and the environmental strategy of the enterprise are determinants of Green IT importance, which should be considered. Green IT can be a powerful initiative to align the activities of the IT department with the overall environmental strategy. On the other hand, if the business needs and the environmental strategy are not congruent with the ideas of Green IT, the chances of adoption seem to be limited. Corporate management as well as environmental and sustainability managers can push the topic of Green IT by actively approaching the IT department and creating the appropriate setting in the context of an environmental strategy.

The findings also indicate the existence of an experience curve (Ghemawat, 1985). Increasing experience with Green IT raises its importance and decreases its uncertainty. CIOs and IT managers should consider this effect when thinking about initial Green IT activities. Additional workshops or training on Green IT could support these activities.

Standards and measurements are needed to decrease the uncertainty about Green IT. Special consortiums, such as The Green Grid or the Uptime Institute, are working on standards and measurements in the scope of Green IT (The Green Grid, 2010a; Uptime Institute, 2010). Still, there are only a few generally accepted standards and measurements (Erek et al., 2009). Therefore, CIOs and IT managers, as well as researchers, have to develop or adapt new metrics and standards.

The discussion about Green IT being a hyped topic creates confusion and uncertainty. CIOs and IT managers should focus on facts, not on marketing slogans and political agendas. As the findings indicate, personal experience with Green IT seems to be the best marketing for Green IT.

Environmental and sustainability managers, as well as corporate management, should consider the advantages of IT staff initiatives. This reduces the uncertainty that can potentially lead to a greater adoption of Green IT practices. Planning and implementing Green IT should therefore be facilitated by a business wide task force, including corporate management, environmental and sustainability managers, and IT executives.

The sample selection and the applied statistical methods impose specific limitations on the findings. Due to the sample selection, the results of this study are only representative of German IT departments. The perception of Green IT might vary from region to region (Molla et al., 2008). Nevertheless, Green IT has been a topic on an international scale with comparable awareness, as indicated. Limitations also derive from the application of regression analysis. Conclusions are restricted to the sample collected and generalizations of the results can be achieved only if analysis of different samples reveals the same outcome (Field, 2009). Furthermore, it has to be considered that there are important underlying predictors that have not been included in this analysis, such as the image or the perceived ease of implementation of Green IT.

Despite the given limitations, these results provide insights and guidelines for CIOs, IT managers, as well as environmental and sustainability managers to promote implementation of Green IT projects.

8.7 Conclusion and Further Research

In this research, we provide a set of predictors of Green IT adoption. We deliver an initial conceptual framework and make practical recommendations. Our findings enable CIOs, IT managers, as well as environmental and sustainability managers to gain further insights about Green IT and to take the appropriate actions to link Green IT with the IT and business strategy.

The results demand further investigation and validation. To refine the suggested model, a cross-validation of the proposed conceptual framework is necessary. Therefore, future research should replicate the survey in other countries to determine if the results are repeatable. The findings should be refined and evaluated further, using in-depth case study analysis (Eisenhardt, 1989; Yin, 2002). Since uncertainty plays an important role in Green IT, further investigations from the perspective of principal-agent theory offer promise of new insights (Pavlou et al., 2007).

The findings indicate that there is a need for the development of standards and measurements. Further research should therefore provide key performance indicators for internal and external reporting. This could be done within the concept of an IT balanced scorecard. Also, the organizational context of Green IT should be investigated, since actors from different divisions are involved. An ideal reference model, defining processes, tasks, roles, and responsibilities in the scope of Green IT for the entire enterprise seem useful.

IT departments must be aware that environmental topics need to be addressed in order to remain competitive in the future. Given the rising prices of energy and other resources, and the increasing awareness of all stakeholders of environmental issues, the relevance of ecological oriented IT is destined to rise in the future. As a result, we reason that following the outlined recommendations can have a positive impact on Green IT management and the business performance.

9 Towards a Contingency Model for Green IT Governance

Title of Article	Towards a Contingency Model for Green IT Governance
Authors	Nils-Holger Schmidt nschmid@uni-goettingen.de Lutz M. Kolbe lkolbe@uni-goettingen.de Georg-August-Universität Göttingen Chair of Information Management Platz der Göttinger Sieben 5 37073 Göttingen
Published	Proceedings of the 19th European Conference on Information Systems (ECIS 2011) (Schmidt & Kolbe, 2011)
Abstract	Although practitioners have begun to implement Green IT in their companies, Green IT governance varies significantly. No research has been done to explain these differences in Green IT governance. Building on contingency theory and IT governance, we develop a contingency model for Green IT governance that demonstrates the fit between contingencies and the company-specific configuration of Green IT. In the first step, three archetypes of Green IT governance are presented, reaching from centralized, over federal to decentralized. In the second step, we identify from literature competitive strategy, firm size, organization structure, performance strategy, environmental impact of industry, environmental strategy, IT infusion, and IT diffusion, as contingency factors that determine the ideal type of Green IT governance. The contingency model for Green IT governance is validated by insights from five case studies. With the enhanced understanding of how Green IT governance is shaped by contingency factors, organizations are able to select the most successful Green IT governance form.

Table B.39: Fact Sheet of Publication No. 9

9.1 Introduction

In information systems (IS) research, the environmental impact of information technology (IT) and related measures for its reduction and management are being discussed under the heading "Green IT" (Kuo & Dick, 2010; Schmidt et al., 2009a; Watson et al., 2010; Yi & Thomas, 2007). Green IT incorporates measures and activities of an enterprises' IT department to achieve environmental sustainability (Chen et al., 2008; Molla et al., 2009; Schmidt et al., 2009b).

Although practitioners have begun to implement Green IT in their companies, the governance of Green IT varies significantly (Molla et al. 2009). No research has been done so far to explain these differences in Green IT governance or to provide a framework to determine the ideal type of Green IT governance in a given context. Many researchers have investigated and explained how organizations structure their general IT governance (e.g. Brown, 1997, 1999; Tavakolian, 1989; Wetherbe & Whitehead, 1977; Xue et al., 2008). Building upon this, we want to extend this research to the specific case of Green IT governance.

Studies on IT governance indicate that the decision rights for IT management differ between companies, depending on contingency factors such as competitive strategy, firm size and organization structure (Ein-Dor & Segev, 1982; Olson & Chervany, 1980; Tavakolian, 1989). Based on the IT governance findings, we assume that the differences in Green IT governance depend on certain contingency factors. To analyze organizational structures in the context of IS sustainability research, Melville (2010) suggests the application of contingency theory.

Consequently, contingency theory and case study research are used in this paper to increase our knowledge of Green IT governance. Specifically, we want to answer the following two questions:

1. What Green IT governance patterns exist?
2. How do contingency factors influence Green IT governance patterns?

This paper proposes a flexible Green IT governance approach, which demonstrates the fit between contingencies and the company-specific configuration of Green IT. In this respect, competitive strategy, firm size, organization structure, performance strategy, environmental impact of industry, environmental strategy, IT infusion, and IT diffusion have been identified as contingency factors.

While this paper focuses on the coordination aspect of Green IT governance, it does not examine guidelines and compliance facets. The paper outlines the first results from case studies on Green IT governance, which the authors conducted with five companies of different size and from different industries.

With an enhanced understanding of how Green IT governance is shaped by contingency factors, organizations might be able to select the most appropriate Green IT governance form to achieve desired outcomes within specified contexts.

This paper is organized as follows: we begin with a literature review on IT governance and contingency theory. Thereafter, we develop a contingency model for Green IT governance from literature. Then, the applied case study research design is described from which we draw our findings. The conducted case studies provide information to validate the proposed contingency approach for Green IT governance. We conclude with implications and a discussion of future research opportunities.

9.2 Developing a Contingency Model for Green IT Governance

9.2.1 IT Governance and Contingency Theory

Many researchers have investigated the link between IT and organizational structure. The organizational structure describes the ways in which an organization divides its labor into distinct tasks and achieves coordination among them (Melville, 2010). Organizational aspects of IT are associated with IT governance. Effective IT governance is potentially the single most important predictor of the value an organization generates from IT (Weill & Ross, 2004). IT governance is the practice that allocates decision rights and establishes the accountability framework for IT decisions to ensure alignment with strategic objectives (Weill & Ross, 2005).

With respect to the distribution of decision rights, IT governance has been categorized into different archetypes, such as centralized, federal, hybrid, and decentralized (Brown 1997; Magill & Brown, 1994). Weil and Ross (2005) identify six archetypal approaches to IT decision-making, ranging from highly centralized to highly decentralized. Organizational centralization specifies the level of concentration in decision-making rights (Xue et al. 2008).

From a scientific perspective, researchers highlight the importance of aligning IT governance with the overall organizational context. Scholars investigate the relationship between organizations' IT governance design and contingency factors, using contingency theory (Brown, 1997; Grant & Brown, 2005; Sambamurthy & Zmud, 1999; Weber et al., 2009b; Weill & Ross, 2005; Xue et al., 2008).

Firms govern IT very differently, depending on a number of contingency factors (Weill & Woodham, 2002). The underlying assumption is that there is no general IT governance design that fits all organizations and that the contingency factors affect the contribution of IT governance in improving the organization's success (Figure B.16). The model illustrates the two main concepts of contingency theory. First, the characteristics of an organization, for example the allocation of decision rights, affect the organization's success. Second, the ideal organizational configuration is determined by specific contingency factors.

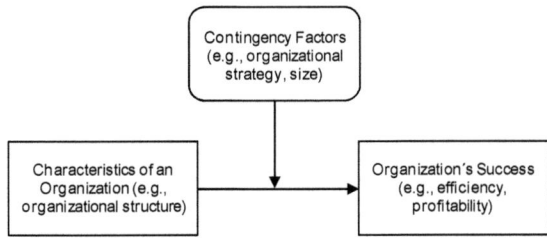

Figure B.16: Contingency Model (Adapted from Weber et al. (2009b) and Umanath (2003))

Many IT governance studies that apply contingency theory have identified various elements that influence the ideal shape of IT governance that leads to success. Contingency factors are, for example competitive strategy (Tavakolian, 1989), diversification breadth (Brown, 1997; Sambamurthy & Zmud, 1999), firm size (Ein-Dor & Segev, 1982), organization structure (Ein-Dor & Segev, 1982; Olson & Chervany, 1980), performance strategy (Weill & Ross, 2005), IT infusion and IT diffusion (Sullivan, 1985; Ward & Peppard, 2002), and line IT knowledge (Sambamurthy & Zmud, 1999). It seems reasonable to think that these contingency factors would also be relevant in Green IT governance.

9.2.2 Green IT

Green IT is a systematic application of environmental sustainability criteria to the design, production, sourcing, use, and disposal of the IT infrastructure in order to reduce IT, business processes, and supply chain related emissions and waste, as well as improve energy efficiency (Molla et al., 2009). Green IT also comprises managerial aspects to control and monitor the effectiveness of implemented measures, as well as marketing measures to communicate success to important stakeholders (Erek et al., 2009). Examples of concrete Green IT measures are provided by Schmidt et al. (2009a) and by Kumar and Mieritz (2007), who describe ideas such as efficient cooling concepts, server virtualization and thin clients. These measures can be structured regarding their strategic, operational and technical impact, and along the IT activity chain of IT departments, covering a *source*, *make* (data center, office environment), *deliver* and *return* process (Molla, 2008; Schmidt et al., 2009a).

9.2.3 Archetypes of Green IT Governance

Green IT governance can be defined as an operating model that describes the administration of Green IT initiatives (Molla et al., 2009). Adapting the IT governance definition of Weil and

Woodham (2002), Green IT governance specifies the decision rights and accountability framework to encourage environmentally desirable behavior in the sourcing, use and disposal of IT. To achieve this, roles, responsibilities, accountability, and control of Green IT initiatives need to be clearly established (Molla et al., 2009).

Desirable behavior is different in every company. Businesses need to determine whether the responsibility for Green IT initiatives should be assigned to CIOs (Chief Information Officers) or to environmental managers (Molla et al., 2009). Current Green IT governance practices vary significantly. Some organizations allocate the responsibility to govern Green IT more centralized to IT managers; others consider Green IT as part of enterprise wide sustainability initiatives and follow a more decentralized approach (Molla et al., 2009).

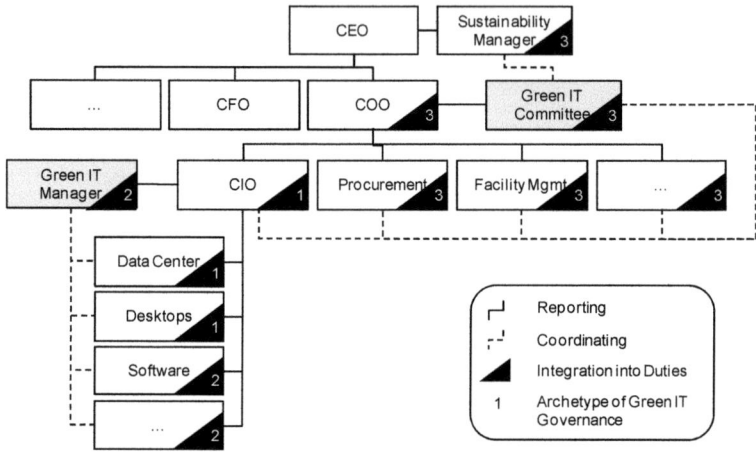

Figure B.17: Archetypes of Green IT Governance Patterns

Regarding these insights from literature and the presented case studies, we assume that there are three ideal Green IT governance archetypes that differ regarding their level of centralization of Green IT decision-making (Figure B.17). This answers our first research question.

The Green IT governance archetypes represent a continuum of coordination arrangements, reaching from centralized (1) over federal (2) to decentralized (3) types (Table B.40). In practice, Green IT governance is likely to occur in a specific form along the continuum, thereby varying slightly from the proposed archetypes. Nevertheless, the archetypes are a first attempt at structuring Green IT governance.

Archetype of Green IT Governance		Description
1	Centralized	Green IT is centralized within few domains of the IT department. The coordination of Green IT is done by extending job responsibilities, for example in the data center or the office environment. The CIO has primary authority. Green IT measures are treated like other IT projects. They mainly focus on cost reduction by lowering the energy consumption in the data center and/or the office environment. Green IT is of low importance to the company.
2	Federal	Green IT is coordinated by a designated Green IT manager. Typically, the Green IT manager is a member of the IT department and keeps track of all initiatives, proposes new ideas and reports to the CIO. The Green IT manager might be a contact partner for the sustainability or environmental manager. Green IT is addressed in the entire IT department and provides initial contacts to other domains. Green IT is of medium importance to the company.
3	Decentralized	Green IT is coordinated by a designated Green IT committee throughout the various business units of the company, following a matrix approach. It consists of a Green IT manager, members of various business units and the sustainability or environmental manager, who reports to the CEO (Chief Executive Officer). The committee holds periodic meetings. The committee reports to a COO (Chief Organization Officer). Green IT activities are an integral part of the company's sustainability strategy. All aspects of Green IT are considered and evaluated. The Green IT committee might also impact the company's strategy by developing new Green IT-related products or services that potentially lead to a competitive advantage. Green IT is of high importance to the company.

Table B.40: Description of Green IT Governance Archetypes

There is no single best model of Green IT governance. Specific external and internal factors of the company, deriving from the organizational, regulatory-market, socio-cultural, ecological, and technological environment influence the organization's actions (Jenkin et al., 2011). Research indicates that the importance of and uncertainty about Green IT and its level of implementation differs for every organization (Schmidt et al., 2010b).

Therefore, every organization will encourage different behaviors. This also determines the ideal type of Green IT governance coordination and the allocation of decision rights. It is important to understand how Green IT governance archetypes are shaped by contingency factors because they may affect desired outcomes of Green IT. The evaluation of contingency factors and their impact on the best fit for Green IT governance is done in the next section.

9.2.4 A Contingency Model of Green IT Governance

Contingency theory respects the fact that each enterprise needs a specific Green IT governance configuration that fits a set of external and internal factors. Green IT governance helps companies structure their Green IT responsibilities. Contingencies and their influence determine which configuration of Green IT governance fits a company best. Finding the best configuration ensures that Green IT contributes to the business objectives of an enterprise.

In the next section, we answer the second research question by outlining how contingency factors influence Green IT governance patterns. From a literature review, we identify competitive strategy, firm size, organization structure, performance strategy, environmental impact of the industry, environmental strategy, IT infusion, and IT diffusion, as potential contingency factors for allocation of decision rights in Green IT governance (Figure B.18).

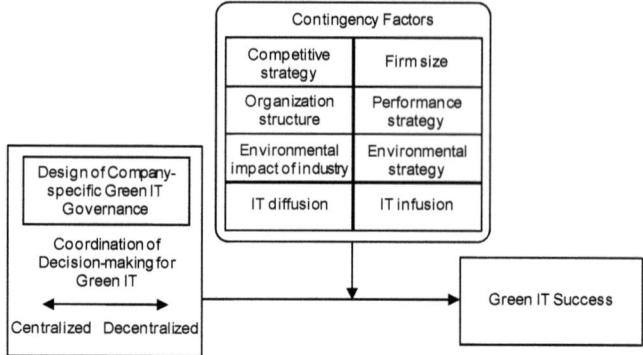

Figure B.18: Contingency Model of Green IT Governance

Most contingency factors are adopted from research on IT governance because they proof to be also relevant for Green IT governance. Other contingency factors come from environmental research (Table B.41).

The competitive strategy of a company has an influence on the degree of centralization of IT decision-making (Tavakolian, 1989). Tavakolian (1989) distinguishes between three main strategies: defender, analyzer, and prospector. A defender is an organization that has a conservative competitive strategy and a tendency to rely on centralized decision-making. Organizations with a moderate competitive strategy, relying on federal decision-making, are called analyzers. A prospector is an organization that has an aggressive competitive strategy and attempts to pioneer in product or market development. A prospector displays the tendency to rely on decentralized decision-making (Tavakolian, 1989). It seems reasonable that this also applies to Green IT governance. While conservative companies will do what is necessary, aggressive companies will try to gain a competitive advantage from Green IT. Decentralized Green IT governance holds promise as potentially the best way to develop such an advantage.

The firm size is associated with the degree of IT governance centralization (Ein-Dor & Segev, 1982). A larger firm is likely to possess a greater potential for Green IT and might be more aware of current IT trends, which makes decentralized Green IT governance more favorable.

It has been shown that the organization structure and the degree of IT governance are related (Ein-Dor & Segev, 1982; Olson & Chervany, 1980; Sambamurthy & Zmud, 1999). It seems reasonable that this characteristic also affects Green IT governance.

Weill and Ross (2005) differentiate between three performance strategies: profit, asset utilization, and growth. They assign these strategies to a continuum of governance modes that reach from more centralized to more decentralized. A profit oriented strategy aligns well with centralized Green IT governance, which focuses on the biggest energy consumers, such as the data center and the office environment. Growth is associated with innovation, which is likely to be achieved through decentralized Green IT governance, gathering multiple business units in a Green IT committee.

Each industry's environmental impact is different, which implies specific regulations, stakeholder pressures, technological developments, and environmental risks for the companies (Schaltegger & Synnestvedt, 2002). Companies from disparate industries, for example a transportation company vs. a software company, might have different perspectives on environmental management. We assume that companies from industries with a higher environmental impact tend to be more control oriented in their environmental management and their Green IT governance than companies from industries with a lower environmental impact.

Contingency Factor	Definition	References	Green IT Governance Archetypes		
			1. Centralized	2. Federal	3. Decentralized
Competitive strategy	Type of engagement in product/market development and commitment to stability	(Tavakolian, 1989)	Defender	Analyzer	Prospector
Firm size	For example, number of employees or revenue	(Ein-Dor & Segev, 1982; Sambamurthy & Zmud, 1999)	Small	Medium	Large
Organization structure	Degree of centralization of the organization	(Ein-Dor & Segev, 1982; Olson & Chervany, 1980; Sambamurthy & Zmud, 1999)	Centralized	Federal	Decentralized
Performance strategy	Emphasized performance objective by the company	(Weill & Ross, 2005)	Profit	Asset utilization	Growth
Environmental impact of industry	Level of environmental impact by industry	(Schaltegger & Synnestvedt, 2002)	High	Medium	Low
Environmental strategy	Enterprise approach towards regulations and stakeholder pressures	(Aragón-Correa & Sharma, 2003)	Reactive	Balanced	Proactive
IT infusion	Degree to which an organization is dependent on IT to carry out core operations	(Sullivan, 1985; Ward & Peppard, 2002)	Low	Medium	High
IT diffusion	Degree to which IT is dispersed throughout the organization	(Sullivan, 1985; Ward & Peppard, 2002)	Low	Medium	High

Table B.41: *Contingency Factors and Their Assumed Influence on Green IT Governance*

Strategies for managing environmental activities can be classified along a continuum that ranges from reactive to proactive (Aragón-Correa & Sharma, 2003). At one end of the continuum, a reactive posture responds to changes in environmental regulations and stakeholder pressures (Aragón-Correa & Sharma, 2003). Proactive organizations are more likely to decentralize decision-making about environmental issues (Aragón-Correa & Sharma, 2003). According to Jenkin et al. (2011), a more proactive environmental orientation induces an elaborated Green IT strategy to which the organization will strive. Therefore, it can be concluded that proactive organizations implement more decentralized Green IT governance, while reactive organizations tend towards a more centralized configuration.

The level of IT infusion and IT diffusion define the importance and the dispersion of IT (Sullivan, 1985; Ward & Peppard, 2002). They both relate to the centralization level of IT governance (Sullivan, 1985; Ward & Peppard, 2002). It seems reasonable that this also applies to Green IT governance. If IT is of high importance (e.g., in a software company) then Green IT will probably be too. A high level of diffusion implies a high level of energy consumption by IT, and makes more Green IT measures useful. Greater importance and more benefits are likely to be accommodated by decentralized Green IT governance. The developed contingency model for Green IT governance is validated in the next section by case study research.

9.3   Case Study Research Design

Given the objective of addressing "how" and "why" questions about a present phenomenon within a complex natural setting, we selected a case research design for this study (Benbasat et al., 1987). Case study research is a widely acknowledged and used methodology in IS research (Dubé & Paré, 2003). It is suitable for exploration of new topics that lack empirical validation (Crane, 1999; Eisenhardt, 1989a; Robertson, 1993). It can serve multiple purposes: describing phenomena, testing theories, and developing new theories and hypotheses (Benbasat et al., 1987; Eisenhardt, 1989a). This applies to the given situation and corresponds with the paper's intention to explain Green IT governance patterns by contingency theory.

The specific research design is based on multiple case studies. Between December 2009 and September 2010, interviews with SMEs (Subject Matter Experts) from five different companies were carried out, using a structured interview guideline. The case sites – referred to here as company A to E – were selected, based on company size and industry, ensuring a cross-sectoral analysis (Table B.42). They became accessible to the author as part of a book project on sustainability in IT. All the companies consider themselves experts in Green IT. Profit, size, and the lack of financial problems suggested that major structural differences in Green IT governance would not occur due to a turnaround situation (Brown, 1997).

Characteristics	Company				
	A	B	C	D	E
Industry	Transportation	Computer software	Financial services	Newspaper, media	Pharmaceuticals, chemicals
Revenue (2009)	€0.17 Bn	€10.67 Bn	€27.95 Bn	€2.61 Bn	€31.17 Bn
Number of Employees (2009)	1,886	47,578	81,929	10,740	108,400
Market served	national	global	global	international	global
SME roles	CIO, Environmental Manager, Director Data Center Operations	Vice President Sustainability, Director Global IT Client, Vice President Green IT, Director Data Center Operations	Global Lead Eco-Efficient IT, Vice President Corporate Social Responsibility	Project Manager Green IT, Director Newspaper Publishing Applications, Director Sustainability	Director Global Data Center Operations, Green IT Coordinator, Director Procurement & Transport
Time	Dec 2009	Jun 2010	Sep 2010	Mar 2010	Sep 2010

Table B.42: Description of Case Studies

The development of the structure and questions was based on a literature review and the developed contingency model of Green IT governance in Section B.9.2. The interview guideline's questions were structured as follows: 1. introduction: position, responsibilities and experiences of the SME; 2. characteristics of the company and the IT department; 3. environmental management; 4. structure of Green IT governance; and 5. closing, feedback, and additional documents. The interviews were recorded and transcribed. All information was used to assess each contingency factor and to determine the existing form of Green IT governance.

9.4 Findings from Case Studies

To illustrate the validity of the proposed approach, the results from one company are described in detail (Table B.43). The findings from all five cases are summarized in Table B.44.

Contingency Factor	Assessment for Company A
Competitive strategy	The public transport company defends its regional monopoly to provide services. Other markets are not supposed to be served.
Firm size	With little more than 10,000 employees, the company is a regional player. Compared to other companies, it is rather small.
Organization structure	The company is located in one city in one prime headquarter and has various outposts that manage the vehicles. The organizational structure is assessed as centralized.
Performance strategy	The company is owned by the state. The main objective is neither profit nor growth, but the efficient utilization of all assets.
Environmental impact of industry	The company belongs to the transportation industry, which can be considered to have a high environmental impact.
Environmental strategy	The company issues annual environmental reports and follows a necessary environmental management process in reaction to stakeholder pressures.
IT infusion	Core operation is passenger transportation by trams or busses. IT is only needed to support these activities and to provide basic office applications.
IT diffusion	Most employees work in trams or busses. IT is used in the offices and the control center. Compared to other companies, the IT diffusion is low.
Observed Green IT governance	Green IT is the centralized responsibility of the CIO and the director of data center operations. The importance of Green IT to the company is low.

Table B.43: Influence of Contingency Factors on the Green IT Governance Design of Company A

Following the contingency model in Section B.9.2, the observed contingency factors from companies A to E determine the theoretical Green IT governance archetype, which is compared to each company's observed type of Green IT governance (Table B.44). From this comparison, a confirmation level of the contingency model is derived.

Contingency Factors	Company				
	A	B	C	D	E
Competitive strategy	Defender (c)	Prospector (d)	Prospector (d)	Analyzer (f)	Analyzer (f)
Firm size	Small (c)	Large (d)	Large (d)	Medium (f)	Large (d)
Organization structure	Centralized (c)	Decentralized (d)	Decentralized (d)	Centralized (c)	Decentralized (d)
Performance strategy	Asset utilization (f)	Growth (d)	Profit (c)	Profit (c)	Asset utilization (f)
Environmental impact of industry	High (c)	Low (d)	Low (d)	Medium (f)	High (c)
Environmental strategy	Reactive (c)	Proactive (d)	Balanced (f)	Reactive (c)	Balanced (f)
IT infusion	Low (c)	High (d)	High (d)	Medium (f)	Low (c)
IT diffusion	Low (c)	High (d)	High (d)	High (d)	Medium (f)
Theoretical Green IT governance	Centralized	Decentralized	Decentralized	Centralized / Federal	Federal
Observed Green IT governance	Centralized	Decentralized	Federal	Federal	Federal
Confirmation level	High	High	Low	Medium	High

Table B.44: Summary of Findings (Trend Towards: (c) Centralized, (f) Federal, (d) Decentralized)

9.5 Theoretical and Practical Implications

The above findings provide support for our proposed contingency model of Green IT governance. From this, we draw theoretical and practical implications for researchers and companies within the scope of Green IT.

The flexible Green IT governance model presented allows a company-specific design of Green IT governance. Based on insights from five case studies, this article adds to the scientific knowledge about Green IT and its governance within organizations. Green IT belongs in the context of environmental sustainability (Molla et al., 2009). Therefore, this study contributes to the important field of research on environmental sustainability and IS (Melville, 2010; Watson et al., 2010). Furthermore, the paper proves the applicability of contingency theory in the scope of Green IT, as suggested by Melville (2010).

While the nature of this study is descriptive and explanatory, we offer some prescriptive insights about Green IT governance archetypes, based on theory and our observations. With the enhanced understanding of how Green IT governance is shaped by contingency factors, organizations are able to select the most promising Green IT governance form.

This has implications for companies that have not yet adopted Green IT. For them, the framework provides a reference for coordinating decision-making when implementing Green IT. By assessing each contingency factor in its situation, the model suggests a Green IT governance archetype that should lead to the greatest likelihood of Green IT success. This helps managers to avoid initial mistakes and to get a realistic perspective on the significance of Green IT for their company. Companies that have already adopted Green IT can benchmark their existent Green IT governance against the proposed archetype in the model. This should either confirm the applied strategy or provide a strategic direction for future development of Green IT governance.

Furthermore, the model provides a framework for implementing Green IT in IT departments and whole organizations. This helps COOs, CIOs, and sustainability managers to define roles and responsibilities, and to create the relevant relationships within the organization. The outlined archetypes provide examples on what Green IT governance could look like.

9.6 Conclusion and Further Research

Although we provided a first qualitative evaluation of the contingency factors and the suggested contingency model for Green IT governance, a number of limitations need to be considered.

This article transfers knowledge from IT governance research to Green IT governance. Green IT governance is not fully comparable to IT governance. Nevertheless, IT governance research pursues similar objectives. Research on contingencies influencing IT governance models is used as a starting point for the Green IT governance contingency model. Other contingency factors that were not regarded could also play an important role. Furthermore, the effect of each contingency factor on Green IT governance was not assessed. It can be assumed that different factors have a different level of impact on Green IT governance. Some factors might also be interdependent. Although the scaling and measurement of each contingency factor was done to the best of our knowledge, inconsistencies cannot be fully excluded. Each company provided different SMEs, documents, and information. This limits the comparability of the cases and might have an influence on the findings. Because of the small sample, conclusions are limited to the interviewed enterprises. Nevertheless, the results describe possible relationships and results that could be relevant for other enterprises.

Further research should be done to validate the proposed model. Although we provided a first qualitative evaluation of the contingency factors, the suggested contingency model should be validated and refined in a quantitative empirical survey in order to demonstrate generalizability of the factors and their influence on Green IT governance design. Therefore, future research should develop a survey, based on the proposed model. Also, an analysis of the guidelines and policy aspects of Green IT governance is recommended. Though the contingency model has not been tested empirically, its suitability could be demonstrated with five case studies. These results provide insights and guidelines for COOs, CIOs, IT managers, and sustainability managers to implement adequate Green IT governance. Companies that understand the relationships in the contingency model can design a Green IT governance configuration that fits their specific requirements, thereby maximizing the positive contribution of Green IT to their business objectives.

10 Strategic Green IT Planning: Lessons from a Financial Services Case

Title of Article	Strategic Green IT Planning: Lessons from a Financial Services Case
Authors	Nils-Holger Schmidt nschmid@uni-goettingen.de Tobias F. Langkau tlangka@uni-goettingen.de Thierry J. Ruch truch@uni-goettingen.de Lutz M. Kolbe lkolbe@uni-goettingen.de Georg-August-Universität Göttingen Chair of Information Management Platz der Göttinger Sieben 5 37073 Göttingen
Published	Proceedings of the 8th European, Mediterranean and Middle Eastern Conference on Information Systems (EMCIS 2011) (Schmidt et al., 2011)
Abstract	The increasing energy consumption by IT and new demands from stakeholders require a reorientation of IT management. Until now, only little research has focused on strategic Green IT planning. The purpose of this paper is to refine and test a procedural model for strategic Green IT planning. This is done with a case study at a Polish bank. As a contribution to the ongoing research on Green IT, we provide a practical management framework with concepts, procedures, and tools that can be applied by executives and IT managers. The model provides a first attempt at including Green IT in daily business operations and is a basis for further research within the scope of Green IT and Green IS management.

Table B.45: Fact Sheet of Publication No. 10

10.1 Introduction

Nowadays, companies are challenged to integrate sustainability into day-to-day management decisions (Porter & Reinhardt, 2007). In the field of information systems (IS), Piotrowicz and Cuthbertson (2008) see an "increasing trend showing that IT/IS leaders incorporated sustainability aspects into their business."

In spite of this focus on sustainability, the concept is still rather fuzzy. It is generally acknowledged that environmental protection is an integral part of it (Molla et al., 2009). In IS research, the negative environmental impact of information technology (IT) and related measures for its reduction and management are discussed under the heading "Green IT" (Kuo & Dick, 2010; Schmidt et al., 2009a; Watson et al., 2010; Yi & Thomas, 2007).

Although environmental strategies have been discussed extensively in management literature, very little research has been conducted on Green IT strategies (Jenkin et al., 2011). The existent literature is largely conceptual and focuses primarily on the benefits of Green IT practices (Jenkin et al., 2011).

A coherent framework for strategic Green IT planning is still absent. Initial research on this topic, for example by Schmidt et al. (2009a), who proposed a procedural model for sustainability management in IS, is rather generic and has not been practically validated.

Strategic planning is supported by a set of concepts, procedures, and tools (Bryson, 2004). The purpose of this paper is to develop a framework for strategic Green IT planning by refining Schmidt et al.'s (2009a) work.

This paper aims to answer the following research questions:

- What is the possible shape of a strategic Green IT planning framework?
- Which concepts, procedures, and tools support strategic Green IT planning?

These two questions are answered through a thorough literature review and a case study with the Polish CSD Bank[14]. First, we develop and refine a strategic Green IT planning framework. Then we demonstrate the feasibility of the strategic Green IT planning framework and related methods by employing it at the bank's Chief Operating Officer (COO) division and IT department. Through triangulation by interviews, observations and questionnaires, we verify our findings and derive implications for research and practice. This research contributes to the body of knowledge on the management of Green IT in IT organizations.

---

[14] Name changed

10.2 Developing a Strategic Green IT Framework

10.2.1 Green IT

In 2007, the Environmental Protection Agency (2007) published a report for the US Congress on the expected energy consumption of data centers. Since then, the importance of Green IT has steadily increased. The overall objective of Green IT is to increase energy efficiency and reduce CO_2 emissions (Watson et al., 2010).

Green IT is the systematic application of sustainability criteria to the design, production, sourcing, use, and disposal of IT in order to reduce related emissions and waste and to improve energy efficiency (Molla et al., 2009). Hedwig, Malkowski, and Neumann (2009) propose that the term "Green IT", "denotes all activities and efforts incorporating ecologically friendly technologies and processes into the entire life cycle of information and communication technology." Green IT also includes management aspects for controlling and monitoring the effectiveness of implemented measures and marketing strategies to communicate success to key stakeholders (Erek et al., 2009).

Besides the contribution to environmental protection, Green IT has other advantages, such as cost reduction, reputational improvements and marketing possibilities (Mines & Davis, 2007; Molla et al., 2008; Schmidt et al., 2010a).

Examples of specific Green IT measures are provided by Schmidt et al. (2009a), as well as Kumar and Mieritz (2007), and cover ideas such as efficient cooling concepts, server virtualization and thin clients.

Green IT measures can be assigned to the strategic, operational and technical level of an IT organization. They could also be structured according to the *source, make* (data center, office environment), *deliver* and *return* process of the IT value chain of IT departments (Molla, 2008; Schmidt et al., 2009a). In each of these areas, measures within the scope of Green IT can be implemented (Schmidt et al., 2009a).

Up to now, no detailed strategic Green IT planning process has been described that shows how measures are evaluated and introduced into the mentioned processes.

10.2.2 Strategic Planning

To understand strategic planning, it is necessary to define the key terms first. According to Porter (1980), strategy can be defined as "an integrated set of actions aimed at increasing the long-term well-being and strength of the enterprise relative to competitors." Fayol (1947) described a first strategic process. In his opinion, strategic management consists of five subsequent tasks, which add up to a management process (Gray & Fayol, 1987). These tasks are: planning, organizing, guiding, coordinating and controlling. Many slight variations have evolved from this initial model, according to the scope of application.

Goodstein, Nolan, and Pfeiffer (1993) define strategic planning as "the process by which the guiding members of an organization envision its future and develop the necessary procedures and operations to achieve that future."

Ward and Peppard (2002) stress the need for analysis by defining strategic planning as a "systematic, comprehensive analysis to develop a plan of action."

A more comprehensive definition is provided by Bryson (2004), who states that "strategic planning is simply a set of concepts, procedures, and tools designed to help executives, managers, and others think, act and learn strategically on behalf of their organizations and their organizations' stakeholders."

All strategic planning processes have in common that they repeatedly apply similar types of tasks (see for example Bryson, 2004, Luftman & Bullen, 2004 or Ward & Peppard, 2002). They usually begin by defining key objectives. After that, they perform a gap analysis by comparing the current and desired situation in order to derive measures to get there. This is usually followed by some kind of prioritization algorithm that determines the order of implementation. A periodic review measures the success of the undertaken actions and provides data for future goals.

10.2.3 A Framework for Strategic Green IT Planning

In relation to the definitions above, we define strategic Green IT planning as a process supported by a set of concepts, procedures and tools to help executives, IT managers and others to develop a plan of action in the scope of environmental protection and IT.

A first strategic management process for sustainability and Green IT was introduced by Schmidt et al. (2009a). An adapted and refined version of this model is illustrated in Figure B.19.

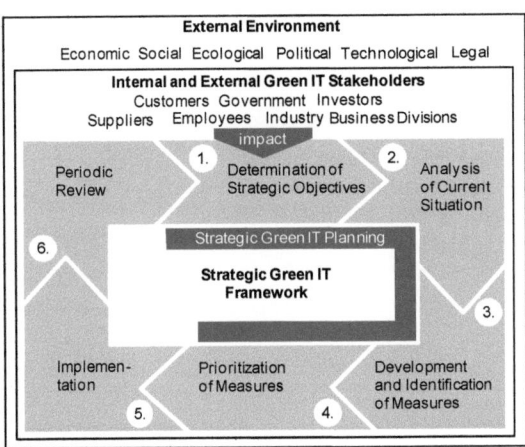

Figure B.19: Strategic Green IT Framework (Developed from Schmidt et al. (2009a) and Ward and Peppard (2002))

The starting point for formulating any strategy must be derived from the firm's identity and purpose (Grant, 1991). In the case of IT, the strategy should align with the overall organizational strategies (Jenkin et al., 2011). Green IT is a response of the IT department to the demands of important stakeholders (Watson et al., 2010). A stakeholder is "any group or individual who can affect or is affected by the achievement of the organization's objectives" (Freeman, 1984). They include consumers, suppliers, society, government, industry and alliances, organizations, and employees (Elliot, 2011; Watson et al., 2010). For this reason, we have integrated stakeholders and their demands into the strategic Green IT framework (Figure B.19).

In the first step of the strategic Green IT planning process, the strategic objectives of the IT department are determined (Figure B.19 [1]). The next step (Figure B.19 [2]) is an assessment of the current situation in the IT department. This comprises, for example, an analysis of the energy consumption in the data center and the office environment. Following this (Figure B.19 [3]), appropriate measures are identified or developed. Concerning energy consumption, measures such as server virtualization and efficient cooling equipment provide ways to improve energy efficiency. These measures are evaluated regarding their contribution to the strategic objectives of the IT department (Figure B.19 [4]), and the most promising measures are implemented (Figure B.19 [5]). After implementation, success is periodically reviewed and evaluated before the strategic Green IT planning process restarts (Figure B.19 [6]).

10.3 Methodology

The refined framework was applied in a case study of the Polish CSD Bank to prove the feasibility of the strategic Green IT planning process (Section B.10.5). Case study research is a widely acknowledged and used methodology in IS research (Dubé & Paré, 2003). It generates insights by examining a phenomenon in its natural setting (Benbasat et al., 1987; Yin, 2002).

Case study research can serve multiple purposes: to describe phenomena, to test theories, and to develop new theories and hypotheses (Benbasat et al., 1987; Eisenhardt, 1989). This corresponds with the paper's intention to test and refine the proposed strategic Green IT planning process.

Phase	Tasks	Purpose
1. Kick-off Presentation	• On-site presentation and joint meeting with experts from the COO division and the IT department (45 min.)	• Gaining support from management and employees • Introducing the topic of „Green IT" • Presentation of the Green IT strategy process model
2. Prioritization	Interviews with • Member of the Management Board and Chief Operations and IT Officer (COO) (73 min.), • Director of Business Management COO Division (28 min.) and • Head of Operations and IT department (CIO) and Director of IT infrastructure department (125 min.)	• Defining Green IT objectives for the CSD Bank • Strategically prioritizing Green IT objectives and relevant Green IT stakeholders
3. Evaluation	Interviews with • Director of Information Systems (71 min.), • Director of Banking Systems (72 min.), • Director of IT Development (32 min.), • Environmental Officer (69 min.), • Director of Purchasing and Exploitation (Procurement) (60 min.). • On-site measurements of energy consumption by PCs, Monitors, Laptops, Printers and Servers • Collection of documents	• Evaluating the current "as-is" situation in the IT department according to the source, make (office environment, data centers) and deliver phase of IT departments (Hochstein et al., 2006) • Collecting potential Green IT measures from interviews
4. Compilation	• Preparation and analysis of the obtained information and data	• Designing and analyzing possible Green IT solutions • Prioritizing of identified Green IT measures
5. Final Presentation	• On-site final presentation of the results to experts from the COO division and IT department	• Outlining possible short- and medium-term measures for the IT department • Evaluating and prioritizing of Green IT measures • Feedback about the overall approach

Table B.46: Summary of the Data Collection Analysis Process at the CSD Bank

In terms of data collection, methodological triangulation was used (Denzin, 1978). Data was gathered using semi-structured interviews, observations, questionnaires, documents and technical measurements. Documents such as organizational mission and vision statements, objectives, annual reports, industry reports, in-house presentations, and training materials were also collected and used for this case. Technical measurements were gathered to estimate the energy consumption of PCs, monitors, laptops, printers, and servers. Interviews were conducted at the COO division and the IT department of the CSD Bank.

The case study reported here is one of twelve IT departments that were examined in a multiple cross-sectoral research project. It was conducted over a period of four months, from January to April 2009. The Polish CSD Bank was selected for this research because it was at an early stage of Green IT implementation. Therefore, the results are assumed to be unbiased by influencing factors. The overall approach of the study is shown in Table B.46. It is recommended that, at every step of a strategy planning process, people are informed and involved (Goodstein et al., 1993). Therefore, all results were continuously discussed and rechecked with the corresponding experts at the CSD Bank.

The research approach of this paper is primarily exploratory. Stebbins (2001) defines the outcome of exploratory research in social sciences as follows: "The emergent generalizations are many and varied; they include the descriptive facts, folk concepts, cultural artifacts, structural arrangements, social processes, and beliefs and belief systems normally found there." This applies to the development of a strategic Green IT framework and the enhancement of each process step with concepts, procedures, and tools.

The work also adopts an initial confirmatory approach by validating the framework with a single case study at the CSD Bank. Though this procedure might provide initial hints, the results have only limited significance because confirmatory research requires a quantitative analysis with a larger sample size to achieve greater confidence in its findings (Straub, 1989).

10.4 The Case

The CSD Bank is part of a foreign banking group and an important player in Central and Eastern Europe. In recent years, the CSD Bank has been one of the market growth leaders in Poland. In December 2008, the CSD Bank belonged to the three largest banks listed on the Warsaw Stock Exchange (by assets, the portfolio of credits and loans to non-financial clients, and the public sector). The bank is divided into two branches: corporate banking with over 10,000 customers, and retail banking with over 2.5 million customers. In 2008, the entire bank generated an untaxed profit on continued and discontinued operations of over US$300 million. At the end of 2008, around 6,000 persons were employed at the CSD Bank, about 1000 persons more than at the end of 2007 (Table B.47). The bank's employees are mainly college and university graduates (68%), and are mostly younger than 35 years (74%).

Name	CSD Bank
Foundation	1986
Headquarter	Warsaw
Industry	Banking
Balance Sheet Total	2008: US$22.5 Bn.
Employees	2008: 5,877
Classification of the IT Department	Cost center
Data Centers	5 (2 primary, 1 secondary and 2 backup data centers)

Table B.47: Company Overview

The CSD Bank's IT is coordinated under the responsibility of a COO, who is member of the bank's executive board. The core IT department of the CSD Bank consists of Group IT & Ops, but a broader view also includes responsibilities from Group Logistics, Group Security and Business Management (Figure B.20).

Figure B.20: Interviewees and Organizational Structure of the CSD Bank's COO Division

The CSD Bank cares about corporate social responsibility (CSR) and wants to join the United Nations Global Compact by 2011 – a strategic policy initiative to align their operations and strategies with ten universally accepted principles in the areas of human rights, labor, the environment, and anti-corruption (United Nations Global Compact, 2011).

The calculation of indirect CO_2 emissions was performed with data from the World Resources Institute for Poland (World Resources Institute, 2009). The World Resources Institute provides figures about the average CO_2 emissions produced to generate electrical power in each country. In 2008, the CSD Bank paid around US$3.5 million for electricity. The electricity accounts for approximately 18,000 tons of indirect CO_2 emissions, and falls into "Scope 2", according to the World Resources Institute.

10.5 Strategic Green IT Planning at the CSD Bank

In this section, we aim to validate the strategic Green IT planning process of the framework in Section B.10.2.2 by applying it to the CSD Bank case study. The sections that follow are structured according to this model. The starting point is the CSD Bank's strategic objectives.

For each step of the strategic Green IT planning process, we apply explorative concepts, procedures, and tools, and illustrate them in the selected case.

10.5.1 Defining the Strategic Objectives

It is typical in a bank for IT to be one of the largest energy consumers. Green IT has been initiated at the CSD Bank due to high electricity costs. This was confirmed by the COO: "Every half a year I have to pay an enormous electricity bill and I do not know where that comes from." Obviously, one strategic Green IT objective is to reduce IT-related costs. To determine other strategic objectives, the COO, CIO and the responsible person from Business Management were asked to prioritize a given list of possible Green IT objectives. The achievement of Green IT goals depends on a blend of external forces that are shaped by major stakeholders (Watson et al., 2010). Therefore, the same approach was applied to prioritize the most important stakeholders for the COO division and its IT department.

Priority ranking	Green IT Objectives	Green IT Stakeholders
1.	Saving costs	CSD Bank's business divisions
2.	Improving corporate reputation	Customers
3.	Complying with legislative or industrial regulations	Banking industry
4.	Gaining competitive advantage	Investors
5.	Reducing social based risk	Suppliers
6.	Preserving the environment	Employees
7.		Government

Table B.48: Priority Ranking of Green IT Objectives and Stakeholders

The prioritization of Green IT objectives shows that the IT department wants to implement Green IT primarily to save costs (Table B.48). The second most important objective is to improve the corporate reputation of the IT department within the CSD Bank. An interesting finding is that preserving the environment is the least important objective. The ranking also corresponds with the COO's personal interest. His personal remuneration system includes cost reduction as a major objective: "I committed myself to achieve certain defined cost targets. I think Green IT could contribute to this."

The ranking of objectives matches the stakeholders' ranking. The business division sees the IT department of the CSD Bank as a cost center. Owing to the financial crisis, the pressure to cut costs has grown. Contrary to common opinions (e.g., Elliot, 2011) employees' influence as internal stakeholders is of low importance.

A tool that can be applied in this step is Molla's (2009) "Green IT Reach-Richness Framework". This tool can be used to assess both the breadth and focus of Green IT adoption. It indicates different strategic positions and directions in greening IT (Molla, 2009). The IT department of the CSD Bank has not yet implemented any Green IT measures and therefore can be considered a Green IT starter (Figure B.21).

The strategic direction is expressed by a manager saying: "We heard about Green IT. We do not know exactly what it is about, but we heard it is possible to save costs with it. Maybe we could also communicate our efforts to our customers and our employees. That's why we want to do Green IT."

The objective is to explore the potential of Green IT in various areas of the IT value chain. According to the Green IT Reach-Richness Framework, the IT department wants to move towards becoming a Green IT pioneer (Figure B.21).

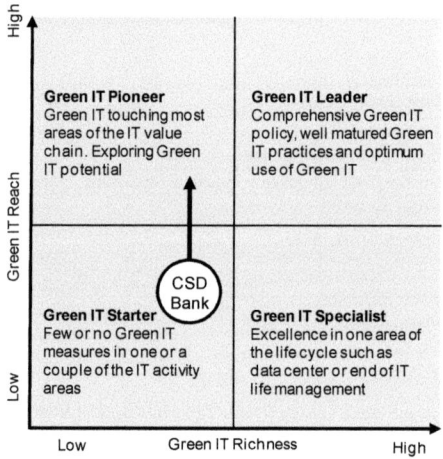

Figure B.21: Strategic Direction of the CSD Bank in the Green IT Reach-Richness Framework (Adapted from Molla (2009))

10.5.2 Analysis of Current Situation

Every strategic planning process demands a gap analysis (Section B.10.2.2); therefore, the current situation at the CSD Bank was examined. We applied a top-down approach to evaluate the relevant resource consumption. In 2008, the bank spent over US$4 million on water, gas, oil and electricity (Table B.49).

Consumption per Resource		Costs in Thousand US$ per Year	Share of Costs
Water	51,515,000 liters	107	2,5%
Gas/Oil	442,486 m³	707	16,5%
Electricity	27 GWh	3,467	81,0%
Total		4,281	100,0%

Table B.49: Consumption of Basic Resources at the CSD Bank

The biggest share of costs resulted from electricity consumption. Electricity consumption is connected to the IT infrastructure: IT at the CSD Bank accounted for 52% of the total electricity consumption and generated costs of more than US$1.8 million a year. The CSD Bank's IT infrastructure can be divided into the data center and the office environment, which mainly comprises PCs, laptops, and printers (Table B.50).

	Electricity Consumption (kWh) per Year	Costs in Thousand US$ per Year	Indirect CO_2 Emissions (Tons per Year)	Share
Data Centers (Servers, Auxiliary)	10,409,694	1,327	6,859	38%
Office IT (PCs, Printers, Laptops)	3,834,645	489	2,527	14%
Total	14,244,339	1,816	9,386	52%

Table B.50: IT-related Electricity Consumption and Environmental Impact

Two primary, one secondary and two backup data centers provide computational power for all operations of corporate and retail banking. This structure historically evolved parallel to the business development. A project to consolidate the data centers into just one primary and one backup data center is scheduled for 2011. The data centers' electricity consumption is provided by internal measurements and estimations, done by the IT department (Table B.51). All data centers are assumed to have power usage effectiveness (PUE) of 2.0. PUE is the ratio of the total amount of power used by a computer data center facility to the power delivered to computing equipment (The Green Grid, 2010b).

Corporate (Location: Warsaw)	Power Capacity of Servers (kW)	Electricity Consumption (kWh) per Year	Costs in Thousand US$ per Year	Share
Data Center 1	180	1,892,672	241	18%
Data Center 2	160	1,682,375	214	16%
Backup Data Center	250	2,628,711	335	26%
Retail (Location: Lodz)				
Data Center 1	200	2,102,968	268	20%
Backup Data Center	200	2,102,968	268	20%
Total		10,409,694	1,326	100%

Table B.51: Estimations for the Energy Consumption of Data Centers

Dell, HP and IBM are the prevalent manufacturers of PCs and laptops for the office environment. All desktop services at the CSD Bank are managed entirely by the IT department.

The electricity consumption of PCs, laptops and printers was estimated using random sampling, utilization approximations and switch-off rates. Interviewees at the bank's IT department indicated that 40% of the IT infrastructure in the office environment was not switched off after work. Questioned about the low switch-off rate of PCs at the CSD Bank, a technical employee stated: "They [PCs] have to run so we can run updates, for security reasons."

This high value of 40% was confirmed by the Environmental Officer, stating: "A lot of people leave their PCs running over night because they do not care."

PCs were the biggest consumers of electricity in the office environment (Table B.52). Laptops were very energy efficient. The per capita rate indicated that there were more PCs and laptops than employees. Most employees used more than one device.

	Units	Per Capita Rate	Electricity Consumption (kWh) per Year	Costs in Thousand US$ per Year	Indirect CO_2 Emission (Tons per Year)	Share
PCs	8,385	1.43	3,054,521	389	2,013	80%
Laptops	1,905	0.32	172,924	22	400	5%
Printers	2,215	0.38	607,200	77	114	15%
Total			3,834,645	489	2,527	100%

Table B.52: IT in the Office Environment and Its Estimated Environmental Impact

The paper consumption was also related to the environmental impact of the office environment. At the bank, approximately 40,000,000 sheets of paper were consumed and accounted to a little more than US$290,000. Correspondingly, printer cartridges were procured for around US$880,000. These costs were mainly caused by the high number and the variety of printers. In this context, the behavior of the employees played an important role. One employee said: "Everybody uses a lot of paper. They [employees] print everything. I think we could do something there."

There were 202 tons of paper waste and 28 tons of electronic waste per year. The disposal of paper waste cost around US$7,000 per year, while electronic waste needing special treatment added extra costs of US$22,000 per year.

10.5.3 Development and Identification of Measures

The biggest cost saving potential was found in the data center and the office environment (Section B.10.5.2). Therefore, measures that specifically focus on these two areas were developed and identified. In IS research, many possible Green IT measures are mentioned (Erek et al., 2009; Molla, 2009). Employees of the CSD Bank were asked to complement these measures with their own ideas. A list of all the measures was then presented to the COO, who selected what he considered the most promising measures. These were further investigated. The complexity of each measure was estimated, analyzing:

- the estimated time to implement it;
- the extensiveness of the need for company-wide coordination and therefore effort; and
- the certainty of a positive business case.

The relevant Green IT measures are described in detail in Table B.53. In this table, waste reduction comprises waste from paper usage, electronic components and indirect CO_2 emissions from electricity consumption. Total cost savings were calculated from expected cost savings and necessary investments. Expected cost savings were derived from the approximated reduction of electricity, paper, cartridges and equipment consumption. Necessary investments comprise cost for hardware, software and labor to implement and manage initiatives.

Measure	Description	Objectives	Activities and Investments	Project Risks
1. Reorganization of printers (Office Environment)	• Reduction of printer/employee ratio to 1 per 8 employees (from 2,215 to 735) • Setting up printer rooms • The transition phase will last 2 years • Fewer multifunctional printers are procured	• Reducing the consumption of paper and cartridges by 40% • Reducing the number of printers by 40% • Lowering procurement costs for printers by 67% • Creating a healthier and cleaner work environment • Improving document security	Reorganization project, requiring: • Project management • Facility management • Procurement management • Service management	• Technical difficulties • Employee non-acceptance • Coordination problems
2. Reducing paper consumption (Office Environment)	• Employees at the CSD Bank are encouraged via newsletter and intranet to save paper by doing double-sided printing, and to minimize printing	• Reducing consumption of paper from 33 pages to 25 pages per employee per day • Reducing the consumption of printer cartridges • Supporting the digitalization of data management	• Information campaign (newsletter, intranet, and FAQs)	• Lack of employee support
3. Presetting printer configurations (Office Environment)	• All printers at the CSD Bank are preset to double-sided printing • Users can manually switch to other configurations	• Reducing consumption of paper by 15% • Reducing the consumption of printer cartridges	• Configuration of all PCs and laptops • Developing a script that sets the printer configuration at start-up • Answering questions from employees	• Technical difficulties due to the variety of printers: not all printers support double-sided printing
4. Achieving a PUE of 1.7 (Data Center)	• Various measures contribute to a reduction of energy consumption in the data center to a PUE of 1.7	• Lowering the overall energy consumption of all data centers by 15% • Building high quality data centers • Increasing capacity flexibility	Optimization of data centers: • Searching for optimization potential • Evaluating solutions (e.g., server virtualization, and efficient cooling) • Applying solutions	• Time consuming • Demands high level of technical knowledge
5. Remote shut down of PCs (Office Environment)	• Remote shut down of PCs using Wake-on-LAN (PCs are shut down after a specified period of inactivity or at a certain time of day)	• Increasing the shut down rate of PCs to 90% • Saving electricity costs (reducing electricity consumption in the office environment by 42%) • Lowering the wear out of IT equipment	• Selecting or developing a shut down solution • User support	• PCs might not support Wake-on-LAN
6. Extending lifecycle (Office Environment)	• The lifecycle of PCs and laptops is extended from 3.25 years to 3.5 years	• Reducing procurement costs for PCs and laptops • Reducing dangerous waste		• Employee non-acceptance • Technical difficulties
7. Switch them off (Office Environment)	• Employees at the CSD Bank are encouraged via newsletter and intranet to switch off their PCs, laptops, printers, and other equipment after work or when they are not in use	• Increasing the switch-off rate by 10% • Reducing the electricity consumption of PCs by 14%, printers by 10% and laptops by 12%	• Information campaign (newsletter, intranet, and FAQs) • Answering questions from employees	• Employee non-acceptance due to computer booting delays
8. Increasing temperature in data centers (Data Center)	• Climate control units in the data centers are turned down to save energy • Targeted temperature for the data centers in Warsaw (22 C°) and Lodz (25 C°) would be 26 C°	• Reducing electricity consumption for cooling in Warsaw and Lodz	Increasing temperatures: • Introducing new guidelines • Checking with hardware suppliers • Checking with security department	• Warranty of servers might not cover all temperatures • Higher server failure rate is possible
9. Enable remote work via VPN (Office Environment)	• By developing a Virtual Private Network for the CSD Bank, employees would be enabled to work at remote locations	• Reducing the physical presence of employees by 5% • Reducing the consumption of basic resources by 2% • Enabling flexible work methods, such as using a home office • Saving office space	VPN development: • Developing a technical solution • Selecting vendors • User support	• Technical difficulties • Security issues impose risks

Table B.53: Assessment of Possible Green IT Measures

10.5.4 Prioritization of Measures

Given the primary objective of cost saving, a clear ranking of the proposed Green IT measures evolved (Table B.54). The first three measures related to printing. Employees considered it convenient to have their own printers, because it was considered flexible and a help to save time. At the CSD Bank, eight employees shared three printers, on average (Section B.10.5.2). However, in contrast to PCs, printers do not just consume electricity but also cartridges and paper. Therefore, when the mentioned measures were implemented, it would have a positive effect in multiple dimensions: electricity consumption, waste reduction and procurement costs.

Nr.	Measure	Total Cost Savings (Thousand US$)	Waste Reduction (t)	Complexity
1	Reorganization of printers	726	356	high
2	Reducing paper consumption	279	50	low
3	Presetting printer configurations	174	31	medium
4	Achieving a PUE of 1,7	159	1,029	medium
5	Remote shut down of PCs	142	845	high
6	Extending life cycle	126	1.2	low
7	Switching PCs off	59	337	low
8	Increasing temperature in data centers	47	245	low
9	Enable remote work via VPN	17	376	medium
Total		1,729	3,270	

Table B.54: Overview and Ranking of the Proposed Green IT Measures

When the measures are placed in a business case-environment framework that considers the business case and the environmental contribution, it becomes obvious that the biggest environmental contributions derive from measure 4 and 5 (Figure B.22). If all measures were implemented, a total waste reduction of 3,270 tons could be achieved. This would have constituted more than 20% of the electricity related carbon footprint. Figure B.22 also illustrates that the CSD Bank aimed at cost-driven Green IT. The other option would have been environmentally driven Green IT. In this case, the IT department would also implement measures with a negative business case but a positive environmental contribution. Here cost-driven Green IT projects fund environmental-driven Green IT projects.

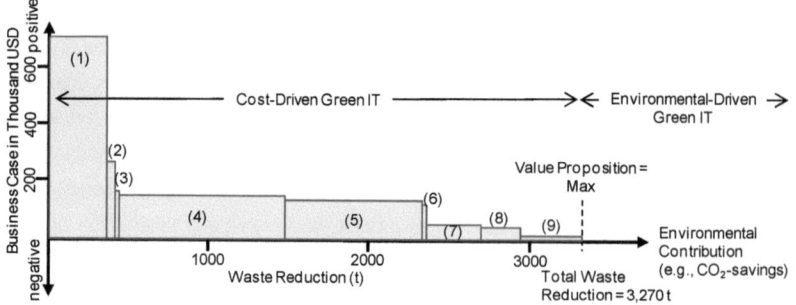

Figure B.22: Evaluation of Green IT Measures in a Business Case-Environment Framework

The final prioritization was done using a portfolio. Generally, portfolio planning models represent a two-dimensional, matrix-based framework that can be used to evaluate business unit performance, to formulate business unit strategies, and to set performance targets (Grant, 2005). In our portfolio, we matched cost savings with the estimated complexity of each measure (Figure B.23).

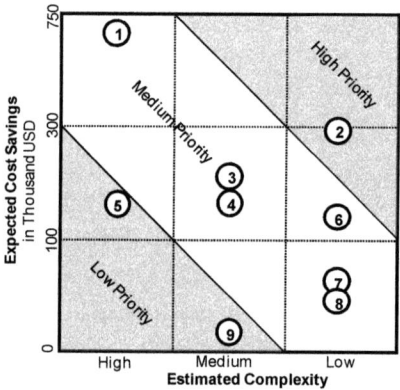

Figure B.23: Prioritization of Green IT Measures by a Cost Saving-Complexity Portfolio

The portfolio prioritized measures that were easy to implement. Therefore, reducing paper consumption had the highest priority, followed by extending the life cycle of equipment. Reorganizing the printers was expected to save most costs but was complex because rooms needed to be allocated, employees needed to change their behavior, and new printers needed to be procured.

The portfolio ranking was the final result of the strategic Green IT planning process and provided the starting point for the implementation of the proposed measures.

10.6 Business and Research Implications

The case of the CSD Bank illustrates that at a bank, IT can account for more than 50% of all electricity costs. The data centers consume tremendous amounts of energy, and in the office environment, PCs are the biggest consumers of electricity. Interviews indicated that many employees do not switch off their PCs after work. Printers use not only electricity but also costly cartridges and paper. At the end of their life cycle, IT produces more costs through the disposal of dangerous waste. To reduce and manage these negative effects, the CSD Bank went through a strategic green planning process. The findings from this case lead to implications for business and research.

The case of the CSD Bank proves the feasibility of the strategic Green IT framework and its concepts, procedures, and tools. The model provides a structured approach for the implementation of Green IT. It helps IT managers and CIOs to introduce Green IT into their daily business. Every step is described in detail but leaves enough space for customization to every IT department's specific situation. The methods and tools that were developed provide useful hints on how to process collected data, how to break it down to an operational level, and how to illustrate the results. Graphics and tables can serve as templates. Some of the measures might be transferable to other IT departments. The detailed figures from the CSD Bank provide other companies with a reference against which they can benchmark their own activities.

The precise determination of the objectives and stakeholders at the beginning of the strategic Green IT planning process is particularly important. The case shows that these findings significantly affect all subsequent steps and influence the selection of Green IT measures. Therefore, the framework supports the alignment with the overall organizational strategies, as is recommended by Jenkin et al. (2011).

In this context, top management's personal views play an important role. As the COO of the CSD Bank will be judged on the goal of cost reduction, he pursues Green IT for his purpose. A COO with a stronger interest in environmental protection could come to a different conclusion that might, for example, lead to an environmentally driven selection of Green IT projects.

Although the bank's employees were rated as unimportant stakeholders, their behaviors influence the success of Green IT measures. Especially in the field of printers and PCs, this is very apparent. Small changes in behavior can have a big impact. IT departments need to involve employees in the strategic Green IT planning process. In the best case scenario, the Environmental Officer takes on this responsibility by communicating, coordinating and guiding Green IT projects.

There are also implications for policy-makers. Since the government is seen as an irrelevant stakeholder, it does not play any role in the strategic Green IT planning process. To pursue an environmentally oriented policy for IT, policy-makers must encourage and support companies in implementing Green IT. Financial support, consulting or regulations provide incentives for companies. Mandatory guidelines, such as the efficiency of data centers, exert additional pressure on them.

From an IS research perspective, this paper contributes to the body of knowledge on the management of Green IT in IT organizations. It closes the gap between theoretical Green IT concepts and technical Green IT measures. The paper illustrates initial tools, concepts, and procedures, showing how economic and environmental questions can be answered in practice. These findings demand further validation in future research. There is also a need to develop more methods that are especially suitable for Green IT. An interesting question is whether there is an infinite number of Green IT strategies or a limited number (e.g., Porter's (1980) three generic strategies). In this connection it is interesting how context factors shape these strategies.

10.7 Conclusion and Limitations

This paper's findings belong to the emerging research branch of sustainable IS, which investigates social and environmental questions, as well as other aspects, in the scope of IS (Schmidt et al., 2009; Watson et al., 2010).

In this paper, we developed and refined a strategic Green IT planning framework. It closes the research gap between conceptual and technical research on Green IT. Its feasibility was demonstrated with a case study at the Polish CSD Bank. The results provide a structured procedure for implementing Green IT measures. Our approach supports executives, IT managers and CIOs in their daily business.

Although the CSD Bank case is a good representation of a larger study, the derived conclusions are limited to this individual case and cannot be generalized to all IT departments. Nevertheless, this case proved the applicability of the strategic Green IT planning process. Future research needs to verify the developed framework and its concepts, procedures, and tools by further rounds of case studies and expert interviews.

The implications from the case provide first hints. To establish greater confidence, a quantitative analysis with a larger sample size is recommended (Straub, 1989).

Given the rising prices of energy and the environmental awareness of stakeholders, Green IT is destined to gain greater importance in the future. The strategic Green IT framework provides a useful tool for dealing with this challenge.

C. Contributions

This final part concludes the outlined research activities. It discusses the contributions, significance and limitations of the study and its outcomes. This part starts with a short recapitulation of the findings (Section C.1). Thereafter, the implications for research and practice, based on the findings, are highlighted (Section C.2). Finally, the conclusion describes limitations of the research and presents further research possibilities (Section C.3).

1 Findings

The findings summarize the results of each publication, as well as the two sections in Part A and give answer to every research question. The findings are then combined to develop a model for environmentally sustainable information management, which represents the overall finding of the thesis.

1.1 Findings Regarding Sustainability and IS

Sustainability is becoming an important topic for IS, owing to the increasing dissemination and utilization of IT in every sphere of life, which leads to growing ecological and social impacts. Legislation, practice and theory must respond to this development and integrate IT into their sustainability agenda. This section provides a summary of the main findings of each of the publications related to sustainability and IS. The title and the related core research questions are highlighted.

- **Publication B.1** *"Sustainable Information Systems Management"*
- **Research question 1** *"What theories and concepts provide a foundation for incorporating sustainability into IS?"*

Sustainability can be incorporated into IS by focusing on stakeholders and resources. The stakeholder theory and the resource-based view provide the theoretical foundations for this. Stakeholders' needs must be at the core of all planning considerations. Examples of stakeholders that are relevant for IT organizations are business units, policy-makers, employees, and investors. Corresponding to their significance and power of influence, and based on the triple bottom line of sustainability, weighted short and long-term economical, ecological and social objectives are derived. These sustainability objectives are achieved by obtaining, applying and securing essential IT resources. Economical, ecological and social oriented measures contribute to meeting stakeholders' demands.

- **Publication B.2** *"Towards a Procedural Model for Sustainable Information Systems Management"*
- **Research question 2** *"How can sustainability be managed in IS?"*

Sustainability in IS can be managed by following a procedural model for sustainable IS management. The model outlines the most important steps that will lead to the implementation of sustainability within IT organizations. The model provides IT executives with a structured framework for including and managing sustainability in business operations. Sustainability initiatives can be structured along IT organizations' value chain in line with the industrialized information management model. This helps decision-makers and theorists to structure the scope of sustainability and IS.

1.2 Findings Regarding Green IS

This thesis focuses on the environmental dimension of sustainability by investigating aspects of Green IS and Green IT. Green IS can enable a multitude of economical and environmental benefits (e.g., business activities, processes, and reporting) in all types of industries. This section provides a summary of the main findings of each of the Green IS publications. These consist of IT-enabled green marketing (Publication B.3), green business models (Publication B.4), and green processes (Publication B.5). They provide a first impression of the multitude of possible Green IS research topics. Besides the title, the related core research question is highlighted.

- **Publication B.3** *"Influence of Green IT on Consumers' Buying Behavior of Personal Computers: Implications from a Conjoint Analysis"*
- **Research question 3** *"What is the market potential of IT with green features?"*

The estimated market potential of IT with green features is 26.6%, based on a survey with 500 participants in a conjoint-analysis of PCs. While price and performance are the dominant criteria, disposal and energy consumption are also important determinants of consumers' buying behavior. The findings show that the marketing mix should focus on disposal, rather than on energy attributes, and more on female than on male customers. These findings are, however, limited to the German PC market and can only be generalized to a certain extent. Nevertheless, this example demonstrates the overall market relevance of environmentally sustainable IT and clearly shows that IT products with green attributes possess market relevance.

- **Publication B.4** *"Search Engines and Social Business – Implications from the Case of Ecosia"*
- **Research question 4** *"What is the potential of IT-enabled green business models?"*

IT-enabled green business models can make a positive contribution to the environment, stay competitive due to customers valuing their environmental orientation, and can influence a market in which companies compete over environmental standards in a "race to the top". An example of an IT-enabled green business model is provided by the environmentally friendly search engine, Ecosia, which follows the social business concept. Ecosia donates at least 80% of its revenues to the World Wildlife Fund. An increasing number of users support this behavior, which influences competitors' environmental engagement. IT-enabled green business models can conquer a market niche, even in tough markets. Social businesses and IT-enabled green business models have only received limited scientific attention. This work is therefore a starting point for further IS research.

- **Publication B.5** *"Ökobilanzierung in der Informationstechnik – Zwei Distributionsformen der Musikindustrie im Vergleich"*
- **Research question 5** *"What is the green advantage of IT-enabled processes?"*

IT's greatest environmental contribution might be as a result of its ability to change physical processes into digital processes. It has been assumed that this dematerialization and digitalization leads to lower emissions. This facet is investigated by comparing the physical form with the digital form of music distribution via a life cycle assessment (LCA). Owing to IT's energy consumption, the results indicate only a slight advantage of digital music distribution (578.8 gCO_2) over physical distribution via CD (862.5 gCO_2). This example illustrates the environmental advantage of IT-enabled processes. Furthermore, it illustrates the advantage of LCA. LCAs' results help decision-makers in developing and improving products and services, supports political decision processes and provides additional arguments for marketing. LCA is a relevant tool for analyzing IT-related products and services.

1.3 Findings Regarding Green IT

This section provides a summary of the main findings of each of the publications and sections related to Green IT. Explanatory and descriptive research illustrates the Green IT scope (Publication B.6), the Green IT objectives (Publication B.7), the Green IT adoption (Publication B.8), the Green IT measures (Section A.3.3.3.3), and the Green IT metrics (Section A.3.3.3.4). Design oriented research findings are related to Green IT governance (Publication B.9), and also to strategic Green IT planning (Publication B.10). Besides the title, the related core research question is highlighted.

- **Publication B.6** *"Sustainability in Information Systems: Assortment of Current Practices in IS Organizations"*
- **Research question 6** *"What is Green IT's scope in practice?"*

The scope of Green IT covers the following phases: source, make, deliver, return, and govern, according to the value chain of IT organizations, which is based on industrialized information management. This perspective is confirmed by 15 expert interviews with CIOs, IT and environmental managers from IT organizations of major companies. Green IT measures are implemented throughout these IT organizations processes. The industrialized information management model provides practitioners and researcher with a suitable framework to map the scope of Green IT.

- **Publication B.7** *"Examining the Contribution of Green IT to the Objectives of IT Departments: Empirical Evidence from German Enterprises"*
- **Research question 7** *"What Green IT objectives are pursued by IT departments?"*

Green IT pursues similar objectives to those of corporate social responsibility (CSR). A survey with 116 IT executives confirms that Green IT contributes to the objectives of efficient internal operations, reputational management, and market competitiveness. In particular, reputational management plays a major role in Green IT engagement.

- **Publication B.8** *"Predictors of Green IT Adoption: Implications from an Empirical Investigation"*
- **Research question 8** *"Why is Green IT adopted by IT departments?"*

The adoption of Green IT depends positively on the perceived importance and negatively on the perceived uncertainty related to Green IT, as shown in a survey with 116 IT executives. Importance derives from corporate management's focus on Green IT, the company's environmental engagement, and experience with Green IT. Uncertainty relates to the absence of experience, measurements, standards, and support of the IT staff in relation to Green IT. The perception of Green IT as a hyped topic contributes further to this uncertainty.

- **Publication B.9** *"Towards a Contingency Model for Green IT Governance"*
- **Research question 9** *"How should Green IT governance be designed?"*

The design of Green IT governance should be based on contingency factors of the IT organization. Building upon contingency theory and IT governance, a contingency model for Green IT governance is developed. Green IT governance reaches over a continuum from centralized over federal to decentralized archetypes. It is possible to determine the Green IT governance type by assessing the competitive strategy, firm size, organization structure, performance strategy, environmental impact of industry, environmental strategy, IT infusion, and IT diffusion. The model is then validated using the insights gained from five case studies. With the enhanced understanding of how Green IT governance is shaped by contingency factors, IT organizations can select the most successful for of Green IT governance.

- **Publication B.10** *"Strategic Green IT Planning: Lessons from a Financial Services Case"*
- **Research question 10** *"How should Green IT planning be conducted?"*

Green IT planning should follow a structured, six step, strategic process, based on the procedural model for sustainable IS management. This model is refined and validated, using a Polish banking industry case study. Each step is supported by concepts, procedures, and tools, which can instantly be applied by executives and IT managers.

- **Section A.3.3.3.3** *"Exemplary Measures"*
- **Research question 11** *"What Green IT measures are applicable?"*

Applicable Green IT measures include behavioral and technological measures. Behavioral measures relate to changes in the organizational processes, in the use of IT, or in the IT organization's relationships. They are generally less expensive than technological measures but depend on employee support. Technological measures relate to changes in the infrastructures and in the applications of the IT organization.

- **Section A.3.3.3.4** *"Performance Metrics"*
- **Research question 12** *"What metrics are available to evaluate Green IT success?"*

A great variety of metrics are available to evaluate Green IT success. These metrics reach from the organizational level down to the technical level of single circuits and CPUs. Metrics help to establish objectives and to monitor the achievement level. Furthermore, they enable benchmarking practices, locations, and organizations. For practical relevance, each Green IT metric should be meaningful, understandable, and easy to measure.

Finally, the thesis findings on sustainability and IS, Green IS, and Green IT, are consolidated in the model of environmentally sustainable information management (ESIM). This practical concept distinguishes between the different roles and responsibilities of Green IS and Green IT. It aims to support IT executives in their daily work and provides IS scientists with a theoretical basis for further research in this emerging field.

1.4 Towards Environmentally Sustainable Information Management

This section answers the central research question of the thesis:

"How should environmentally sustainable information management be incorporated into IT organizations?"

As mentioned in Publication B.8, it would be useful to develop a reference model that defines Green IS and Green IT processes, tasks, roles, and responsibilities for the entire enterprise. Therefore, the single publications' findings and the results of the introductory section are combined to produce the ESIM model. This artifact integrates the findings regarding sustainability and IS, Green IS, and Green IT into a holistic, applicable management framework.

Similar to the underlying concept of information management (Section A.3.4), ESIM is responsible for applying Green IS and Green IT to enable and align the corporate strategy. Figure C.1 illustrates the role of ESIM by emphasizing the differences between Green IS and Green IT.

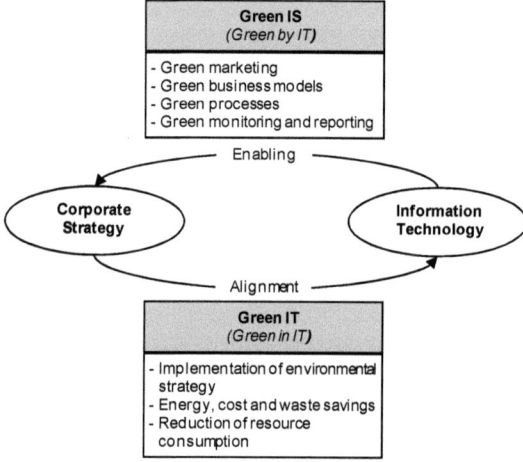

Figure C.1: Environmentally Sustainable Information Management Between Enabling and Alignment Using Green IS and Green IT (Adapted from Krcmar (2005))

Green IS enables green opportunities in marketing, business models, processes, and reporting. These initiatives actively contribute to the corporate strategy. Green IS aims to enhance the corporation's competitive advantage, legitimacy, and reputation (Thambusamy & Salam, 2010).

However, corporate strategy demands an integrated implementation of the corporate environmental strategy, as well as the efficient use of IT and associated resources. Green IT measures help to align IT with the corporate strategy, goals, and needs (Corbett, 2010; Luftman et al., 1999).

C.1 Findings

Based on the findings of Part B, as well as the definition of information management (Section A.3.4), the following definition of ESIM is derived.

> **Environmentally Sustainable Information Management (ESIM)** is the management of Green IS and Green IT. ESIM supervises the development of IT-enabled IS in organizations, to support and enable green business activities, green reporting, and green processes.
>
> Furthermore, it manages the governance, planning, development, and implementation of behavioral and technological measures throughout the value chain of IT organizations, which aim at an environmentally friendlier utilization of IT.
>
> The objective of ESIM is to ensure the best use of Green IS and Green IT in relation to the corporate strategy, the demands of relevant stakeholders and the environment.

The ESIM model, shown in Figure C.2, is an extension of the industrialized information management model (Section A.3.4).

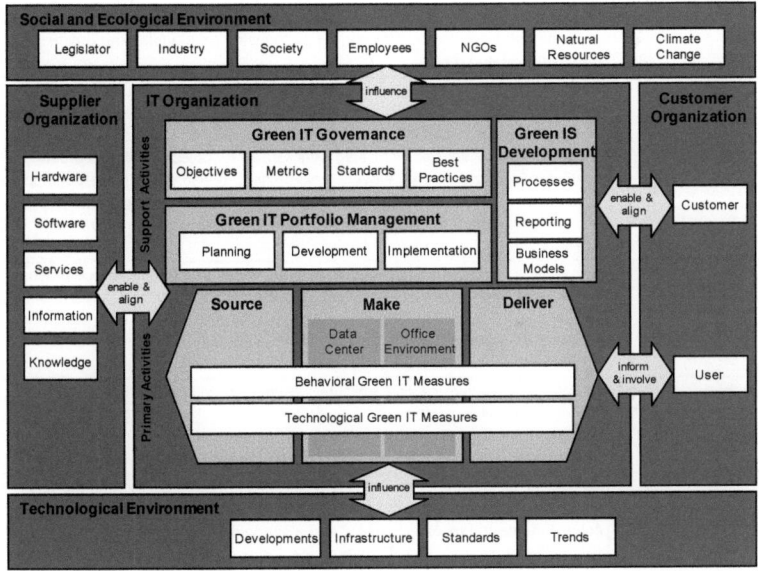

Figure C.2: Model of Environmentally Sustainable Information Management Consolidated from the Individual Findings

The model integrates a clear stakeholder orientation, due to the findings on sustainability (Publications B.1 and B.2) and the adoption of Green IT (Publication B.8). This is represented in ESIM by the social, ecological, and technological environment. ESIM is influenced by the demands, objectives and support of stakeholder groups, which include supplier and customer organizations.

In line with Porter (1998), ESIM divides its responsibilities into primary and support activities within the IT organization. Primary activities relate to Green IT measures (Section A.3.3.3.3) that are implemented in the IT value chain (Publication B.6). Support activities are divided into Green IT governance (Publication B.9), Green IT portfolio management, and Green IS development.

Role	Description of Responsibilities
Green IT governance	Green IT governance supervises Green IT initiatives. It aligns Green IT objectives with the customer organization and with the relevant stakeholders' needs. It chooses suitable performance metrics, and defines the targeted outcomes. Furthermore, it monitors and reports the achievement level. Green IT governance defines standards and collects best practices that are disseminated throughout the entire IT organization. The organizational design of Green IT governance depends on contingency factors. Green IT governance is practiced in close accord with stakeholders and Green IT portfolio management, and tracks the social, ecological and technological environment.
Green IT portfolio management	Green IT portfolio management conducts the Green IT planning process, collects and develops possible Green IT projects, evaluates them according to Green IT objectives, and determines priorities. It creates an implementation order and manages the implementation of Green IT measures by focusing on the following processes: source, make, deliver and govern.
Green IS development	Green IS development engineers innovate IT-enabled IS to facilitate and support green business activities, green reporting, and green processes. During Green IS development, the customer organization is developed to diagnose environmental action areas. Green IS development also sets Green IS objectives in accordance with the customer organization and relevant stakeholders. It also works closely with sourcing to get support for initiatives. It implements production solutions; it communicates activities and achievements through delivery; and it coordinates its work with Green IT governance.
Source	Its role is to implement and execute Green IT measures for the source process, and to ensure sourcing alignment with Green IT objectives. Furthermore, suppliers (hardware, software, services, information, and knowledge) are tracked to enable and support Green IT and Green IS initiatives. It works closely with suppliers and Green IT portfolio management, as well as Green IS development.
Make	Its role is to implement and execute Green IT measures for the production (make) process, focusing on the office environment and the data center. Furthermore, it provides the infrastructure to run Green IS solutions. It works closely with sourcing and delivery, as well as Green IT portfolio management and Green IS development.
Deliver	Its role is to implement and execute Green IT measures for the delivery process, informing and involving users, communicating all Green IT and Green IS efforts and achievements to customers, users and stakeholders. It works closely with the "make" part of the process, Green IT governance, Green IT portfolio management, and Green IS development.

Table C.1: Roles and Responsibilities of the ESIM Model

Green IT governance defines Green IT objectives (Publication B.7), and measures Green IT performance with adequate metrics (Section A.3.3.3.4). Green IT portfolio management manages the implementation of Green IT projects (Publication B.10).

Green IS development is responsible for creating IT-enabled green business activities (Publications B.3 and B.4), green reporting (Section A.3.3.2.2), and green processes (Publication B.5).

The ESIM model defines the roles and responsibilities of each of the above-mentioned elements (Table C.1). It integrates sustainability, Green IS, and Green IT aspects into information management. The ESIM model outlines possible roles and responsibilities to ensure the best use of Green IS and Green IT in relation to the corporate strategy, relevant stakeholders' demands, and the environment. It is a comprehensive, applicable approach for IT organizations, and a conceptual basis for further research on environmental sustainability and IS.

2 Implications

The previous sections describe a multitude of findings and insights on sustainability, Green IS, and Green IT. Based on these finding, policy implications (Section C.2.1), managerial implications (Section C.2.2), and research implications (Section C.2.3) are derived.

2.1 Policy Implications

Globally, governments are working towards environmental sustainability. For example, they have agreed to keep the rise in global temperature below 2° C, especially by reducing greenhouse gas emissions (United Nations Environment Programme, 2011).

The European Union (EU) has set the "20-20-20" targets to be achieved by the year 2020. These targets include a reduction in EU greenhouse gas emissions of at least 20% below 1990 levels; 20% of EU energy consumption to come from renewable resources; and a 20% reduction in primary energy use, compared with projected levels, to be achieved by improving energy efficiency (European Commission, 2010).

Research Level	Implications
Sustainability	• Governance of social and environmental issues related to IT is increasingly important • Laws, regulations, and incentives are adequate instruments for affecting IT organizations' emphasis on sustainability • IT organizations anticipate governmental behavior and try to benefit by implementing voluntary efforts in order to get ahead of the development. This demands a long-term sustainability strategy • Research funding should be provided to support research on environmental and social aspects related to IT • Educational policy should include sustainability issues, and the related role of IT, in curricula
Green IS	• Green IS is inevitable for achieving the environmental objectives • IT organizations, entrepreneurs and researchers should be encouraged in their endeavors to develop, implement, and disseminate Green IS • Research funding should not only focus on specific industries (e.g., automotive, energy, and transportation), but should also support universally applicable IT solutions, because many challenges (e.g., optimization of network flows) are similar in different industries and require transferable types of IT solutions
Green IT	• Green IT must be incorporated in the political endeavors to reduce electricity consumption and CO_2 emissions • Policy-makers should encourage, support, and force companies to implement Green IT (e.g., by governmental aid, knowledge transfer, or mandatory guidelines for IT operations) • The development of Green IT standards should be supported to increase the adoption of Green IT • The ESIM model and all related Green IT findings can be applied to manage Green IT in the public administration

Table C.2: Policy Implications

The German government pursues even more ambitious objectives. It aims to reduce primary energy consumption by 20% by 2010 (in relation to the 2008 consumption), and by 50% by 2050. Electricity consumption is projected to decline by 10% by 2020 and by 25% by 2050, compared to 2008 (BMWi and BMU, 2010). In its own administration, the German government aims to reduce the IT induced energy consumption by 40% by 2013, compared to the highest consumption level before 2009 (Rat der IT-Beauftragten, 2008).

These facts summarize the potential contribution and political importance of sustainability, Green IS, and Green IT. Based on the findings of this thesis (Section C.1), implications for legislators arise (Table C.2).

Governments can play a key role in establishing standards, providing economic incentives, and influencing social norms to change environmental behaviour in a desirable direction (Watson et al., 2010). Policy-makers understand the societal demands regarding environmental protection and respond to this by shaping an adequate legislative framework, which should also be supported by research and education.

Environmental protection will remain an important topic in the 21st century. It is therefore essential to build up a knowledge base and develop solutions in all areas. To achieve this, people should become experts at schools and universities.

Policy-makers should embrace the opportunities that IT offers for working towards environmental sustainability. This also means dealing with the negative aspects of IT. The outlined implications and recommendations provide a guideline for political decision-makers to take advantage of the thesis findings.

2.2 Managerial Implications

Ecological and social changes transform IT organizations' market environments. External stakeholders put pressure on IT organizations to incorporate sustainability. Businesses aim to reduce CO_2 emissions and costs by applying Green IS in their functions, such as production, logistics, buildings, and power (Climate Group and Global eSustainability Initiative, 2008). IT departments spend a lot of their budgets on electricity (Symantec, 2009) and must align with the corporate environmental strategy.

These facts summarize the importance of sustainability, Green IS, and Green IT for practice. Based on the findings of this thesis (Section C.1), the following managerial implications arise (Table C.3).

Research Level	Implications
Sustainability	• IT executives have to increasingly manage social and environmental issues • IT organizations should focus on their most valuable IT resources and relevant stakeholders • IT executives can manage sustainability by following the procedural model for sustainable IS management, and they can structure sustainability initiatives along the value chain of IT organizations

Green IS	• Decision-makers should encourage Green IS initiatives in order to improve environmental performance and to cut costs
	• IT-enabled green products and services have a promising market potential
	  - Green products and services should be developed or enhanced
	  - The marketing mix needs to be adapted, focusing on the target group
	• IT-enabled green business models have a promising market potential
	  - Decision-makers must consider that the perceived value of IT products or IT services is also determined by the provider's underlying business model
	  - When social and environmental aspects are included into the traditional business model, this leads to an emergence of new business models
	  - Entrepreneurs should be encouraged to initiate new businesses
	• Decision-makers should encourage the digitalization of processes for environmental reasons
	• Product and service developers should apply LCA to improve products and services and to illustrate the environmental benefits of Green IS solutions

Green IT	• IT executives should be aware of the factors that influence the adoption of Green IT (importance and uncertainty) to avoid mistakes
	• Decision-makers should manage Green IT in organizations with the ESIM model
	  - IT executives need to decide which objectives they want to pursue with Green IT: efficient internal operations, reputation management, and/or market competitiveness
	  - The ideal company-specific design of Green IT governance is determined by contingency factors
	  - Green IT metrics help IT executives to set and monitor targets
	  - Strategic Green IT planning provides applicable concepts, procedures, and tools
	  - The value chain of IT organizations defines the scope for behavioral and technological Green IT measures
	  - The ESIM model defines roles and responsibilities related to Green IS and Green IT
	• IT executives can use the thesis findings to compare and evaluate their own Green IT activities
	• Decision-makers should apply the outlined concepts and methods to maximize Green IT's positive contribution to the business objectives

Table C.3: Managerial Implications

Successful and well managed companies know that they are dependent on the natural environment and that they must address the needs of the environment and society to ensure long-term market relevance. Therefore, these companies approach sustainability proactively. Such an approach can achieve credibility by applying integrated sustainability management in all areas. Therefore, sustainability also applies to IT organizations.

Green IS should be developed and applied to reduce the company's environmental impact. Green IT minimizes IT's environmental impact. The outlined implications and recommendations provide a guideline for decision-makers. Although the ideal shape of Green IS and Green IT differs from

2.3 Research Implications

Research on environmental sustainability in IS has received considerable attention in recent years. It is an important topic for academia, and is likely to receive more attention in the future (Section A.3.1). The theoretical and conceptual basis of environmental sustainability and IS is still limited, due to the novelty of the topic (Section A.3.3). This thesis contributes to the body of knowledge by deriving the following implications (Table C.4), based on the findings from Section C.1.

Research Level	Implications
Sustainability	• Sustainability and IS is a relevant IS research branch that investigates environmental and social issues related to IT • Environmental and social aspects' inclusion into IS research leads to a multitude of research questions • Stakeholder theory, the resource-based view, and the value chain of IT organizations provide a theoretical basis and prove to be applicable for conceptualizing sustainability in IS research • The procedural model for sustainable IS management is an applicable artifact • Many large-scale organizations specify sustainability targets for their IT, and manage sustainability with IT • Sustainability, Green IS, and Green IT should become part of the IS curricula at universities

Green IS	• Similar to other industries (e.g., automotive), green attributes of IT products and services influence customer perception
	   - Conjoint analysis proves to be an appropriate method for evaluating the market potential of Green IS
	   - Researchers should derive an adequate marketing mix for IT products and services
	• Social business is a new concept for IS research
	   - The phenomenon of a "race to the top" helps to explain behavior of IT organizations
	   - IT-enabled green business models possess the potential for success
	• Digital processes appear to be environmentally friendlier than physical processes
	• Many environmental challenges (e.g., optimization of network flows) in different industries are similar and require transferable types of IT solutions
	• The environmental impact of digital processes positively correlates with the amount of processed data
	• LCA is an appropriate method to evaluate the environmental impact of IT products and IT services
	• Green IS provides a multitude of new research questions (Section C.3.2.2)

Green IT	• Industrialized information management, contingency theory, and CSR provide an applicable theoretical basis for Green IT research • The awareness of Green IT in IT organizations enables large empirical studies • The illustrated tools, concepts, procedures, metrics, measures, and standards provide a starting point for further research • The ESIM model provides an ideal reference model for defining processes, tasks, roles, and responsibilities in the Green IS and Green IT scope • Green IT has been researched extensively from multiple perspectives (Section A.3.3.3.2). This suggests a consolidation of research findings

Table C.4: Research Implications

The outlined implications provide references for academics. Based on these implications, IS researchers are encouraged to pursue further research topics, which are outlined in Section C.3.2.

The implications also highlight the fact that sustainability, Green IS, and Green IT should become part of the IS curricula at universities. Owing to the fact that many researchers are also lecturers at universities, the insights of this thesis and the referenced literature provide substantial course contents. Students should be taught Green IS and Green IT principles. Therefore, researchers should approach policy-makers and practitioners to support their activities with funding and practical insights.

3 Conclusion and Further Research

The findings and implications of this thesis have limitations that are summarized in Section C.3.1. The implications and limitations result in suggestions for further research related to sustainability and IS (Section C.3.2). Finally, the thesis closes with a concluding statement about the applied procedure and the significance of the findings (Section C.3.3).

3.1 Limitations

Although this thesis provides a comprehensive overview of sustainability and IS, Green IS, and Green IT, a number of limitations must be considered.

The research publications on sustainability (Publications B.1 and B.2) follow a conceptual argumentative analysis, based on literature findings. Therefore, researchers and practitioners need to critically reflect on the findings and implications derived from this analysis. Other theories than the applied ones might explain sustainability and IS just as well. The procedural model for sustainable IS management might also not be the optimal solution for managing sustainability in IT organizations. Regardless, the limited research on sustainability and IS as well as the lack of practical manifestations of the phenomenon necessitated the applied research process.

The research publications on Green IS have specific shortcomings, related to their applied research design, the method of data collection, and the method of data analysis. With regard to green marketing, green business, and green processes, the investigation into Green IS was very limited. Regarding green marketing (Publication B.3), the empirical data is only representative of the German-speaking area and might be biased due to self-selection. The research on green business (Publication B.4) is based on one case, which is insufficient for generalizable statements. The evaluation of green processes (Publication B.5) by LCA produced a number of assumptions that were based on literature and interviews. Some of these assumptions might be incorrect. Nevertheless, the findings and implications provide the first set of assumptions in the field, as well as important initial concepts for further research.

Specific limitations due to the research design also apply to each Green IT publication. The proposed models and concepts regarding Green IT governance (Publication B.9), Green IT planning (Publication B.10) and ESIM (Section C.1.4) demand further validation and testing. Research on the adoption of Green IT (Publication B.8) is based on single measurements only. Furthermore, important underlying factors might not have been included in the research. The collected data from 15 expert interviews, 116 surveyed CIOs and IT managers, and 6 case studies provide a substantial empirical basis. However, most of the empirical data were collected in the

German-speaking area. Therefore, transferring the findings and implications to other countries must be limited because they are not generalizable beyond the domain that the researcher actually observed (Lee & Baskerville, 2003). Moreover, empirical studies are limited by their dependence on the data quality provided by the respondents.

3.2 Further Research

Research on environmental sustainability and IS will continue to be an important topic for academia. It is, in fact, likely to receive more attention in future (Section A.3.1). Research is recommended in a number of scientific and practical areas, including those proposed here.

3.2.1 Further Research on Sustainability and IS

Further research on sustainability and IS includes, but is not limited to, the following:

- **Theoretical elaboration of sustainability and IS:** The concept and its underlying terms remain vague, and a common understanding as well as a strong theoretical basis are still absent. Sustainability and IS should be investigated by applying other theories, such as the organizational culture theory (Pettigrew, 1979), or the principal agent theory (Alchian & Demsetz, 1972; Eisenhardt, 1989b). Research should contribute to the knowledge base by structuring existing IS research according to sustainability's economic, ecologic and social dimensions. The links between key concepts, such as sustainability, CSR, and corporate sustainability have also not been described adequately (Marrone et al., 2011). Therefore, IS researchers can focus on these relationships, describing them in detail. Furthermore, some researchers suggest that sustainability should include a fourth dimension, culture (Hawkes, 2001; Nurse, 2006). Culture can be examined in terms of IS: Scholars can clarify how it could be integrated.

- **Instruments for sustainable IS management:** Practical solutions are needed to manage sustainability in IT, and to manage sustainability with IT. Researchers can therefore develop and test specific IT artifacts that support practitioners in these endeavors. The procedural model for sustainable IS management (Publication B.2) represents a first attempt, but needs to be tested and refined further. This thesis emphasizes the environmental dimensions of sustainability. Further research should investigate the social dimension of sustainability in IS, for example by developing social key performance indicators. This would allow integrated management concepts, such as an IT sustainability balanced scorecard, to be produced. These concepts would cover economical, environmental and social aspects related to IT.

3.2.2 Further Research on Green IS

Green IS provides a multitude of research opportunities. Many industries (e.g., agriculture, energy, manufacturing, and transportation) and stakeholders (e.g., customers, providers, and legislators) can be combined when the research scope is defined. To create a common ground for Green IS research, academics must develop a theoretical and methodological Green IS toolset by applying and adapting economic theories to Green IS.

Transaction cost theory could, for example, provide a theoretical foundation for Green IS research (Coase, 1937; Williamson, 1985). According to this theory, a transaction can be defined as the transfer of property rights between two contracting parties (Coase, 1937; Williamson, 1985). Transaction cost theory investigates the ideal coordination of these transactions from an economic perspective. The theory is highly relevant in IS research due to IT's ability to reduce transaction costs (Picot et al., 2003). This relevance is highlighted further by Williamson's (1985) original definition of transaction costs: "Transaction costs are the economic equivalent of friction in physical systems." In a physical system, friction produces heat, which is usually undesirable and considered a waste of energy. Hence, if IT can reduce transaction costs, and transaction costs are equivalent to physical friction, IT can reduce physical friction; this implies that IT can reduce wasted energy or resources. This ability of IT is represented by Green IS. Therefore, further research on Green IS can enhance the theoretical knowledge base by:

- **Developing a transaction impact theory:** Based on the aforementioned deliberations, IS researchers can adapt transaction cost theory to develop a transaction impact theory that investigates the coordination of transactions from an environmental perspective. This theory would enable IS researchers to analyze the general role of Green IS in reducing transactions' environmental impact. The theory could be applied in all industries, in single organizations and in corporate networks.

The development of such a transaction impact theory must be accompanied by a strong empirical validation. For this, it is advantageous that IT is disseminated in all types of industries, including agriculture, energy, manufacturing, and transportation. IS researchers are therefore uniquely able to access insights from these different business sectors, enabling comparison of environmental challenges.

Even though these industries have different characteristics, the environmental objectives (e.g., optimization of network flows, processes, and environmental reporting) can often be compared (Watson et al., 2010). This creates the possibility of developing similar and transferable types of Green IS solutions, which can be investigated by:

- **Discovering cross case patterns in Green IS:** As outlined, Green IS can make a positive contribution in various industries, because they experience similar environmental challenges. Scholars can find out what the similarities are, and then propose generic IT concepts as solutions.

For single organizations, IS researchers can develop applicable solutions by:

- **Designing Green IS artifacts:** Researchers can select organizations from a specific industry and then analyze and compare their environmental impact. In the next step, IT-enabled solutions can be designed (e.g., reporting systems, planning algorithms) to improve the organizations' environmental performance.

- **Designing Green IS meter systems:** In many cases the resource consumptions can only be estimated due to missing meter systems that measure and communicate relevant data (e.g., energy consumption, CO_2 emissions). This hampers environmental management on all levels. IS researchers should therefore search for ways to identify possible data sources (e.g., smart meters) and to develop applications that collect, store, and process the data.

More specific research questions are derived from the findings and limitations of green marketing (Publication B.3), green business activities (Publication B.4), and green processes (Publication B.5). Possible research topics include, but are not limited to, the following:

- **Assessing the relevance of IT products and services with green features for internal markets:** While external markets have been investigated, the role of environmental attributes of IT products and services for internal markets has not been researched. It would be valuable to highlight related differences and similarities. This would provide IT organizations, which serve an internal market, with recommendations regarding their internal marketing.

- **Evaluating and developing IT-enabled green business models:** IT-enabled green business models combine certain aspects of IT, environmental protection, and economic success, making them highly socially relevant. Researchers should describe this concept in greater detail, providing practical examples and suitable theories. Moreover, exemplary business models should be developed and tested.

- **Applying LCA to compare the environmental impact of traditional and IT-enabled solutions:** Although the LCA technique is widely used, the process of data collection and data analysis demands intense effort and is often unreliable due to poor data quality. Researchers should develop tools to automate these processes, thereby improving the results' validity. Furthermore, LCA should be applied to IT products and services to improve knowledge about IT's environmental impact.

In future research, scholars should also emphasize the difference between Green IS research and traditional IS research, to highlight Green IS research's relevance.

3.2.3 Further Research on Green IT

Green IT does not have the same environmental potential that Green IS has. However, Green IT's research area is better defined and established. Unlike Green IS, Green IT research must primarily test and refine its findings. This also applies to the models of this thesis, including the ESIM model. Nevertheless, Green IT is important for any credible application of Green IS. Further research on Green IT includes, but is not limited to, the following:

- **Extending the Green IT knowledge base:** This thesis focuses on the scope (Publication B.6), objectives (Publication B.7), adoption (Publication B.8), measures (Section A.3.3.3.3), and metrics (Section A.3.3.3.4) of Green IT. Each of these aspects should be proved, extended, and enhanced by further research, for example by surveys in other countries in order to determine if the results are transferable. Furthermore, research can determine the factors that result in Green IT initiatives' failure. Since Green IT is a new phenomenon, it should also be subject to research on fads and trends in IS research. Researchers can also apply other IS theories (Section A.3.2), such as the principal agent theory, to investigate Green IT in more depth.

- **Validating Green IT concepts:** Further research should be done to validate the proposed models. Although the first evaluations have been done, the suggested Green IT governance model (Publication B.9), the strategic Green IT planning process (Publication B.10), and the ESIM model (Section C.1.4) need to be validated and refined, using case studies and a quantitative empirical survey, to demonstrate generalizability. An interesting research question is whether the ESIM model can be linked to frameworks of IT service management, such as ITIL. All concepts must prove that they make a positive contribution to the success of IT organizations.

- **Designing new Green IT measures and metrics:** Constant technological advances make it possible for researchers to design greener IT solutions than the ones currently in use. Research can integrate Green IT metrics into applied concepts of performance measurement systems, such as the IT balanced scorecard. Scholars must develop a standard procedure to determine IT carbon productivity (number of IT services (e.g., transactions, storage, FLOPS, and IPS) per kg CO_2 emissions). This meaningful metric can then be used to measure IT's environmental impact. For this it is also necessary to identify potential data sources and to install sensors to collect the data needed.

The knowledge base on Green IT has grown rapidly in recent years. Therefore, for any further research on Green IT, IS researchers must carefully review the numerous publications on Green IT in conference proceedings and academic journals.

3.3 Concluding Statements

The thesis aimed to contribute to a better understanding of the relevance and the benefits of sustainability, Green IS, and Green IT. While answering the outlined research questions and developing the ESIM model, some new questions for further research evolved.

The thesis focused on three research topics, rather than just one. This broad approach was not ideal because it produced less clear and concise results than would have been achieved if only one research topic (e.g., Green IT) had been studied. However, the author selected the presented procedure as a necessary tradeoff between formal requirements, completeness, and comprehensibility.

Owing to the broad scope, the thesis provided a holistic view on the topic. The analysis systematically progressed from sustainability and IS, to Green IS, then to Green IT, and consolidated its findings in the ESIM model. A great amount of data has been collected during this research. It is hoped that the knowledge and the tools in this thesis will stimulate practitioners and researchers to engage in the global struggle against climate change in order to positively contribute to environmental protection.

Responsible researchers are aware that their work and teaching can influence others. They are the societal experts who provide knowledge and solutions to enable reasoned decision-making. Therefore, they play a key role in the global struggle against climate change.

Nicholas Carr (2003) once made the provocative statement that "IT doesn't matter." Based on this thesis, it is clear that IT does matter for the environment. And the environment must matter to us. Therefore, we have the responsibility to realize the full potential of IT to save our common future.

References

Agarwal, M. K., & Green, P. E. (1991). Adaptive Conjoint Analysis Versus Self-explicated Models: Some Empirical Result. *International Journal of Research in Marketing, 8*(2), 141-146.

Akamai Technologies Inc. (2009). Report - The State of the Internet (Vol. 2). Retrieved Febuary 26, 2010, from http://www.akamai.com/dl/whitepapers/Akamai_State_Internet_Q2_2009.pdf

Albers, S. (1984). Fully Nonmetric Estimation of a Continuous Nonlinear Conjoint Utility Function. *International Journal of Research in Marketing, 1*(4), 311-319.

Alchian, A. A., & Demsetz, H. (1972). Production, Information Costs, and Economic Organization. *The American Economic Review, 62*(5), 777-795.

Amit, R., & Schoemaker, P. J. H. (1993). Strategic Assets and Organizational Rent. *Strategic Management Journal, 14*(1), 33-46. doi:10.1002/smj.4250140105

Apple Inc. (2009). 13-inch MacBook Pro. Retrieved August 1, 2009, from http://images.apple.com/environment/resources/pdf/MacBook-Pro-13-inch-Environmental-Report.pdf

Applegate, L. M., McFarlan, F. W., & McKenney, J. L. (1999). Corporate Information Systems Management: Text and Cases (5th ed.). McGraw-Hill, Boston, USA.

Aragón-Correa, J. A., & Sharma, S. (2003). A Contingent Resource-based View of Proactive Corporate Environmental Strategy. *Academy of Management Review, 28*(1), 71-88.

Backhaus, K., Erichson, B., Plinke, W., & Weiber, R. (2008). Multivariate Analysemethoden: Eine anwendungsorientierte Einführung (12th ed.). Springer, Berlin.

Barney, J. (1991). Firm Resources and Sustained Competitive Advantage. *Journal of Management, 17*(1), 99-120.

Belady, C., Azevedo, D., Patterson, M., Pouchet, J., & Tipley, R. (2010). Carbon Usage Effectiveness (CUE): A Green Grid Data Center Sustainability Metric (White Paper No. 32). Retrieved April 8, 2011, from http://www.thegreengrid.org/~/media/WhitePapers/CarbonUsageEffectivenessWhitePaper20101202.ashx?lang=en

Belady, C., Rawson, A., Pfleuger, J., & Cader, T. (2008). Green Grid Data Center Power Efficiency Metrics: PUE and DCiE (White Paper No. 6). Retrieved April 8, 2011, from http://www.thegreengrid.org/~/media/WhitePapers/White_Paper_6_-_PUE_and_DCiE_Eff_Metrics_30_December_2008.ashx?lang=en

Benbasat, I., Goldstein, D. K., & Mead, M. (1987). The Case Research Strategy in Studies of Information Systems. *MIS Quarterly, 11*(3), 369-386.

Benbasat, I., & Zmud, R. W. (1999). Empirical Research in Information Systems: The Practice of Relevance. *MIS Quarterly, 23*(1), 3-16.

Benefind (2010). benefind - Wie funktioniert benefind? Retrieved July 28, 2010, from http://fwsd.benefind.de/funktionsweise.html

Bengtsson, F., & Agerfalk, P. J. (2011). Information Technology as a Change Actant in Sustainability Innovation: Insights from Uppsala. *The Journal of Strategic Information Systems, 20*(1), 96-112. doi:10.1016/j.jsis.2010.09.007

Berens, G., van Riel, C. B. M., & van Bruggen, G. H. (2005). Corporate Associations and Consumer Product Responses: The Moderating Role of Corporate Brand Dominance. *Journal of Marketing, 69*(3), 35-18.

Berkhout, F., & Hertin, J. (2001). Impacts of ICT on Environmental Sustainability: Speculations and Evidence. Report to the OECD. Brighton, United Kingdom. Retrieved November 9, 2009, from http://www.oecd.org/LongAbstract/0,3425,en_2649_34499_1897149_119666_1_1_1,00.html

Bharadwaj, A. S., Sambamurthy, V., & Zmud, R. W. (1999). IT Capabilities: Theoretical Perspectives and Empirical Operationalization. *Proceedings of the 20th International Conference on Information Systems (ICIS) 1999*. Atlanta, USA.

Blackle - Heap Media (2010). About Blackle - Energy Saving Search. Retrieved July 28, 2010, from http://www.blackle.com/about/

Bose, R., & Luo, X. (2011). Integrative Framework for Assessing Firms' Potential to Undertake Green IT Initiatives via Virtualization - A Theoretical Perspective. *The Journal of Strategic Information Systems, 20*(1), 38-54. doi:10.1016/j.jsis.2011.01.003

Boudreau, M.-C., Watson, R. T., & Chen, A. (2008). From Green IT to Green IS. *Cutter Benchmark Review, 8*(5), 5-11.

Brenner, W. (1994). Grundzüge des Informationsmanagements (1st ed.). Springer, Berlin.

Brill, K. (2007). Data Center Energy Efficiencyand Productivity (White Paper). Santa Fe, USA. Retrieved July 9, 2008, from http://www.uptimeinstitute.org/symp_pdf/%28TUI3004C%29DataCenterEnergyEfficiency.pdf

Brown, C. V. (1997). Examining the Emergence of Hybrid IS Governance Solutions: Evidence from a Single Case Site. *Information Systems Research, 8*(1), 69-94.

Brown, C. V. (1999). Horizontal Mechanisms under Differing IS Organization Contexts. *MIS Quarterly, 23*(3), 421-454.

Brown, T. J., & Dacin, P. A. (1997). The Company and the Product: Corporate Associations and Consumer Product Responses. *Journal of Marketing, 61*(1), 68-84.

Bryson, J. M. (2004). Strategic Planning for Public and Nonprofit Organizations: A Guide to Strengthening and Sustaining Organizational Achievement. John Wiley & Sons, Hoboken, USA.

Buhl, H. U., & Laartz, J. (2008). Warum Green IT nicht ausreicht – oder: Wo müssen wir heute anpacken, damit es uns übermorgen immer noch gut geht? *WIRTSCHAFTSINFORMATIK, 50*(4), 261-265. doi:10.1365/s11576-008-0058-5

Buhl, H. U., Laartz, J., Löffler, M., & Röglinger, M. (2009). Green IT reicht nicht aus! *WIRTSCHAFTSINFORMATIK & MANAGEMENT, 1*(1), 54-58.

References

Bundesamt für Sicherheit in der Informationstechnik (2009). Die Lage der IT-Sicherheit in Deutschland 2009. Retrieved April 17, 2009, from http://www.bsi.bund.de/literat/lagebericht/Lagebericht2009.pdf

BMWi and BMU (Bundesministerium für Wirtschaft und Technologie and Bundesministerium für Naturschutz und Reaktorsicherheit) (2010). Energy Concept for an Environmentally Sound, Reliable and Affordable Energy Supply. Retrieved May 12, 2011, from http://www.bmu.de/files/english/pdf/application/pdf/energiekonzept_bundesregierung_en.pdf

BITKOM (Bundesverband Informationswirtschaft Telekommunikation und neue Medien e. V.) (2008). Verbraucher achten zunehmend auf Energie- und Umwelteigenschaften. Retrieved November 13, 2009, from http://www.bitkom.org/de/presse/56204_51978.aspx

Bundesverband Musikindustrie e. V. (2009). Musikindustrie in Zahlen 2008. Retrieved Febuary 27, 2010, from http://www.musikindustrie.de/uploads/media/ms_branchendaten_jahreswirtschaftsbericht_2008.pdf

Businessweek (2007). The World's 50 Most Innovative Companies. Retrieved May 16, 2008, from http://www.businessweek.com/interactive_reports/most_innovative.html?chan=innovation_special+report+--+2007+most+innovative+companies_2007+most+innovative+companies

Butler, T., & Daly, M. (2008). Environmental Responsibilty and Green IT: An Institutional Perspective. *Proceedings of the 16th European Conference on Information Systems (ECIS) 2008*. Galway, Irland. Retrieved from http://aisel.aisnet.org/ecis2008/10

Capra, E., & Merlo, F. (2009). Green IT: Everything Starts from the Software. *Proceedings of the 17th European Conference on Information Systems (ECIS) 2009*. Verona, Italy. Retrieved from http://aisel.aisnet.org/ecis2009/221

car2go (2011). car2go: The Mobility Concept. Retrieved January 20, 2011, from http://www.car2go.com/ulm/en/

Carr, N. G. (2003). IT doesn't matter. *Harvard Business Review, 8*(5), 24-38.

Cater-Steel, A., & Tan, W.-G. (2010). The Role of IT Service Management in Green IT. *Australasian Journal of Information Systems, 17*(1), 107-125.

Cattell, R. (1966). The Scree Test for the Number of Factors. *Multivariate Behavioral Research, 1*(2), 245-276. doi:10.1207/s15327906mbr0102_10

Chen, A. J., Watson, R. T., Boudreau, M. C., & Karahanna, E. (2009a). Organizational Adoption of Green IS & IT: An Institutional Perspective. *Proceedings of the 30th International Conference on Information Systems (ICIS) 2009*. Phoenix, USA. Retrieved from http://aisel.aisnet.org/icis2009/142

Chen, A. J. W., Boudreau, M.-C., & Watson, R. T. (2008). Information Systems and Ecological Sustainability. *Journal of Systems and Information Technology, 10*(3), 186 - 201. doi:10.1108/13287260810916907

Chen, A., Watson, R., Boudreau, M.-C., & Karahanna, E. (2009b). Organizational Adoption of Green IS & IT: An Institutional Perspective. *Proceedings of the 30th International Conference on Information Systems (ICIS) 2009*. Phoenix, USA. Retrieved from http://aisel.aisnet.org/icis2009/142

Chitra, K. (2007). In Search of the Green Consumers: A Perceptual Study. *Journal of Services Research, 7*(1), 173-191.

Chou, T. (2008). Seven: Software Business Models. Active Book Press, San Mateo, USA.

Clemons, E. K., & Row, M. C. (1991). Sustaining IT Advantage: The Role of Structural Differences. *MIS Quarterly, 15*(3), 275-292.

Climate Group and Global eSustainability Initiative. (2008). SMART 2020: Enabling the Low Carbon Economy in the Information Age. Retrieved November 5, 2009, from http://www.smart2020.org/

Coase, R. H. (1937). The Nature of the Firm. *Economica, 4*(16), 386-405.

comScore (2010). comScore Reports Global Search Market Growth of 46 Percent in 2009 - comScore, Inc. Retrieved July 5, 2010, from http://www.comscore.com/Press_Events/Press_Releases/2010/1/Global_Search_Market_Grows_46_Percent_in_2009

Constantinides, E. (2006). The Marketing Mix Revisited: Towards the 21st Century Marketing. *Journal of Marketing Management, 22*(3/4), 407-438.

Corbett, J. (2010). Unearthing the Value of Green IT. *Proceedings of the 31st International Conference on Information Systems (ICIS) 2010*. St. Louis, USA. Retrieved from http://aisel.aisnet.org/icis2010_submissions/198

Costello, A. B., & Osborne, J. W. (2005). Best Practices in Exploratory Factor Analysis: Four Recommendations for Getting the Most from Your Analysis. *Practical Assessment, Research & Evaluation, 10*(7), 1-9.

Crane, A. (1999). Are You Ethical? Please Tick Yes ☐ Or No ☐ On Researching Ethics in Business Organizations. *Journal of Business Ethics, 20*, 237-248.

Cyber Rain Inc. (2011). Cyber-Rain. Retrieved May 3, 2011, from http://www.cyber-rain.com/

Dandridge, C. B., Roturier, J., & Norford, L. K. (1994). Energy Policies for Energy Efficiency in Office Equipment: Case Studies from Europe, Japan and the USA. *Energy Policy, 22*(9), 735-747. doi:10.1016/0301-4215(94)90049-3

De Vaus, D. (2001). Research Design in Social Research. SAGE, Thousand Oaks, USA.

Dellaert, B., Borgers, A., & Timmermans, H. (1996). Conjoint Choice Models of Joint Participation and Activity Choice. *International Journal of Research in Marketing, 13*(3), 251-264.

Delone, W. H., & McLean, E. R. (2003). The DeLone and McLean Model of Information Systems Success: A Ten-Year Update. *Journal of Management Information Systems, 19*(4), 9-30.

Denzin, N. K. (1978). Sociological Methods: A Sourcebook. McGraw-Hill, Boston, USA.

DesAutels, P., & Berthon, P. (2011). The PC (Polluting Computer): Forever a Tragedy of the Commons? *The Journal of Strategic Information Systems, 20*(1), 113-122. doi:10.1016/j.jsis.2010.09.003

Deutsches Institut für Normung e.V. (2009). DIN EN ISO 14040 - Umweltmanagement - Ökobilanz - Grundsätze und Rahmenbedingungen. Berlin.

Diaz, M. A., Nickels, G., Kautz, E. B., & Cochran, T. (2008). Current and Potential Green Jobs in the U.S. Economy (The United States Conference of Mayors and the Mayors Climate Protection Center). Lexington, USA. Retrieved April 5, 2011, from http://www.usmayors.org/pressreleases/uploads/greenjobsreport.pdf

Du, S., Bhattacharya, C. B., & Sen, S. (2007). Reaping Relational Rewards from Corporate Social Responsibility: The Role of Competitive Positioning. *International Journal of Research in Marketing, 24*(3), 224-241. doi:10.1016/j.ijresmar.2007.01.001

Dubé, L., & Paré, G. (2003). Rigor in Informations Systems Positivist Case Research: Current Practices, Trends, and Recommendations. *MIS Quarterly, 27*(4), 597-635.

Dürr, B. (2010). Umkämpftes Coltan: Der Stoff, aus dem die Handys sind. Retrieved May 4, 2011, from http://www.stern.de/digital/telefon/umkaempftes-coltan-der-stoff-aus-dem-die-handys-sind-1551021.html

Dyllick, T., & Hockerts, K. (2002). Beyond the Business Case for Corporate Sustainability. *Business Strategy and the Environment, 11*(2), 130-141. doi:10.1002/bse.323

Earl, M. J. (1998). Information Management: The Organizational Dimension. Oxford University Press, New York, USA.

Ecocho (2010). Ökosuche FAQs: Antworten zu den häufigsten Fragen an Ecocho. Retrieved July 28, 2010, from http://www.ecocho.eu/faqs.php

Ecosia (2010a). FAQ - Ecosia. Retrieved July 5, 2010, from http://ecosia.org/faq.php?id=31#33

Ecosia (2010b). Ecosia Payments. Retrieved July 5, 2010, from http://ecosia.org/_files/donations.pdf

Ecosia (2010c). Statistik - Ecosia. Retrieved July 5, 2010, from http://ecosia.org/statistics.php

Eder, S. W. (1994). Grüne Computer. *WIRTSCHAFTSINFORMATIK, 36*(6), 600-603.

Eder, S. W. (2009). Green Computers. *Business & Information Systems Engineering, 1*(1), 123-125. doi:10.1007/s12599-008-0012-5

Ein-Dor, P., & Segev, E. (1982). Organizational Context and MIS Structure: Some Empirical Evidence. *MIS Quarterly, 6*(3), 55-68.

Eisenhardt, K. M. (1989a). Building Theories from Case Study Research. *The Academy of Management Review, 14*(4), 532-550.

Eisenhardt, K. M. (1989b). Agency Theory: An Assessment and Review. *The Academy of Management Review, 14*(1), 57-74.

El-Gayar, O., & Fritz, B. D. (2006). Environmental Management Information Systems (EMIS) for Sustainable Development: A Conceptual Overview. *Communications of the Association for Information Systems, 17*(1), 756-784.

Elkington, J. (1997). Cannibals with Forks: The Triple Bottom Line of 21st Century Business. Capstone Publishing, Oxford, United Kingdom.

Elliot, S. (2007). Environmentally Sustainable ICT: A Critical Topic for IS Research? *Proceedings of the 11th Pacific Asia Conference on Information Systems (PACIS) 2007*. Auckland, New Zealand. Retrieved from http://www.pacis-net.org/file/2007/1302.pdf

Elliot, S. (2011). Transdisciplinary Perspectives on Environmental Sustainability: A Resource Base and Framework for IT-enabled Business Transformation. *MIS Quarterly, 35*(1), 197-236.

Elliot, S., & Binney, D. (2008). Environmentally Sustainable ICT: Developing Corporate Capabilities and an Industry-Relevant IS Research Agenda. *Proceedings of the 12th Pacific Asia Conference on Information Systems (PACIS) 2008*. Suzhou, China. Retrieved from http://aisel.aisnet.org/pacis2008/209/

Emerson, J. (2003). The Blended Value Proposition: Integrating Social and Financial Returns. *California Management Review, 45*(4), 35-51.

Enkvist, P., Naucler, T., & Rosander, J. (2007). A Cost Curve for Greenhouse Gas Reduction. *McKinsey Quaterly, 1*(2007), 34-45.

Environmental Protection Agency (2007). Report to Congress on Server and Data Center Energy Efficiency - Public Law 109-431. Retrieved December 10, 2010, from http://www.energystar.gov/ia/partners/prod_development/downloads/EPA_Datacenter_Report_Congress_Final1.pdf

Environmental Protection Agency (2009). About ENERGY STAR. Retrieved January 30, 2009, from http://www.energystar.gov/ia/partners/prod_development/downloads/EPA_Datacenter_Report_Congress_Final1.pdf

Epstein, M. J. (2008). Making Sustainability Work: Best Practices in Managing and Measuring Corporate Social, Environmental and Economic Impacts. Berrett-Koehler, San Francisco, USA.

Epstein, M. J., & Roy, M.-J. (2001). Sustainability in Action: Identifying and Measuring the Key Performance Drivers. *Long Range Planning, 34*(5), 585-604. doi: 10.1016/S0024-6301(01)00084-X

Erek, K., Schmidt, N.-H., Zarnekow, R., & Kolbe, L. M. (2009). Sustainability in Information Systems: Assortment of Current Practices in IS Organizations. *Proceedings of the 15th Americas Conference on Information Systems (AMCIS) 2009*. San Francisco, USA. Retrieved from http://aisel.aisnet.org/amcis2009/123

Esty, D. C., & Winston, A. S. (2006). Green to Gold: How Smart Companies Use Environmental Strategy to Innovate, Create Value, and Build Competitive Advantage. Yale University Press, New Haven, USA.

European Commission (2008a). Impact of Information and Communication Technologies on Energy Efficiency (Final report). Retrieved December 1, 2010, from ftp://ftp.cordis.europa.eu/pub/fp7/ict/docs/sustainable-growth/ict4ee-final-report_en.pdf

References

European Commission (2008b). Code of Conduct on Data Centres Energy EfficiencyVersion 1.0. Ispra, Italy. Retrieved December 1, 2010, from http://ec.europa.eu/information_society/activities/sustainable_growth/docs/datacenter_code-conduct.pdf

European Commission (2009). Code of Conduct on Data Centres Energy EfficiencyVersion 2.0 - Endorser Guidelines and Registration Form. Ispra, Italy. Retrieved December 12, 2010, from http://re.jrc.ec.europa.eu/energyefficiency/pdf/CoC%20DC%20new%20rep%20form%20and%20guidelines/Endorser%20Guidelines%20v2%200%201.pdf

European Commission (2010). The EU climate and energy package - Policies - Climate Action - European Commission. Retrieved February 3, 2011, from http://ec.europa.eu/clima/policies/brief/eu/package_en.htm

Fabrigar, L. R., Wegener, D. T., MacCallum, R. C., & Strahan, E. J. (1999). Evaluating the Use of Exploratory Factor Analysis in Psychological Research. *Psychological Methods*, *4*(3), 272-299. doi:10.1037/1082-989X.4.3.272

Facebook - Ecosia (2010). Facebook - Ecosia. Retrieved October 8, 2010, from http://www.facebook.com/profile.php?id=1262181419#!/ecosia

Fayol, H. (1947). Administration Industrielle et Générale: Prévoyance, Organisation, Commandement, Coordination, Contrôle. Dunod, Paris, France.

Field, A. (2009). Discovering Statistics Using SPSS (3rd ed.). SAGE, Thousand Oaks, USA.

Figge, F. (2005). Value-based Environmental Management. From Environmental Shareholder Value to Environmental Option Value. *Corporate Social Responsibility and Environmental Management*, *12*(1), 19-30. doi:10.1002/csr.74

Figge, F., Hahn, T., Schaltegger, S., & Wagner, M. (2002). The Sustainability Balanced Scorecard - Linking Sustainability Management to Business Strategy. *Business Strategy and the Environment*, *11*(5), 269-284. doi:10.1002/bse.339

FOCUS Online (2009). Ecosia: Suchmaschine will Regenwald retten. Retrieved July 28, 2010, from http://www.focus.de/digital/internet/ecosia-suchmaschine-will-regenwald-retten_aid_460358.html

Fombrun, C. J. (2005). Building Corporate Reputation Through CSR Initiatives: Evolving Standards. *Corporate Reputation Review*, *8*(1), 7-11.

Forestle. (2010). Fragen zu Forestle. Retrieved July 28, 2010, from http://forestle.org/_lang/de/faq.php#1

Forge, S. (2007). Powering Down: Remedies for Unsustainable ICT. *Foresight*, *9*(4), 3-21.

Fox-Penner, P. (2010). Smart Power: Climate Change, the Smart Grid, and the Future of Electric Utilities (1st ed.). Island Press, Washington, USA.

Fraunhofer IZM and Fraunhofer ISI (2009). Abschätzung des Energiebedarfs der weiteren Entwicklung der Informationsgesellschaft - Abschlussbericht an das Bundesministerium für Wirtschaft und Technologie. Retrieved September 2, 2010, from http://www.bmwi.de/Dateien/BMWi/PDF/abschaetzung-des-energiebedarfs-der-weiteren-entwicklung-der-informationsgesellschaft,property=pdf,bereich=bmwi,sprache=de,rwb=true.pdf

Freeman, R. E. (1984). Strategic Management: A Stakeholder Approach. Pitman, Boston, USA.

Fuchs, C. (2006). The Implications of New Information and Communication Technologies for Sustainability. *Environment, Development and Sustainability, 10*(3), 291-309. doi:10.1007/s10668-006-9065-0

Fuhrmanns, V., & Crawford, D. (2011). Siemens Division to Focus on Green Infrastructure. *The Wall Street Journal*. Retrieved April 5, 2011, from http://online.wsj.com/article/SB10001424052748703696704576222730939679172.html?mod=googlenews_wsj

Fujitsu Australia. (2009). Green IT: The Convenient Truth. Retrieved November 13, 2009, from https://www-s.fujitsu.com/au/whitepapers/convenient_truth.html

Gable, G. G. (1994). Integrating Case Study and Survey Research Methods: An Example in Information Systems. *European Journal of Information Systems, 3*(2), 112-126.

Gadatsch, A., & Juszczak, J. (2009). Ergebnisse der Kurzumfrage zum Stand von Green IT im deutschsprachigen Raum. Schriftenreihe des Fachbereiches Wirtschaftswissenschaften Sankt Augustin (Vol. 24). Sankt Augustin. Retrieved September 30, 2009, from http://www.fb01.h-brs.de/wirtschaftsanktaugustinmedia/Downloads/Schriftenreihe/bd24web.pdf

Galliers, R. D., & Land, F. F. (1987). Viewpoint: Choosing Appropriate Information Systems Research Methodologies. *Communications of the ACM, 30*(11), 901-902. doi:10.1145/32206.315753

Galliers, R. D., & Leidner, D. E. (2003). Strategic Information Management, Challenges and Strategies in Managing Information Systems (3rd ed.). Butterworth-Heinemann, Oxford, UK.

Gantz, J. F., Chute, C., Manfrediz, A., Minton, S., Reinsel, D., Schlichting, W., & Toncheva, A. (2008). The Diverse and Exploding Digital Universe - An Updated Forecast of WorldwideInformation Growth Through 2011. Retrieved March 17, 2010, from http://www.emc.com/collateral/analyst-reports/diverse-exploding-digital-universe.pdf

Gartner Inc. (2009). Gartner's 2009 Hype Cycle Special Report Evaluates Maturity of 1,650 Technologies. Retrieved March 1, 2010, from http://www.gartner.com/it/page.jsp?id=1124212

Gartner Inc. (2007). Gartner Estimates ICT Industry Accounts for 2 Percent of Global CO2 Emissions. Press Release. Retrieved March 31, 2008, from http://www.gartner.com/it/page.jsp?id=503867

Ghemawat, P. (1985). Building Strategy on the Experience Curve. *Harvard Business Review, 63*(2), 143-149.

Gibbs, M. (2008). Desktop Virtualization for the Enterprise. Retrieved January 30, 2009, from http://www.networkworld.com/columnists/2008/091108-gearhead.html

Glass, R. (2009). Google Emissions Study Borders on the Absurd. *Information Systems Management*, *26*(3), 302-303. doi:10.1080/10580530903018227

Global Reporting Initiative (2006). Sustainability Reporting Guidelines (Version 3.0). Amsterdam, Netherlands. Retrieved March 21, 2009, from http://www.globalreporting.org/NR/rdonlyres/ED9E9B36-AB54-4DE1-BFF2-5F735235CA44/0/G3_GuidelinesENU.pdf

GoodSearch (2010). About GoodSearch. Retrieved July 28, 2010, from http://www.goodsearch.com/about.aspx#faq2

Goodstein, L. D., Nolan, T. M., & Pfeiffer, J. W. (1993). Applied Strategic Planning: A Comprehensive Guide. McGraw-Hill, Boston, USA

Google Inc. (2011). Data center efficiency measurements · Google Data Centers · About. Retrieved April 11, 2011, from http://www.google.com/corporate/datacenter/efficiency-measurements.html

Grant, G. G., & Brown, A. E. (2005). Framing the Frameworks: A Review of IT Governance Research. *Communications of the Association for Information Systems*, *15*(1), 696-712.

Grant, R. M. (1991). The Resource-based Theory of Competitive Advantage: Implications for Strategy Formulation. *California Management Review*, *33*(3), 114-135.

Grant, R. M. (2005). Contemporary Strategy Analysis. John Wiley & Sons, Hoboken, USA.

Gray, I., & Fayol, H. (1987). General and Industrial Management. Pitman, London, UK.

Greenpeace International. (2009). Guide to Greener Electronics (No. 14). Retrieved from http://www.greenpeace.org/raw/content/international/press/reports/guide-to-greener-electronics-14-edition.pdf

GreenQloud. (2011). GreenQloud - The Worlds First Truly Green Compute Cloud. Retrieved January 19, 2011, from http://www.greenqloud.com/

Gregor, S. (2006). The Nature of Theory in Information Systems. *MIS Quarterly*, *30*(3), 611-642.

Hague, P. N. (2002). Market research. Kogan Page Publishers, London, UK.

Hahn, R. (2009). Multinationale Unternehmen und die "Base of the Pyramid": Neue Perspektiven von Corporate Citizenship und nachhaltiger Entwicklung. Gabler, Wiesbaden.

Hair, J. F., Black, W. C., Babin, B. J., & Anderson, R. E. (2009). Multivariate Data Analysis (7th ed.). Prentice Hall, Upper Saddle River, USA.

Hall, B. H., & Khan, B. (2003). Adoption of New Technology. *SSRN eLibrary*. Retrieved April 20, 2010, from http://papers.ssrn.com/sol3/papers.cfm?abstract_id=410656

Hart, S. L. (1995). A Natural Resource Based View of the Firm. *Academy of Management Review*, *20*(4), 986-1014.

Hauff, V. (Ed.). (1987). Unsere gemeinsame Zukunft: Der Brundtland-Bericht der Weltkommission für Umwelt und Entwicklung. Eggenkamp Verlag, Greven.

Hawkes, J. (2001). The Fourth Pillar of Sustainability: Culture's Essential Role in Public Planning. Common Ground, Champaign, USA.

Hedwig, M., Malkowski, S., & Neumann, D. (2009). Taming Energy Costs of Large Enterprise Systems Through Adaptive Provisioning. *Proceedings of the 30th International Conference on Information Systems (ICIS) 2009*. Phoenix, USA. Retrieved from http://aisel.aisnet.org/icis2009/140

Heidbrink, M. (2006). Reliabilität und Validität von Verfahren der Präferenzmessung - Ein meta-analytischer Vergleich verschiedener Verfahren der Conjoint-Analyse (Dissertation). Westfälischen Wilhelms-Universität Münster, Münster.

Heinrich, L. J., & Lehner, F. (2005). Informationsmanagement (8th ed.). Oldenbourg.

Heng, M. S. H., & De Moor, A. (2003). From Habermas's Communicative Theory to Practice on the Internet. *Information Systems Journal*, *13*(4), 331-352. doi:10.1046/j.1365-2575.2003.00144.x

Heng, S. (2009). Green IT: IT is not green and never ever will be! Retrieved May 26, 2009, from http://www.dbresearch.de/PROD/DBR_INTERNET_DE-PROD/PROD0000000000238000.pdf

Hevner, A. R., March, S. T., Jinsoo, P., & Ram, S. (2004). Design Science in Information Systems Research. *MIS Quarterly*, *28*(1), 75-105.

Hewlett, S. A., Sherbin, L., & Sumberg, K. (2009). How Gen Y & Boomers Will Reshape Your Agenda. *Harvard Business Review*, *87*(7/8), 71-76.

Hilty, L. M., Coroama, V., Eicker, M. O. de, Ruddy, T., & Muller, E. (2009). The Role of ICT in Energy Consumption and Energy Efficiency (ICT-ENSURE: European ICT Environmental Sustainability Research; call identifier FP7-ICT-2007-2). Retrieved January 6,2010, from http://ict-ensure.tugraz.at/en/var/plain_site/storage/original/application/2447eaa3b6d3b5a407c220c5955df1ac.pdf

Hintemann, R., & Fichter, K. (2010). Materialbestand der Rechenzentren in Deutschland - Eine Bestandsaufnahme zur Ermittlung von Ressourcen- und Energieeinsatz. Umweltbundesamt (Eds.). Retrieved November 16, 2010, from http://www.umweltdaten.de/publikationen/fpdf-l/4037.pdf

Hintemann, R., & Pfahl, S. (2008). Energy Efficiency in the Data Center - A Guide to the Planning, Modernization and Operation of Data Centers (No. 2). Environment & Energy. Retrieved March 21, 2009, from http://www.bitkom.org/files/documents/Energy_Efficiency_in_the_Data_Center_Volume_2.pdf

Hischier, R. (2007). Life Cycle Inventories of Packaging and Graphical Paper (No. 11 v2.0). St. Gallen, Schweiz: Swiss Centre for Life Cycle Inventories, EMPA. Retrieved January 24, 2010, from http://www.ecoinvent.org

Hochstein, A., Uebernickel, F., & Brenner, W. (2006). Operations Management and IS: Using the SCOR-Model to Source Make and Deliver IS Services. *Proceedings of the 12th Americas Conference on Information Systems (AMCIS) 2006*. Acapulco, Mexiko. Retrieved from http://aisel.aisnet.org/amcis2006/5

Hubbard, D. W. (2007). How to Measure Anything. John Wiley & Sons, Hoboken, USA.

van Huikstee, M., & de Haan, E. (2009). E-Waste: Policy Paper. Amsterdam: Centre for Research on Multinational Corporations. Retrieved January 15, 2010, from http://goodelectronics.org/publications-en/Publication_3289/

Hülsmann, M., & Grapp, J. (2005). Recursivity and Dilemmas of a Sustainable Strategic Management - New Visions for a Corporate Balancing Efficiency and Sustainabilitythrough Autonomous Co-operation in Decision Making Processes. Retrieved March 2, 2009, from http://citeseerx.ist.psu.edu/viewdoc/download?doi=10.1.1.164.2018&rep=rep1&type=pdf

Hutcheson, D. G. D., & Sofroniou, D. N. (1999). The Multivariate Social Scientist: Introductory Statistics Using Generalized Linear Models (1st ed.). SAGE, Thousand Oaks, USA.

IDC (2010). PC Market Rebound Will Drive Double-Digit Growth Through 2014. Retrieved May 4, 2011, from http://www.idc.com/getdoc.jsp?containerId=prUS22247710

ifu Hamburg GmbH (2011). Umberto - Know the Flow. Retrieved January 19, 2011, from http://www.umberto.de/en/index.htm

Ijab, M. T., Molla, A., Kassahun, A. E., & Teoh, S. Y. (2010). Seeking the "Green" in "Green IS": A Spirit, Practice and Impact Perspective. *Proceedings of the 14th Pacific Asia Conference on Information Systems (PACIS) 2010*. Taipei, Taiwan. Retrieved from http://aisel.aisnet.org/pacis2010/46

Itami, H., & Roehl, T. W. (1991). Mobilizing Invisible Assets. Harvard University Press, Cambridge, USA.

Jenkin, T. A., Webster, J., & McShane, L. (2011). An Agenda for "Green" Information Technology and Systems Research. *Information and Organization, 21*(1), 17-40. doi:10.1016/j.infoandorg.2010.09.003

Jiang, J. J., & Klein, G. (1999). Project Selection Criteria by Strategic Orientation. *Information & Management, 36*(2), 63-75. doi: 10.1016/S0378-7206(99)00009-9

Johnson, G., & Scholes, K. (2006). *Exploring Corporate Strategy: Text and Cases* (7th ed.). Prentice Hall, London, UK.

Kaiser, H. F. (1960). The Application of Electronic Computers to Factor Analysis. *Educational and Psychological Measurement, 20*(1), 141-151. doi:10.1177/001316446002000116

Kaiser, H. F. (1970). A Second Generation Little Jiffy. *Psychometrika, 35*(4), 401-415. doi:10.1007/BF02291817

Kaiser, H. F. (1974). An Index of Factorial Simplicity. *Psychometrika, 39*(1), 31-36. doi:10.1007/BF02291575

Kaplan, J. M., Forrest, W., & Kindler, N. (2008). Revolutionizing Data Center Energy Efficiency. Retrieved April 5, 2009, from http://www.mckinsey.com/clientservice/bto/pointofview/pdf/Revolutionizing_Data_Center_Efficiency.pdf

Kawamoto, K., Koomey, J. G., Nordman, B., Brown, R. E., Piette, M. A., Ting, M., & Meier, A. K. (2002). Electricity Used by Office Equipment and Network Equipment in the US. *Energy, 27*(3), 255-269. doi:10.1016/S0360-5442(01)00084-6

Kawamoto, K., Shimoda, Y., & Mizuno, M. (2004). Energy Saving Potential of Office Equipment Power Management. *Energy and Buildings, 36*(9), 915-923. doi:10.1016/j.enbuild.2004.02.004

Klein, J., & Dawar, N. (2004). Corporate Social Responsibility and Consumers' Attributions and Brand Evaluations in a Product-harm Crisis. *International Journal of Research in Marketing, 21*(3), 203-217. doi:10.1016/j.ijresmar.2003.12.003

Koomey, J. G. (2007). Estimating Total Power Consumption by Servers in the U.S. and the World (Final Report). Stanford University, Stanford, USA. Retrieved November 13, 2008, from http://enterprise.amd.com/Downloads/svrpwrusecompletefinal.pdf

Krcmar, H. (2005). Informationsmanagement (4th ed.). Springer, Berlin.

Krcmar, H. (2009). Informationsmanagement (5th ed.). Springer, Berlin.

Kroll, C. (2010). Darstellung von Ecosia. Interview.

Kumar, R., & Mieritz, L. (2007). Conceptualizing "Green" IT and Data Center Power and Cooling Issues. Gartner Inc. Research Paper.

Kuo, B. N., & Dick, G. N. (2010). The Greening of Organisational IT: What Makes a Difference? *Australasian Journal of Information Systems, 16*(2), 81-92.

Kurp, P. (2008). Green Computing. *Communications of the ACM, 51*(10), 11-13. doi:10.1145/1400181.1400186

Leake, J., & Woods, R. (2009, January 11). Revealed: The Environmental Impact of Google Searches. *The Times (UK)*. Retrieved July 28, 2010, from http://technology.timesonline.co.uk/tol/news/tech_and_web/article5489134.ece

Lee, A. S., & Baskerville, R. L. (2003). Generalizing Generalizability in Information Systems Research. *Information Systems Research, 14*(3), 221-243.

Lee, K. (2009). Gender Differences in Hong Kong Adolescent Consumers' Green Purchasing Behavior. *Journal of Consumer Marketing, 26*(2), 87-96.

Lehr, U., Lutz, C., Khoroshun, O., Edler, D., O'Sullivan, M., Nitsch, J., Nienhaus, K., Breitschopf, B., et al. (2010). Erneuerbar beschäftigt! Kurz und langfristige Arbeitsplatzwirkungen des Ausbaus der erneuerbaren Energien in Deutschland. Retrieved April 5, 2011, from http://www.bmu.de/files/pdfs/allgemein/application/pdf/broschuere_erneuerbar_beschaefti gt_bf.pdf

Lichtenstein, D. R., Drumwright, M. E., & Braig, B. M. (2004). The Effect of Corporate Social Responsibility on Customer Donations to Corporate-Supported Nonprofits. *The Journal of Marketing, 68*(4), 16-32.

Lin, D. (2011). Blood Phones, Coltan and Gorillas. Retrieved May 4, 2011, from http://animalrights.about.com/b/2010/03/25/blood-phones-coltan-and-gorillas.htm

Long, J. S. (1997). Regression Models for Categorical and Limited Dependent Variables. SAGE, Thousand Oaks, USA.

Löscher, P. (2011). Speech of Annual Shareholders' Meeting of Siemens AG. Speech presented at the Annual Shareholders' Meeting of Siemens AG, Munich, Germany. Retrieved April 5, 2011, from http://www.siemens.com/press/pool/de/events/2011/corporate/2011-q1/2011-hv-speech-loescher.pdf

Luce, R. D., & Tukey, J. W. (1964). Simultaneous Conjoint Measurement: A New Type of Fundamental Measurement. *Journal of Mathematical Psychology, 1*(1), 1-27. doi: 10.1016/0022-2496(64)90015-X

Luftman, J. N., & Bullen, C. V. (2004). Managing the Information Technology Resource: Leadership in the Information Age. Prentice Hall, Upper Saddle River, USA.

Luftman, J., Papp, R., & Brier, T. (1999). Enablers and Inhibitors of Business-IT Alignment. *Communications of the AIS, 1*(11), 1-32.

Luo, X., & Bhattacharya, C. B. (2006). Corporate Social Responsibility, Customer Satisfaction, and Market Value. *Journal of Marketing, 70*(4), 1-18. doi:10.1509/jmkg.70.4.1

Magill, S., & Brown, C. (1994). Alignment of the IS Function with the Enterprise: Toward a Model of Antecedents. *MIS Quarterly, 18*(4), 371-403.

Magretta, J. (2002). Why Business Models Matter. *Harvard Business Review, 80*(5), 86-93.

Mani, D., Barua, A., & Whinston, A. (2010). An Empirical Analysis of the Impact of Information Capabilities Design on Business Process Outsourcing Performance. *MIS Quarterly, 34*(1), 39-62.

Mann, H., Grant, G., & Mann, I. J. S. (2009). Green IT: An Implementation Framework. *Proceedings of the 15th Americas Conference on Information Systems (AMCIS) 2009*. San Francisco, USA. Retrieved from http://aisel.aisnet.org/amcis2009/121

March, S. T., & Smith, G. F. (1995). Design and Natural Science Research on Information Technology. *Decision Support Systems, 15*(1995), 251-266. doi:10.1016/0167-9236(94)00041-2

March, S. T., & Storey, V. C. (2008). Design Science in the Information Systems Discipline: An Introduction to the Special Issue on Design Science Research. *MIS Quarterly, 32*(4), 725-730.

Marcus, A. A. (2005). Research in Strategic Environmental Management. In Sharma, S. & Aragón-Correa, J. A. (Eds.), Corporate Environmental Strategy and Competitive Advantage. Edward Elgar Publishing, Cheltenham, UK.

Margolus, N., & Levitin, L. B. (1998). The Maximum Speed of Dynamical Evolution. *Physica D: Nonlinear Phenomena, 120*(1-2), 188-195. doi:10.1016/S0167-2789(98)00054-2

Marrewijk, M. van. (2003). Concepts and Definitions of CSR and Corporate Sustainability: Between Agency and Communion. *Journal of Business Ethics, 44*(2-3), 95-105. doi:10.1007/s10551-004-1898-6

Marrone, M., Schmidt, N.-H., Kossahl, J., & Kolbe, L. M. (2011). Creating a Taxonomy of Corporate Social Responsibility, Sustainability, Stakeholders, Environment, Green IS, and Green IT: A Literature Review. *Proceedings of SIGGreen Workshop - Sprouts: Working Papers on Information Systems, 11*(17). Retrieved from http://sprouts.aisnet.org/11-17

Mason, M. (1997). A Look Behind Trend Data in Industrialization: The Role of Transnational Corporations and Environmental Impacts. *Global Environmental Change, 7*(2), 113-127. doi:10.1016/S0959-3780(96)00038-6

McCarthy, E. J. (1960). Basic Marketing: A Managerial Approach. Irwin, Homewood, USA.

McKeen, J. D., & Smith, H. A. (2003). Making IT Happen: Critical Issues in IT Management. John Wiley & Sons, Hoboken, USA.

McNurlin, B., & Sprague, R. H. (2006). Information Systems Management in Practice (7th ed.). Prentice Hall, Upper Saddle River, USA.

Melville, N. P. (2010). Information Systems Innovation for Environmental Sustainability. *MIS Quarterly, 34*(1), 1-21.

Metrolight Ltd. (2011). Metrolight. Retrieved May 3, 2011, from http://www.metrolight.com/about.php

Mines, C., & Davis, E. (2007). Topic Overview: Green IT. Retrieved November 5, 2009, from http://www.forrester.com/Research/Document/Excerpt/0,7211,43494,00.html

Mingay, S. (2007). Green IT: A New Industry Shock Wave. Retrieved August 12, 2008, from http://www.ictliteracy.info/rf.pdf/Gartner_on_Green_IT.pdf

Mingers, J., & Walsham, G. (2010). Toward Ethical Information Systems: The Contribution of Discourse Ethics. *MIS Quarterly, 34*(4), 833-854.

Mitchell-Jackson, J., Koomey, J. G., Nordman, B., & Blazek, M. (2003). Data Center Power Requirements: Measurements from Silicon Valley. *Energy, 28*(8), 837-850. doi:10.1016/S0360-5442(03)00009-4

Mithas, S., Khuntia, J., & Roy, P. (2010). Green Information Technology, Energy Efficiency, and Profits: Evidence from an Emerging Economy. *Proceedings of the 31st International Conference on Information Systems (ICIS) 2010*. St. Louis, USA. Retrieved from http://aisel.aisnet.org/icis2010_submissions/11

Mithas, S., Ramasubbu, N., & Sambamurthy, V. (2011). How Information Management Capability Influences Firm Performance. *MIS Quarterly, 35*(1), 237-256.

Molla, A., Cooper, V. A., & Pittayachawan, S. (2009). IT and Eco-sustainability: Developing and Validating a Green IT Readiness Model. *Proceedings of the 30th International Conference on Information Systems (ICIS) 2009*. Phoenix, USA. Retrieved from http://aisel.aisnet.org/icis2009/141

Molla, A. (2008). GITAM: A Model for the Adoption of Green IT. *Proceedings of the 19th Australasian Conference on Information Systems (ACIS) 2008*. Christchurch, New Zealand.

Molla, A. (2009). The Reach and Richness of Green IT: A Principal Component Analysis. *Proceedings of the 20th Australasian Conference on Information Systems (ACIS) 2009*. Melbourne, Australia.

Molla, A., Cooper, V., Corbitt, B., Deng, H., Peszynski, K., Pittayachawan, S., & Teoh, S. Y. (2008). E-Readiness to G-Readiness: Developing a Green Information TechnologyReadiness Framework. *Proceedings of the 19th Australasian Conference on Information Systems (ACIS) 2008*. Christchurch, New Zealand.

Montiel, I. (2008). Corporate Social Responsibility and Corporate Sustainability: Separate Pasts, Common Futures. *Organization & Environment, 21*(3), 245-269. doi:10.1177/1086026608321329

Moore, G. E. (1998). Cramming More Components onto Integrated Circuits. *Proceedings of the IEEE, 86*(1), 82-85.

Mungwititkul, W., & Mohanty, B. (1997). Energy Efficiency of Office Equipment in Commercial Buildings: The case of Thailand. *Energy, 22*(7), 673-680. doi:10.1016/S0360-5442(97)00162-X

Murugesan, S. (2008). Harnessing Green IT: Principles and Practices. *IT Professional, 10*(1), 24-33. doi:10.1109/MITP.2008.10

Nguyen, R., Bidault, S., & Nahal, S. (2009). Green IT - Energy Efficiency: The Silent Killer & Enabler - Data Centres, Semis & the Smart Grid (Equity Research). Retrieved April 6, 2011, from http://www.samsung.com/global/business/semiconductor/products/dram/DDR3/swf/download_file/green_it/SGCrossAssetResearch_Green_IT.pdf

Nielsen Wire. (2010). Top U.S. Search Sites for May 2010. Retrieved July 5, 2010, from http://blog.nielsen.com/nielsenwire/online_mobile/top-u-s-search-sites-for-may-2010/

Nonaka, I. (1994). A Dynamic Theory of Organizational Knowledge Creation. *Organization Science, 5*(1), 14-37.

Nurse, K. (2006). Culture as the Fourth Pillar of Sustainable Development, 32-48. Commonwealth Secretariat, London, UK.

Olsen, M., & Boxenbaum, E. (2009). Bottom-of-the-Pyramid: Organizational Barriers to Implementation. *California Management Review, 51*(4), 100-125.

Olson, M. H., & Chervany, N. L. (1980). The Relationship Between Organizational Characteristics and the Structure of the Information Services Function. *MIS Quarterly, 4*(2), 57-68.

Österle, H., & Blessing, D. (2000). Business Engineering Model. In Österle, H., & Winter, R. (Eds.), Business Engineering: Auf dem Weg zum Unternehmen des Informationszeitalters, 61-80. Springer, Heidelberg.

Österle, H., Brenner, W., & Hilbers, K. (1992). Unternehmensführung und Informationssystem. Der Ansatz des St. Galler Informationssystem-Managements (2nd ed.). Vieweg+Teubner, Wiesbaden.

Otten, J. (2010). Öko-Suchmaschinen: Grüner als Google. *taz.de*. Retrieved July 28, 2010, from http://www.taz.de/1/netz/netzoekonomie/artikel/1/gruener-als-google/

Palvia, P., En Mao, P., Salam, A. F., & Soliman, K. S. (2003). Management Information Systems Research: What's there in a Methodology? *Communications of AIS, 11*(2003), 289-309.

Parker, M. M., Benson, R. J., & Trainor, H. E. (1988). Information Economics: Linking Business Performance to Information Technology (1st ed.). Prentice Hall, Upper Saddle River, USA.

Patterson, M., Azevedo, D., Belady, C., & Pouchet, J. (2011). Water Usage Effectiveness (WUE): A Green Grid Data Center Sustainability Metric (White Paper No. 35). Retrieved April 8, 2011, from http://www.thegreengrid.org/~/media/WhitePapers/CarbonUsageEffectivenessWhitePaper 20101202.ashx?lang=en

Pavlou, P. A., Liang, H., & Xue, Y. (2007). Understanding and Mitigating Uncertainty in Online Exchange Relationships: A Principal Agent Perspective. *MIS Quarterly, 31*(1), 105-136.

Pettigrew, A. M. (1979). On Studying Organizational Cultures. *Administrative Science Quarterly, 24*(4), 570-581. doi:10.2307/2392363

Picot, A., Reichwald, R., & Wigand, R. T. (2003). Die grenzenlose Unternehmung (5th ed.). Gabler, Wiesbaden.

Piotrowicz, W., & Cuthbertson, R. (2008). Sustainability - A New Dimension in Information Systems Evaluation. *Proceedings of the 5th European and Mediterranean Conference on Information Systems (EMCIS) 2008*. Al Bostan Rotana, Dubai, UAE.

Poppo, L., & Zenger, T. (2002). Do Formal Contracts and Relational Governance Function as Substitutes or Complements? *Strategic Management Journal, 23*(8), 707-725.

Porter, M. E. (1980). Competitive Strategy: Techniques for Analyzing Industries and Competitors: with a new Introduction. Simon and Schuster, New York, USA.

Porter, M. E. (1998). Competitive Advantage: Creating and Sustaining Superior Performance: With a New Introduction. Simon and Schuster, New York, USA.

Porter, M. E., & Kramer, M. R. (2006). Strategy & Society: The Link Between Competitive Advantage and Corporate Social Responsibility. *Harvard Business Review, 84*(12), 78-92.

Porter, M. E., & van der Linde, C. (1995). Green and Competitive: Ending the Stalemate. *Harvard Business Review, 73*(5), 120-134.

Porter, M. E., & Reinhardt, F. (2007). Grist: A Strategic Approach to Climate. *Harvard Business Review, 85*(10), 22-26.

Pozzebon, M., Vu, T., Fleury, A., & Petrini, M. (2006). Information Management Models for Corporate Social Responsibility Practices. *Proceedings of the 12th Americas Conference on Information Systems (AMCIS) 2006*. Acapulco, Mexico. Retrieved from http://aisel.aisnet.org/amcis2006/482

Proto, M., Malandrino, O., & Supino, S. (2007). Eco-labels: A Sustainability Performance in Benchmarking? *Management of Environmental Quality: An International Journal, 18*(6), 669-683. doi:10.1108/14777830710826702

Rasmussen, N. (2006a). Implementing Energy Efficient Data Centers (White Paper). Retrieved Febuary 9, 2010, from http://www.apcmedia.com/salestools/NRAN-6LXSHX_R0_EN.pdf

Rasmussen, N. (2006b). Electrical Efficiency Modeling for Data Centers (White Paper). Retrieved March 15, 2010, from http://www.apcmedia.com/salestools/NRAN-6LXSHX_R0_EN.pdf

Rat der IT-Beauftragten. (2008). Green-IT in der Bundesverwaltung (Beschluss des Rates der IT-Beauftragten No. 8). Retrieved November 12, 2010, from http://www.cio.bund.de/SharedDocs/Publikationen/DE/Ueber_uns/IT_Rat_Beschluesse/beschluss_08_2008_download.pdf;jsessionid=BCC8DF11FC0159FAC6EDC2C4426C8C47.2_cid102?__blob=publicationFile

Ray, P. H., & Anderson, S. R. (2001). The Cultural Creatives: How 50 Million People are Changing the World. Three Rivers Press, New York, USA.

RMIT University. (2009). Green IT Observatory. Retrieved September 14, 2009, from http://greenit.bf.rmit.edu.au/index.php

Robertson, D. C. (1993). Empiricism in Business Ethics: Suggested Research Directions. *Journal of Business Ethics, 12*(1993), 585-599.

Roland Berger Strategy Consultants GmbH (2011). Green Growth, Green Profit: How Green Transformation Boosts Business. Palgrave Macmillan, Basingstoke, UK.

Ross, K. (2010). Facebook Under Pressure to Be Greener. *The New York Times*. Retrieved April 10, 2011, from http://www.nytimes.com/2010/11/04/business/energy-environment/04ihtrbogface.html

Rudd, C., & Lloyd, V. (2007). ITIL Service Design. TSO, Norwich, UK.

Russo, M. V. (2003). The Emergence of Sustainable Industries: Building on Natural Capital. *Strategic Management Journal, 24*(4), 317-331. doi:10.1002/smj.298

Sambamurthy, V., & Zmud, R. W. (1999). Arrangements for Information Technology Governance: A Theory of Multiple Contingencies. *MIS Quarterly, 23*(2), 261-290.

Sanchez, R., Heene, A., & Thomas, H. (1996). Dynamics of Competence-based Competition: Theory and Practice in the New Strategic Management. Pergamon, Oxford, UK.

Schaltegger, S., & Synnestvedt, T. (2002). The Link between "Green" and Economic Success: Environmental Management as the Crucial Trigger between Environmental and Economic Performance. *Journal of Environmental Management, 65*(4), 339-346.

Schaltegger, S., & Wagner, M. (2006). Managing the Business Case for Sustainability: The Intergration on Social, Environmental and Economic Performances. Greenleaf Publishing, Sheffield, UK.

Scheer, A.-W. (1992). Architektur integrierter Informationssysteme. Grundlagen der Unternehmensmodellierung (2nd ed.). Springer, Berlin.

Schendler, A. (2002). Where's the Green in Green Business? *Harvard Business Review, 80*(6), 28-29.

Schlager, E. (2009). Coltan: Ein seltenes Erz und die Folgen seiner Nutzung. Retrieved May 4, 2011, from http://www.scinexx.de/dossier-443-1.html

Schlomann, B., Gruber, E., Eichhammer, W., Kling, N., Diekmann, J., Ziesing, H.-J., Rieke, H., & Wittke, F. (2004). Energieverbrauch der privaten Haushalte und des Sektors Gewerbe, Handel, Dienstleistung (GHD) - Abschlussbericht an das Bundesministerium für Wirtschaft und Arbeit. Projektnummer 17/02. Karlsruhe, Berlin. Retrieved from http://www.bmwi.de/BMWi/Redaktion/PDF/E/energieverbrauchsstudie-hauptbericht,property=pdf,bereich=bmwi,sprache=de,rwb=true.pdf

Schmidt, M., & Häuslein, A. (1996). Ökobilanzierung mit Computerunterstützung: Produktbilanzen und betriebliche Bilanzen mit dem Programm Umberto (1st ed.). Springer, Berlin.

Schmidt, N.-H. (2011). Search Engines and Social Business - Implications from the Case of Ecosia. In Haton, J.-P., Sidhom, S., Ghenima, M., & Benzakour, K. (Eds.), *Proceedings of the 4th. International Conference on Information Systems & Economic Intelligence (SIIE) 2011*, 248-254. Marrakech, Morocco.

Schmidt, N.-H., Erek, K., Kolbe, L. M., & Zarnekow, R. (2009a). Towards a Procedural Model for Sustainable Information Systems Management. *Proceedings of the 42nd Hawaii International Conference on System Sciences (HICSS) 2009*. Hawaii, USA. doi:http://doi.ieeecomputersociety.org/10.1109/HICSS.2009.984

Schmidt, N.-H., Erek, K., Kolbe, L. M., & Zarnekow, R. (2009b). Sustainable Information Systems Management. *Business & Information Systems Engineering, 1*(5), 400-402. doi:10.1007/s12599-009-0067-y

Schmidt, N.-H., Erek, K., Kolbe, L. M., & Zarnekow, R. (2010a). Examining the Contribution of Green IT to the Obejctives of IT Departments: Emprical Evidence fro German Enterprises. *Australasian Journal of Information Systems, 1*(17), 127-140.

Schmidt, N.-H., Erek, K., Kolbe, L. M., & Zarnekow, R. (2010b). Predictors of Green IT Adoption: Implications from an Empirical Investigation. *Proceedings of the 16th Americas Conference on Information Systems (AMCIS) 2010*. Lima, Peru. Retrieved from http://aisel.aisnet.org/amcis2010/367

Schmidt, N.-H., & Kolbe, L. M. (2011). Towards a Contingency Model for Green IT Governance. *Proceedings of the 19th European Conference on Information System (ECIS) 2011*. Helsinki, Finnland.

Schmidt, N.-H., Langkau, T., Ruch, T., & Kolbe, L. M. (2011). Strategic Green IT Planning: Lessons from a Financial Services Case. *Proceedings of the 8th European, Mediterranean and Middle Eastern Conference on Information Systems (EMCIS) 2011*. Athens, Greece.

Schmidt, N.-H., Schmehl, M., Thies, F., Kolbe, L. M., & Geldermann, J. (2010c). Ökobilanzierung in der IT - Distributionsformen der Musikindustrie im Vergleich. (Gomez, J. M., Strahringer, S., & Teuteberg, F. Eds.) *HMD - Praxis der Wirtschaftsinformatik, 274* (2010), 65-73.

Schmidt, N.-H., Schmidtchen, T., Erek, K., Kolbe, L. M., & Zarnekow, R. (2010d). Influence of Green IT on Consumers' Buying Behavior of Personal Computers: Implications from a Conjoint Analysis. *Proceedings of the 18th European Conference on Information System (ECIS) 2010*. Pretoria, South Africa.

Schwab, W. (2011). Experton Group: Der Markt für Green IT in Deutschland 2010 bis 2012. Retrieved April 5, 2011, from http://www.experton-group.de/research/ict-news-dach/news/article/der-markt-fuer-green-it-in-deutschland-2010-bis-2012.html

Schwaiger, M. (2004). Components and Parameters of Corporate Reputation - An Empirical Study. *Schmalenbach Business Review, 56*(1), 46-71.

Sen, S., & Bhattacharya, C. B. (2001). Does Doing Good Always Lead to Doing Better? Consumer Reactions to Corporate Social Responsibility. *Journal of Marketing Research, 38*(2), 225-243.

Sijpheer, N. C. (2008). Energy Saving at Data Hotels: Doing More with Less (No. ECN-E--08-035). ECN Energy in the Built Environment. Retrieved April 5, 2011, from http://www.ecn.nl/docs/library/report/2008/e08035.pdf

Singleton, J., McLean, E., & Altman, E. (1988). Measuring Information Systems Performance: Experience with the Management by Results System at Security Pacific Bank. *MIS Quarterly, 12*(2), 325-337.

Smerdon, G. (2000). Designing Energy-efficient PCs Using Integrated Power Management. In Goldberg, L. (Eds.), Green Electronics, Green Bottom Line: Environmentally Responsible Engineering, 15-28. Butterworth-Heinemann, Oxford, UK.

Smith, D. (1992). Strategic Management and the Business Environment: What Lies Beyond the Rhetoric of Greening? *Business Strategy and the Environment, 1*(1), 1-9. doi:10.1002/bse.3280010103

Smith, H. J. (2003). The Shareholders vs. Stakeholders Debate. *MIT Sloan Management Review, 44*(4), 85-90.

Smith, J. H. (2011). Tantalus in the Digital Age: Coltan Ore, Temporal Dispossession, and "Movement" in the Eastern Democratic Republic of the Congo. *American Ethnologist, 38*(1), 17-35. doi:10.1111/j.1548-1425.2010.01289.x

Som, C., Hilty, L. M., & Köhler, A. R. (2009). The Precautionary Principle as a Framework for a Sustainable Information Society. *Journal of Business Ethics, 85*(3), 493-505. doi:10.1007/s10551-009-0214-x

Spielmann, M., Dones, R., & Bauer, C. (2007). Life Cycle Inventories of Transport Services (Final report ecoinvent v2.0 No. 15). Dübendorf, Schweiz: Swiss Centre for Life Cycle Inventories, EMPA. Retrieved from http://www.ecoinvent.org

Srivastava, R. K., Shervani, T. A., & Fahey, L. (1998). Market-Based Assets and Shareholder Value: A Framework for Analysis. *Journal of Marketing, 62*(1), 2-18.

Starik, M., & Rands, G. P. (1995). Weaving an Integrated Web: Multilevel and Multisystem Perspectives of Ecologically Sustainable Organizations. *The Academy of Management Review, 20*(4), 908-935.

Stebbins, R. A. (2001). Exploratory Research in the Social Sciences. SAGE, Thousand Oaks, USA.

Stenmark, D., Espenkrona, K., & Svensson, M. (2010). Design Implications for Personal Information Management: A Theoretical Evaluation of a Prototype Interface. *Proceedings of the 16th Americas Conference on Information Systems (AMCIS) 2010*. Lima, Peru. Retrieved from http://aisel.aisnet.org/amcis2010/85

Stiftung Warentest. (2009a). Spargeräte PC-Heimvernetzung - Marathon für Router. Retrieved December 8, 2009, from http://www.test.de/themen/umwelt-energie/test/Spargeraete-PC-Heimvernetzung-Marathon-fuer-Router-1791786-2791786/

Stiftung Warentest. (2009b). Net- und Notebooks: Erstmals gute Netbooks. *Stiftung Warentest, 11*.

Straub, D. W. (1989). Validating Instruments in MIS Research. *MIS Quarterly, 13*(2), 147-169. doi:10.2307/248922

Sullivan, J. (1985). Systems Planning in the Information Age. *Sloan Management Review, 26*(2), 3-12.

Supply-Chain Council Inc. (2006). Supply-Chain Operations Reference-model (SCOR): Overview Version 8.0. Retrieved from https://www.supply-chain.org/resources/scor

Symantec. (2009). Green IT Report - Regional Data - United States and Canada: Survey Results. Retrieved April 6, 20110, from http://www.symantec.com/content/en/us/about/media/GreenIT09_Report.pdf

Tavakolian, H. (1989). Linking the Information Technology Structure with Organizational Competitive Strategy: A Survey. *MIS Quarterly, 13*(3), 309-317.

Teece, D. J. (2010). Business Models, Business Strategy and Innovation. *Long Range Planning, 43*(2-3), 172-194. doi: 10.1016/j.lrp.2009.07.003

Tenhunen, M., & Penttinen, E. (2010). Assessing the Carbon Footprint of Paper vs. Electronic Invoicing. *Proceedings of the 21st Australasian Conference on Information Systems (ACIS) 2010*. Brisbane, Australia. Retrieved from http://aisel.aisnet.org/acis2010/95

Teuteberg, F., & Straßenburg, J. (2009). State of the Art and Future Research in Environmental Management Information Systems - A Systematic Literature Review. *Information Technologies in Environmental Engineering, Proceedings of the 4th International ICSC Symposium, ITEE 2009*. Thessaloniki, Greece. May 28-29. doi: 10.1007/978-3-540-88351-7_5

Thambusamy, R., & Salam, A. (2010). Corporate Ecological Responsiveness, Environmental Ambidexterity and IT-Enabled Environmental Sustainability Strategy. *Proceedings of the 31st International Conference on Information Systems (ICIS) 2010*. St. Louis, USA. Retrieved from http://aisel.aisnet.org/icis2010_submissions/191

The Green Grid. (2010a). The Green Grid. Retrieved March 1, 2010, from http://www.thegreengrid.org/

The Green Grid. (2010b). The Green Grid Data Center Power Efficiency Metrics: PUE and DCiE. Retrieved November 1, 2010, from http://www.thegreengrid.org/sitecore/content/Global/Content/white-papers/The-Green-Grid-Data-Center-Power-Efficiency-Metrics-PUE-and-DCiE.aspx

Thomas, D. (2008). Enabling Application Agility–Software as a Service, Cloud Computing and Dynamic Languages. *Journal of Object Technology, 7*(4), 29-32.

Timmers, P. (1998). Business Models for Electronic Markets. *Electronic Markets, 8*(2), 3-8. doi:10.1080/10196789800000016

Treehoo (2010). Treehoo! Good for the planet. Retrieved July 28, 2010, from http://www.treehoo.com/info.html

Tsoutsoura, M. (2004). Corporate Social Responsibility and Financial Performance. UC Berkeley: Center for Responsible Business. Retrieved from http://escholarship.org/uc/item/111799p2

Turban, D. B., & Greening, D. W. (1997). Corporate Social Performance and Organizational Attractiveness to Prospective Employees. *The Academy of Management Journal, 40*(3), 658-672.

TÜV Rheinland (2011). Green IT Analysis and Certification. Retrieved May 7, 2011, from http://www.tuv.com/en/corporate/business_customers/plants_machinery_1/climate_enviro nmental_protection_1/green_it_1/green_it.jsp?null

Umanath, N. (2003). The Concept of Contingency Beyond "It depends": Illustrations from IS Research Stream. *Information & Management, 40*(6), 551-562. doi:10.1016/S0378-7206(02)00080-0

Umweltbundesamt (2009). Entwicklung der spezifischen Kohlendioxid-Emissionen des deutschen Strommix 1990-2007 (Stand April 2009). Retrieved November 10, 2009, from http://umweltfreundliches-unternehmen.de/download/CO2-Strommix-UBA-2009-04.pdf

United Nations Environment Programme (2007). Global Environment Outlook 4. Progress Press Ltd., Valletta, Malta. Retrieved May 17, 2008, from http://www.unep.org/geo/geo4/report/GEO-4_Report_Full_en.pdf

United Nations Environment Programme (2011). UNEP Year Book 2011 Emerging Issues in Our Global Environment. United Nations Environment Programme, Nairobi, Kenya. Retrieved April 5, 2011, from http://www.unep.org/yearbook/2011/pdfs/UNEP_YEARBOOK_Fullreport.pdf

United Nations Global Compact (2011). United Nations Global Compact. Retrieved April 3, 2011, from http://www.unglobalcompact.org/

Uptime Institute (2010). The Uptime Institute - Improving Data Center Uptime and the World's IT Productivity Through Benchmarking and Collaborative Learning. Retrieved March 1, 2010, from http://www.uptimeinstitute.org/

Velte, T., Velte, A., & Elsenpeter, R. C. (2008). Green IT: Reduce Your Information System's Environmental Impact While Adding to the Bottom Line. McGraw-Hill, Boston, USA

Venkatesh, V., & Davis, F. D. (2000). A Theoretical Extension of the Technology Acceptance Model: Four Longitudinal Field Studies. *Management Science, 46*(2), 186-204.

Vensky, H. (2010). Klimaschutz: Öko-Suchen schützen das Gewissen mehr als den Wald. *Die Zeit*. Retrieved July 28, 2010, from http://www.zeit.de/digital/internet/2010-06/ecosia-suchmaschine-oekologisch-klima?page=1

Verdiem (2011). Verdiem :: Home. Retrieved January 19, 2011, from http://www.verdiem.com/

Verron, H., Burkhard, H., Penn-Bressel, G., Röthke, P., Bölke, M., & Hülsmann, W. (2005). Determinanten der Verkehrsentstehung. Retrieved March 21, 2011, from http://www.umweltdaten.de/publikationen/fpdf-l/2967.pdf

Verschoor, C. C., & Murphy, E. A. (2002). The Financial Performance of Large U.S. Firms and Those with Global Prominence: How Do the Best Corporate Citizens Rate? *Business & Society Review, 107*(3), 371-380.

Voß, S., & Gutenschwager, K. (2001). Informationsmanagement (1st ed.). Springer, Berlin.

Vykoukal, J., Wolf, M., & Beck, R. (2009). Does Green IT Matter? Analysis of the Relationship between Green IT and Grid Technology from a Resource-based View Perspective. *Proceedings of the 13th Pacific Asia Conference on Information Systems (PACIS) 2009*. Hyderabad, India. Retrieved from http://aisel.aisnet.org/pacis2009/51

Wade, M., & Hulland, J. (2004). The Resource-based View and Information Systems Research: Review, Extension, and Suggestions for Future Research. *MIS Quarterly, 28*(1), 107-142.

Wagner, M. (2007). Der Sustainable Economic Value von sozialer Nachhaltigkeit und Umweltmanagement: Konzept und empirische Anwendung. In Müller, M. & Schaltegger, S. (Eds.), Corporate Social Responsibility: Trend oder Modeerscheinung? (1st ed.), 229-245. Oekom, München.

Ward, J., & Peppard, J. (2002). Strategic Planning for Information Systems (3rd ed.). John Wiley & Sons, Hoboken, USA.

Watson, R. T., Boudreau, M.-C., & Chen, A. J. (2010). Information Systems and Environmentally Sustainable Development: Energy Informatics and New Directions for the IS Community. *MIS Quarterly, 34*(1), 23-38.

Weber, C. L., Koomey, J. G., & Matthews, H. S. (2009a). The Energy and Climate Change Impacts of Different Music Delivery Methods (Final report to Microsoft Corporation and Intel Corporation). Retrieved March 12, 2009, from http://download.intel.com/pressroom/pdf/CDsvsdownloadsrelease.pdf

Weber, K., Otto, B., & Österle, H. (2009b). One Size Does Not Fit All - A Contingency Approach to Data Governance. *Journal of Data and Information Quality, 1*(1), 1-27. doi:10.1145/1515693.1515696

WebHits (2010). Nutzung von Suchmaschinen. Retrieved July 5, 2010, from http://www.webhits.de/deutsch/index.shtml?webstats.html

Weill, P., & Ross, J. (2004). IT Governance: How Top Performers Manage IT Decision Rights for Superior Results. Harvard Business Press, Boston, USA.

Weill, P., & Ross, J. (2005). A Matrixed Approach to Designing IT Governance. *MIT Sloan Management Review, 46*(2), 26-34.

Weill, P., & Woodham, R. (2002). Don't Just Lead, Govern: Implementing Effective IT Governance. *SSRN eLibrary*. Retrieved from http://papers.ssrn.com/sol3/papers.cfm?abstract_id=317319

Weinhardt, C., Anandasivam, A., Blau, B., Borissov, N., Meinl, T., Michalk, W., & Stößer, J. (2009). Cloud Computing – A Classification, Business Models, and Research Directions. *Business & Information Systems Engineering, 1*(5), 391-399. doi:10.1007/s12599-009-0071-2

Wenzel, E., Kirig, A., & Rauch, C. (2007). Zielgruppe LOHAS - Wie der grüne Lifestyle die Märkte erobert. Zukunftsinstitut, Kelkheim.

Wetherbe, J. C., & Whitehead, C. J. (1977). A Contingency View of Managing the Data Processing Organization. *MIS Quarterly, 1*(1), 19-25.

Wilde, T., & Hess, T. (2007). Forschungsmethoden der Wirtschaftsinformatik. *WIRTSCHAFTSINFORMATIK, 49*(4), 280-287. doi:10.1007/s11576-007-0064-z

References

Williamson, O. E. (1985). The Economic Institutions of Capitalism: Firms, Markets, Relational Contracting. Free Press, New York, USA.

Winter, R. (2009). Interview with Alan R. Hevner on "Design Science." *Business & Information Systems Engineering*, *1*(1), 126-129. doi:10.1007/s12599-008-0004-5

WKWI (Wissenschaftliche Kommission Wirtschaftsinformatik im Verband der Hochschullehrer für Betriebswirtschaft) (2008). WI-Orientierungslisten. *WIRTSCHAFTSINFORMATIK*, *50*(2), 155-163. doi:10.1365/s11576-008-0040-2

Wittink, D., Vriens, M., & Burhenne, W. (1994). Commercial Use of Conjoint Analysis in Europe: Results and Critical Reflections. *International Journal of Research in Marketing*, *11*(1), 41-52. doi:10.1016/0167-8116(94)90033-7

Woods, A. (2010). Cooling the Data Center. *Communications of the ACM*, *53*(4), 36-42.

Woods, E., & Wheelock, C. (2010). Green Data Centers - Power and Cooling Infrastructure, IT Equipment, Monitoring and Management: Business Drivers, Market Analysis and Forecasts. Retrieved April 6, 2011, from https://www.pikeresearch.com/wordpress/wp-content/uploads/2010/08/GDC-10-Executive-Summary.pdf

WBCSD and WRI (World Business Council for Sustainable Development and World Resource Institute (Eds.)) (2004). The Greenhouse Gas Protocol - A Corporate Accounting and Reporting Standard (Revised ed.). Retrieved November 5, 2009, from http://www.ghgprotocol.org/files/ghg-protocol-revised.pdf

World Commission on Environment and Development (1987). Our common future - The Brundtland Report. Oxford University Press, Oxford, UK.

World Information Technology and Service Alliance (2008). Digital Planet 2008 - Executive Summary. Retrieved May 23, 2008, from http://www.witsa.org/kl08/DigitalPlanet2008ExecSummary_cover.pdf

World Resources Institute (2009). The Greenhouse Gas Protocol – A Corporate Accounting and Reporting Standard. Retrieved November 1, 2010, from http://www.ghgprotocol.org/files/ghg-protocol-revised.pdf

WWF (2009). WWF-Deutschland: Suchmaschine rettet Regenwald. Retrieved July 5, 2010, from http://www.wwf.de/presse/details/news/suchmaschine_rettet_regenwald/

Wyner, G. A. (1992). Uses and Limitations of Conjoint Analysis - Part I. *Marketing Research*, *4*(2), 42-44.

Xue, Y., Liang, H., & Boulton, W. R. (2008). Information Technology Governance in Information Technology Investment Decision Processes: The Impact of Investment Characteristics, External Environment, and Internal Context. *MIS Quarterly*, *32*(1), 67-96.

Yi, L., & Thomas, H. (2007). A Review of Research on the Environmental Impact of E-business and ICT. *Environment International*, *33*(6), 841-849. doi:10.1016/j.envint.2007.03.015

Yin, R. K. (2002). Case Study Research: Design and Methods (3rd ed.). SAGE, Thousand Oaks, USA.

Yoon, Y., Gürhan-Canli, Z., & Schwarz, N. (2006). The Effect of Corporate Social Responsibility (CSR) Activities on Companies with Bad Reputations. *Journal of Consumer Psychology*, *16*(4), 377-390.

York University (2011). Theories Used in IS Research Wiki. Retrieved April 20, 2011, from http://www.fsc.yorku.ca/york/istheory/wiki/index.php/Main_Page

Yunus, M. (2006). Social Business Entrepreneurs Are the Solution (Presented at the Skoll World Forum on Social Entrepreneurship). Retrieved August 2, 2010, from http://www.moveyourworld.nl/docs/uploads/Mohammed-Yunus-Social-Entrepreneurs%5B1%5D.pdf

Yunus, M. (2008a). Creating a World Without Poverty: Social Business and the Future of Capitalism. PublicAffairs, New York, USA.

Yunus, M. (2008b). How social business can create a world without poverty. Retrieved August 2, 2010, from http://www.csmonitor.com/Commentary/Opinion/2008/0215/p09s01-coop.html

Zachman, J. A. (1987). A Framework for Information Systems Architecture. *IBM systems journal*, *26*(3), 276-292.

Zarnekow, R., Brenner, W., & Pilgram, U. (2005). Integriertes Informationsmanagement: Strategien und Lösungen für das Management von IT-Dienstleistungen (1st ed.). Springer, Berlin.

Zarnekow, R., Pilgram, U., & Brenner, W. (2006). Integrated Information Management: Applying Successful Industrial Concepts in IT (1st ed.). Springer, Berlin.

Znout (2010). Wie es funktioniert - Znout. Retrieved July 28, 2010, from http://znout.org/_lang/de/how_it_works.php

Zonzoo (2011). About zonzoo. Retrieved May 4, 2011, from http://www.zonzoo.co.uk/about-us

Appendix

Appendix 1: Summary of added publications for Section A.3.1.

Author	Title	Source	Year
Melville, Nigel P.	Information Systems Innovation for Environmental Sustainability	MIS Quarterly	2010
Watson, Richard T.; Boudreau, Marie-Claude; Chen, Adela J.	Information Systems and Environmental Sustainable Development: Energy Informatics and New Directions for the IS Community	MIS Quarterly	2010
Vanessa Cooper and Alemayehu Molla	Conceptualizing Green IT Organizational Learning (GITOL)	AMCIS 2010 Proceedings	2010
Wietske van Osch and Michel Avital	From Green IT to Sustainable Innovation	AMCIS 2010 Proceedings	2010
Robert D. St. Louis and Joseph A. Cazier	Green Business and Online Price Premiums: Will Consumers Pay More to Purchase from Environmentally Friendly Technology Companies?	AMCIS 2010 Proceedings	2010
Gary Hackbarth and Michael B. Pate	Healthcare: Entering the Green Energy Debate	AMCIS 2010 Proceedings	2010
Dirk S. Hovorka and Nancy A. Auerbach	Building Community Sustainability with Geographic Information Systems	AMCIS 2010 Proceedings	2010
Tim S. McLaren, Priscilla R. Manatsa, and Ron Babin	An Inductive Classification Scheme for Green IT Initiatives	AMCIS 2010 Proceedings	2010
Ariyo Maiye and Kathy McGrath	ICTs and Sustainable Development: A Capability Perspective	AMCIS 2010 Proceedings	2010
Yong Seog Kim and Myung Ko	Identifying Green IT Leaders with Financial and Environmental Performance Indicators	AMCIS 2010 Proceedings	2010
Helen Hasan	Was the Copenhagen Summit Doomed from the Start? Some Insights from Green IS Research	AMCIS 2010 Proceedings	2010
Jacqueline Corbett, Jane Webster, Koray Sayili, Ivana Zelenika, and Joshua Pearce	Developing and Justifying Energy Conservation Measures: Green IT under Construction	AMCIS 2010 Proceedings	2010
Nils-Holger Schmidt, Koray Erek, Lutz M. Kolbe, and Rüdiger Zarnekow	Predictors of Green IT Adoption: Implications from an Empirical Investigation	AMCIS 2010 Proceedings	2010
Stoney Brooks, Xuequn Wang, and Saonee Sarker	Unpacking Green IT: A Review of the Existing Literature	AMCIS 2010 Proceedings	2010
Ben N. Kuo	Organizational Green IT: It Seems the Bottom Line Rules	AMCIS 2010 Proceedings	2010
Stefan Seidel, Jan Recker, Christoph Pimmer, and Jan vom Brocke	Enablers and Barriers to the Organizational Adoption of Sustainable Business Practices	AMCIS 2010 Proceedings	2010
Abhijit Datta, Shankha Roy, and Monideepa Tarafdar	Adoption of Sustainability in IT Services: Role of IT Service Providers	AMCIS 2010 Proceedings	2010
Laura B. Iacobelli, Robert A. Olson, and Jeffrey W. Merhout	Green/Sustainable IT/IS: Concepts and Cases	AMCIS 2010 Proceedings	2010
Ali Dada, Thorsten Staake, and Elgar Fleisch	Reducing Environmental Impact in Procurement by Integrating Material Parameters in Information Systems: The Example of Apple Sourcing	AMCIS 2010 Proceedings	2010
Gaurav Bansal	Continuing E-book Use: Role of Environmental Consciousness, Personality and Past Usage	AMCIS 2010 Proceedings	2010
Ravi Thambusamy and A. F. Salam	Corporate Ecological Responsiveness, Environmental Ambidexterity and IT Enabled Environmental Sustainability Strategy	ICIS 2010 Proceedings	2010
Sunil Mithas, Jiban Khuntia, and Prasanto K. Roy	Green Information Technology, Energy Efficiency, and Profits: Evidence from an Emerging Economy	ICIS 2010 Proceedings	2010
Jacqueline Corbett	Unearthing the Value of Green IT	ICIS 2010 Proceedings	2010
Markus Hedwig, Simon Malkowski, and Dirk Neumann	Towards Autonomic Cost-aware Allocation of Cloud Resources	ICIS 2010 Proceedings	2010

Authors	Title	Source	Year
Nils-Holger Schmidt, Timo Schmidtchen, Erek Koray, Lutz M. Kolbe, and Ruediger Zarnekow	Influence of Green IT on Consumers' Buying Behavior of Personal Computers: Implications from a Conjoint Analysis	ECIS 2010 Proceedings	2010
Eugenio Capra, Giulia Formenti, Chiara Francalanci, and Stefano Gallazzi	The Impact of MIS Software on IT Energy Consumption	ECIS 2010 Proceedings	2010
Jens Vykoukal	Grid Technology as Green IT Strategy? Empirical Results from the Financial Services Industry	ECIS 2010 Proceedings	2010
Stan Karanasios, Vanessa Cooper, Hepu Deng, Alemayehu Molla, and Siddhi Pittayachawan	Antecedents to Greening Data Centres: A Conceptual Framework and Exploratory Case Study	ACIS 2010 Proceedings	2010
Maija Tenhunen and Esko Penttinen	Assessing the Carbon Footprint of Paper vs. Electronic Invoicing	ACIS 2010 Proceedings	2010
Mohamad Taha Ijab, Alemayehu Molla, Asmare Emerie Kassahun, and Say Yen Teoh	Seeking the "Green" in "Green IS": A Spirit, Practice and Impact Perspective	PACIS 2010 Proceedings	2010
Kyoung Jun Lee and Federico Casalegno	An Explorative Study for Business Models for Sustainability	PACIS 2010 Proceedings	2010
Lee Hu and Daniel Zeng	IT and the Environment: An Application in Supply Chain Management	PACIS 2010 Proceedings	2010

Appendix 2: Publications of the author in the research area of sustainability and IS, including the 10 presented publications in Part B of this thesis.

Peer-reviewed Journals
Schmidt, N.-H.; Erek, K.; Kolbe, L. M.; Zarnekow, R.: Examining the Contribution of Green IT to the Objectives of IT Departments: Empirical Evidence from German Enterprises, In: Australian Journal of Information Systems (AJIS), Vol. 17 (2010) 1, 127-140
Schmidt, N.-H.; Schmehl, M.; Thies, F.; Kolbe, L. M.; Geldermann, J.: Ökobilanzierung in der Informationstechnik – Zwei Distributionsformen der Musikindustrie im Vergleich, In: HMD - Theorie und Praxis der Wirtschaftsinformatik, Vol. 274 (2010), 65-73
Erek, K.; **Schmidt, N.-H.**; Zarnekow, R.; Kolbe, L. M.: Green IT im Rahmen eines nachhaltigen Informationsmanagements – Status-quo und Handlungsempfehlungen für die Praxis, In: HMD - Theorie und Praxis der Wirtschaftsinformatik, Vol. 274 (2010), 18-27
Schmidt, N.-H.; Erek, K.; Kolbe, L. M.; Zarnekow, R.: Nachhaltiges Informationsmanagement, In: Wirtschaftsinformatik, Vol. 51 (2009) 5, 463-466
Schmidt, N.-H.; Erek, K.; Kolbe, L. M.; Zarnekow, R. (2009): Sustainable Information Systems Management, In: Business & Information Systems Engineering, Vol. 1 (2009) 5, 400-402 *(Translation)*
Peer-reviewed Conferences
Erek, K.; Loeser, F.; **Schmidt, N.-H.**; Zarnekow, R.; Kolbe, L. M.: Green IT Strategies: A Case Study-based Framework for Aligning Green IT with Competitive Environmental Strategies, In: Proceedings of the 15th Pacific Asia Conference on Information Systems (PACIS 2011), July 7-11, Brisbane, Australia
Ruch, J. R.; **Schmidt, N.-H.**; Decker, J.; Kolbe, L. M.: Ecosia – Who Cares About a Green Search Engine?, In: Proceedings of the 17th Americas Conference on Information Systems (AMCIS 2011), August 4-7, Detroit, USA
Loeser, F.; Erek, K.; **Schmidt, N.-H.**; Zarnekow, R.; Kolbe, L. M.: Aligning Green IT with Environmental Strategies: Development of a Conceptual Framework that Leverages Sustainability and Firm Competitiveness, In: Proceedings of the 17th Americas Conference on Information Systems (AMCIS 2011), August 4-7, Detroit, USA
Schmidt, N.-H.; Langkau, T. F.; Ruch, T.; Kolbe, L. M.: Planning a Green IT Strategy: Lessons from a Financial Services Case, In: Proceedings of the 8th European, Mediterranean & Middle Eastern Conference on Information Systems 2011 (EMCIS 2011), May 30-31, Athens, Greece
Schmidt, N.-H.: Search Engines and Social Business - Implications from the Case of Ecosia, In: J. Haton, S. Sidhom, M. Ghenima, & K. Benzakour, eds. Proceeding of the 4th. International Conference on Information Systems & Economic Intelligence (SIIE 2011), February 17-19, Marrakech, Morocco, 248-254 *(Best paper award)*
Schmidt, N.-H.; Kolbe, L. M.: Towards a Contingency Model for Green IT Governance, In: Proceedings of the 19th European Conference on Information System (ECIS 2011), June 9-11, Helsinki, Finland
Schmidt, N.-H.; Erek, K.; Kolbe, L. M.; Zarnekow, R.: Predictors of Green IT Adoption: Implications from an Empirical Investigation, In: Proceedings of the 16th Americas Conference on Information Systems (AMCIS 2010), August 12-15, Lima, Peru
Schmidt, N.-H.; Schmidtchen, T.; Erek, K.; Kolbe, L. M.; Zarnekow, R.: Influence of Green IT on Consumers' Buying Behavior of Personal Computers: Implications from a Conjoint Analysis, In: Proceedings of the 18th European Conference on Information System (ECIS 2010), June 6-9, Pretoria, South Africa
Schmidtchen, T.; **Schmidt, N.-H.**; Kolbe, L. M.; Geldermann, J.: Der Einfluss von ökologischen Produkteigenschaften bei PCs auf die Kaufentscheidung, In: Schumann M. et al., eds. Multikonferenz Wirtschaftsinformatik 2010. Göttingen: Univ.-Verl. Göttingen, 315-326
Erek, K.; **Schmidt, N.-H.**; Zarnekow, R.; Kolbe, L. M.: Nachhaltiges Informationsmanagement - Strategische Optionen und Vorgehensmodell zur Umsetzung, In: Informatik 2009, Workshop: Informatik und Nachhaltigkeitsmanagement, 39. Jahrestagung der Gesellschaft für Informatik e.V. (GI), GI-Edition - Lecture Notes in Informatics (LNI), 2009
Erek, K.; **Schmidt, N.-H.**; Zarnekow, R; Kolbe, L.: Sustainability in Information Systems - Assortment of Current Practices in IS Organizations, In: Proceedings of the 15th Americas Conference on Information Systems (AMCIS 2009), August 6-9, San Francisco, USA
Schmidt, N.-H.; Erek, K.; Kolbe L. M.; Zarnekow, R.: Towards a Procedural Model for Sustainable Information Systems Management, In: Sprague, R. H. (ed.), Proceedings of the 42th Hawaii International Conference on System Sciences 2009 (HICSS-42), Big Island, Hawaii, IEEE Computer Society, Los Alamitos, CA
Other Related Publications
Erek, K.; **Schmidt, N.-H.**; Zarnekow, R.; Kolbe, L. M.: Management Instruments for Sustainable Information Systems Management, In: Teuteberg F & Gomez J. M., eds. Corporate Environmental Management Information Systems: Advancements and Trends. IGI Global, 253-269, 2010
Zarnekow, R.; Kolbe, L. M.; Erek, K.; **Schmidt, N.-H.**: Studie: Nachhaltigkeit und Green IT in IT-Organisationen, Universitätsverlag der TU Berlin, 2010
Zarnekow, R.; Kolbe, L.M.; Erek, K.; **Schmidt, N.-H.**: Der Bund als Vorreiter? – Von Green-IT zum nachhaltigen Informationsmanagement, In: Bundesministerium des Innern (ed.), greenletter - Informationen zur Green-IT-Initiative des Bundes, (1), 7-8

Appendix 3: List of all researched organizations by the author. Some of this information is used in Publications B.4, B.6, B.9, and B.10.

Company
Alcatel-Lucent Deutschland AG
Allianz SE
Axel Springer AG
Bayer Business Services GmbH
BRE Bank SA
Bundesministerium des Innern
Bundesverwaltungsamt
Datev eG
Deutsche Bank AG
Ecosia GmbH
GESIS - Gesellschaft für Informationssysteme mbH
GWDG - Gesellschaft für wissenschaftliche Datenverarbeitung mbH Göttingen
IBM Deutschland GmbH
Infineon Technologies AG
IT-Dienstleistungszentrum Berlin Anstalt des öffentlichen Rechts
Microsoft Corporation
Münchener Rückversicherungs-Gesellschaft
RWE AG
SAP AG
Siemens IT Solutions and Services GmbH
Sun Microsystems, Inc.
T-Systems International GmbH
üstra Hannoversche Verkehrsbetriebe AG
Vodafone D2 GmbH
Yahoo! Inc.

Appendix

Appendix 4: Used questionnaire for Publications B.7 and B.8.

Georg-August-Universität Göttingen

Wirtschaftswissenschaftliche Fakultät
Professur für Informationsmanagement
Prof. Dr. Lutz M. Kolbe

Vielen Dank für Ihre Unterstützung.

Optionale Kontaktdaten zur Zusendung der Forschungsergebnisse

☐ Ich wünsche eine kostenlose Zusendung der Ergebnisse.
Name: _____
E-Mail: _____

☐ Ich habe Interesse an einer vertiefenden Fallstudie.
☐ Ich habe Interesse am vierteljährlichen Newsletter der Professur.

Begriffsverständnis von Green IT in diesem Fragebogen

Green IT umfasst das Management sämtlicher Aktivitäten und Lösungen des IT-Bereichs, die darauf abzielen den Ressourcenverbrauch der IT, z.B. in Form von Energie, Material oder Papier, zu reduzieren. Darüber hinaus beinhaltet Green IT Maßnahmen zur Kontrolle, Steuerung und Kommunikation des Erfolges.

Umweltschutz und Green IT im Unternehmen

1. Wie würden Sie das Engagement Ihres Unternehmens im Bereich Umweltschutz einstufen?
ausreichend engagiert ☐ ☐ ☐ ☐ ☐ sehr stark engagiert

2. Wie wichtig ist das Thema Umweltschutz für Ihr Unternehmen?
☐ Unwichtig ☐ Weniger wichtig ☐ Neutral ☐ Wichtig ☐ Sehr wichtig

3. Wer ist in Ihrem Unternehmen hauptverantwortlich für das Thema Umweltschutz?
☐ Umweltmanager ☐ Vorstand ☐ Aufsichtsrat ☐ COO ☐ CIO ☐ Anderer: _____

4. Green IT Maßnahmen sind in unserem Unternehmen...
☐ ...umgesetzt. ☐ ...geplant. ☐ ...nicht geplant. ☐ Weiß nicht.

5. Wer ist in ihrem Unternehmen hauptverantwortlich für das Thema Green IT?
☐ Aufsichtsrat ☐ Vorstand ☐ COO ☐ CIO ☐ Umweltmanager ☐ Green IT Beauftragter ☐ Anderer: _____

6. Wie wichtig ist das Thema Green IT für den IT-Bereich Ihres Unternehmens?
☐ Unwichtig ☐ Weniger wichtig ☐ Neutral ☐ Wichtig ☐ Sehr wichtig

7. In welchen Bereichen berücksichtigen Sie im Unternehmen Green IT?
☐ Vertrieb ☐ Schulungen ☐ Büroumgebung ☐ Mitarbeiterentlohnung ☐ Kommunikation ☐ Rechenzentrum
☐ Marketing ☐ Entsorgung ☐ Beschaffung Beispielmaßnahmen: _____

8. Woher kam der Anstoß, sich mit Green IT zu beschäftigen?
☐ Konkurrenten ☐ Vorstand ☐ Externe Berater ☐ Geschäftsbereich ☐ Medien ☐ Kunden ☐ IT-Mitarbeiter

9. Wie wird das Thema Green IT bearbeitet?
☐ Vollständig intern im Unternehmen ☐ Eher intern ☐ Eher extern ☐ Vollständig extern des Unternehmens

10. Auf welchen Märkten bietet der IT-Bereich Ihres Unternehmens IT-Produkte/Services an?
☐ Interner Markt ☐ Interner und externer Markt ☐ Externer Markt

Inwieweit stimmen Sie den folgenden Aussagen zu Green IT zu?	Trifft gar nicht zu				Trifft voll und ganz zu
11. Green IT ist ein Hype-Thema dessen Bedeutung überschätzt wird.	☐	☐	☐	☐	☐
12. Durch Green IT können wir bereits bei heutigen IT-Produkten/Services überdurchschnittliche Markt-/Verrechnungspreise durchsetzen.	☐	☐	☐	☐	☐
13. Durch Green IT können wir bei zukünftigen IT-Produkten/Services überdurchschnittliche Markt-/Verrechnungspreise durchsetzen.	☐	☐	☐	☐	☐
14. Mit Green IT können wir bereits heute mehr von unseren IT-Produkten/Services absetzen.	☐	☐	☐	☐	☐
15. Green IT führt zu neuen Alternativen für bestehende Produkte, Prozesse und Kundenbeziehungen, die zukünftig an Wert verlieren.	☐	☐	☐	☐	☐
16. Durch Green IT hat unser Unternehmen einen Konkurrenzvorteil, der schwierig zu imitieren ist.	☐	☐	☐	☐	☐
17. Green IT führt in unserem Unternehmen bei unseren heutigen Prozessen zu niedrigeren Kapitalinvestitionen.	☐	☐	☐	☐	☐
18. Durch Green IT haben wir eine bessere Auslastung vorhandener Anlagen.	☐	☐	☐	☐	☐
19. Green IT führt in unserem Unternehmen zu zeitlich kürzeren Prozessen.	☐	☐	☐	☐	☐
20. Durch Green IT ist der der Anteil fixer Kosten im Unternehmen geringer.	☐	☐	☐	☐	☐
21. Green IT ist für den IT-Bereich notwendig, um als kompetent wahrgenommen zu werden.	☐	☐	☐	☐	☐
22. Bei der Wahl von Vertragspartnern ist Green IT ein Qualitätsmerkmal.	☐	☐	☐	☐	☐

Bitte wenden →

	Trifft gar nicht zu				Trifft voll und ganz zu
23 Green IT ist für den Bezieher von IT-Produkten/Services ein wichtiges Entscheidungskriterium.	☐	☐	☐	☐	☐
24 Mit Green IT sinken die Prozesskosten in unserem Unternehmen.	☐	☐	☐	☐	☐
25 Dank Green IT steigt die Prozessqualität in unserem Unternehmen.	☐	☐	☐	☐	☐
26 Durch Green IT kann unser Unternehmen Kosten genauer vorhersagen.	☐	☐	☐	☐	☐
27 Der IT-Bereich wird von den Geschäftsbereichen häufig auf das Thema Green IT angesprochen.	☐	☐	☐	☐	☐
28 Mit Hilfe von Green IT kann unser Unternehmen Investitionen auf einen späteren Zeitpunkt verschieben.	☐	☐	☐	☐	☐
29 Durch Green IT ist die Laufzeit unserer zurzeit genutzten Anlagen länger.	☐	☐	☐	☐	☐
30 Mit Green IT kann unser Unternehmen seine zukünftigen Investitionen genauer vorhersagen.	☐	☐	☐	☐	☐
31 Durch Green IT wird einer staatlichen Regulierung des Umweltmanagements in der IT entgegengewirkt.	☐	☐	☐	☐	☐
32 Green IT stärkt das Image des IT-Bereichs.	☐	☐	☐	☐	☐
33 Für Green IT gibt es klar definierte und allgemein akzeptierte Standards.	☐	☐	☐	☐	☐
34 Die zukünftige Bedeutung von Green IT für unser Unternehmen ist unsicher.	☐	☐	☐	☐	☐
35 Der Erfolg von Green IT ist schwer messbar.	☐	☐	☐	☐	☐
36 Unser Unternehmen besitzt viel Erfahrung mit Green IT.	☐	☐	☐	☐	☐
37 Durch Verhaltensänderung der Mitarbeiter kann mehr erreicht werden als durch technische Green IT-Lösungen.	☐	☐	☐	☐	☐
38 Unser IT-Bereich besitzt viel Erfahrung im Outsourcing von IT Leistungen.	☐	☐	☐	☐	☐
39 Für die Umsetzung von Green IT ist die genaue Kenntnis des Unternehmens und seiner IT Infrastruktur notwendig.	☐	☐	☐	☐	☐
40 Die Umsetzung von Green IT ist einfach.	☐	☐	☐	☐	☐
41 Die Umsetzung von Green IT erfordert eine unternehmensweite Zusammenarbeit verschiedener Bereiche.	☐	☐	☐	☐	☐
42 Ein vollständiges Outsourcing von Green IT ist denkbar.	☐	☐	☐	☐	☐
43 Wir beraten andere Unternehmen bei Green IT Fragestellungen.	☐	☐	☐	☐	☐
44 Durch Green IT kann der IT-Bereich innovative Technologien schneller einführen.	☐	☐	☐	☐	☐

	Nein	Teilweise	Ja
45 Wird der Erfolg der Green IT Maßnahmen mit Kennzahlen gemessen und gesteuert?	☐	☐	☐
46 Findet eine Einbindung von Green IT in ein Performance Measurement System der IT (z.B. IT-Balanced Scorecard / ITIL) statt?	☐	☐	☐
47 Werden Green IT Aspekte bei der Ausschreibungen für IT-Infrastruktur berücksichtigt?	☐	☐	☐
48 Existieren Anreize für die Mitarbeiter, IT am Arbeitsplatz ressourcenschonend zu nutzen? Wenn ja, welche?	☐	☐	☐
49 Werden die Energiekosten der IT in der Büroumgebung (Desktop-Computer, Drucker, Thin-Clients, Notebook etc.) erfasst? Wie werden diese Kosten verrechnet? ☐ Gemeinkosten ☐ Verursachungsgerecht nach Abteilung Verrechnungsschlüssel nach:	☐	☐	☐
50 Werden die Energiekosten der IT im Rechenzentrum erfasst? Wie werden diese Kosten verrechnet? ☐ Gemeinkosten ☐ Verursachungsgerecht nach Abteilung Verrechnungsschlüssel nach:	☐	☐	☐
51 Der Erfolg unserer Green IT Maßnahmen wird den Mitarbeitern kommuniziert.	☐	☐	☐
52 Der Erfolg unserer Green IT Maßnahmen wird externen Interessenten kommuniziert.	☐	☐	☐

Allgemeine Fragen zum Unternehmen und dem IT-Bereich

53 Wieviele Mitarbeiter sind in Ihrem Unternehmen beschäftigt? ☐ <100 ☐ <500 ☐ <1.000 ☐ <5.000 ☐ ≥ 5.000

54 In welcher Branche ist Ihr Unternehmen aktiv? ☐ Produzierendes Gewerbe ☐ Handel, Verkehr ☐ Baugewerbe
☐ Finanzindustrie ☐ Information und Telekommunikation ☐ Andere: _____

55 Wieviele Mitarbeiter sind im IT-Bereich beschäftigt? ☐ <5 ☐ <10 ☐ <50 ☐ <100 ☐ ≥ 100

56 Wie hoch war der Jahresumsatz Ihres Unternehmens im Jahr 2008 in Mio. Euro? ☐ <5 ☐ <10 ☐ <50 ☐ <500 ☐ ≥ 500

Vielen Dank!

Platz der Göttinger Sieben 5
37073 Göttingen

Telefon: +49 551 39 4440

Telefax: +49 551 39 9735

Appendix 5: Calculation bases for the case in Publication B.10.

Exchange rate of the US-Dollar	1 US-Dollar = 3.2164 Polish Zloty (June 29, 2009)
Price per kilowatt hour electricity for the CSD Bank	0.41 Polish Zloty or 0.12747 US-Dollars
Indirect CO_2 emissions of purchased electricity in Poland	658.899 g CO_2/kWh (WRI, 2009)
Average employees working hours per year	1680 hours
Average electricity consumption of a PC with monitor	85 Watts
Average electricity consumption of a switched off PC, including monitor	5 Watts
Average energy consumption of a notebook	20 Watts
Average energy consumption of a switched off notebook	2.5 Watts
Average electricity consumption of a laser printer during working times (average of idle, stand-by)	84 Watts
Average energy consumption of a switched off printer	5 Watts
Data center utilization	60% of max. capacity
Weight estimations	
Sheet of paper	5 g
PC	6 kg
Printer	20 kg
Cartridge	300g
Laptop	2.5 kg
Cost per kg dangerous waste	2.5 Polish Zloty or 0.78 US-Dollars
Cost per ton of paper waste	541 Polish Zloty or 168.20 US-Dollars
Day of labor	1000 Polish Zloty or 310 US-Dollars
Costs of not switching of a PC after work	0.52 Polish Zloty per day or 0.16 US-Dollar
Switch off rate of PCs, printers, laptops after work	60%
Utilization rate of servers	60% for 365 days a year
Assumption of PUE	2.00 for all data centers
Backup DC in Lodz assumed to equal primary DC	
All data center estimations are based on the findings from the primary data center in Lodz	

Göttinger Wirtschaftsinformatik

Herausgeber: Prof. Dr. J. Biethahn • Prof. Dr. L. M. Kolbe • Prof. Dr. M. Schumann

Band 31: Dr. rer. pol. Christian Stummeyer
Integration von Simulationsmethoden und hochintegrierter betriebswirtschaftlicher PPS-Standardsoftware im Rahmen eines ganzheitlichen Entwicklungsansatzes
ISBN 3-89712-874-8

Band 32: Dr. rer. pol. Stefan Wegert
Gestaltungsansätze zur IV-Integration von elektronischen und konventionellen Vertriebsstrukturen bei Kreditinstituten
ISBN 3-89712-924-8

Band 33: Dr. rer. pol. Ernst von Stegmann und Stein
Ansätze zur Risikosteuerung einer Kreditversicherung unter Berücksichtigung von Unternehmensverflechtungen
ISBN 3-89873-003-4

Band 34: Dr. rer. pol. Gerald Wissel
Konzeption eines Managementsystems für die Nutzung von internen sowie externen Wissen zur Generierung von Innovationen
ISBN 3-89873-194-4

Band 35: Dr. rer. pol. Wolfgang Greve-Kramer
Konzeption internetbasierter Informationssysteme in Konzernen
Inhaltliche, organisatorische und technische Überlegungen zur internetbasierten Informationsverarbeitung in Konzernen
ISBN 3-89873-207-X

Band 36: Dr. rer. pol. Tim Veil
Internes Rechnungswesen zur Unterstützung der Führung in Unternehmensnetzwerken
ISBN 3-89873-237-1

Band 37: Dr. rer. pol. Mark Althans
Konzeption eines Vertriebscontrolling-Informationssystems für Unternehmen der liberalisierten Elektrizitätswirtschaft
ISBN 3-89873-326-2

Band 38: Dr. rer. pol. Jörn Propach
Methoden zur Spielplangestaltung öffentlicher Theater
Konzeption eines Entscheidungsunterstützungssystems auf der Basis Evolutionärer Algorithmen
ISBN 3-89873-496-X

Cuvillier Verlag Göttingen
Nonnenstieg 8 • 37075 Göttingen

Göttinger Wirtschaftsinformatik

Herausgeber: Prof. Dr. J. Biethahn • Prof. Dr. L. M. Kolbe • Prof. Dr. M. Schumann

Band 39: Dr. rer. pol. Jochen Heimann
DV-gestützte Jahresabschlußanalyse
Möglichkeiten und Grenzen beim Einsatz computergeschützter Verfahren zur Analyse und Bewertung von Jahresabschlüssen
ISBN 3-89873-499-4

Band 40: Dr. rer. pol. Patricia Böning Spohr
Controlling für Medienunternehmen im Online-Markt
Gestaltung ausgewählter Controllinginstrumente
ISBN 3-89873-677-6

Band 41: Dr. rer. pol. Jörg Koschate
Methoden und Vorgehensmodelle zur strategischen Planung von Electronic-Business-Anwendungen
ISBN 3-89873-808-6

Band 42: Dr. rer. pol. Yang Liu
A theoretical and empirical study on the data mining process for credit scoring
ISBN 3-89873-823-X

Band 43: Dr. rer. pol. Antonios Tzouvaras
Referenzmodellierung für Buchverlage
Prozess- und Klassenmodelle für den Leistungsprozess
ISBN 3-89873-844-2

Band 44: Dr. rer. pol. Marina Nomikos
Hemmnisse der Nutzung Elektronischer Marktplätze aus der Sicht von kleinen und mittleren Unternehmen eine theoriegeleitete Untersuchung
ISBN 3-89873-847-7

Band 45: Dr. rer. pol. Boris Fredrich
Wissensmanagement und Weiterbildungsmanagement
Gestaltungs- und Kombinationsansätze im Rahmen einer lernenden Organisation
ISBN 3-89873-870-1

Band 46: Dr. rer. pol. Thomas Arens
Methodische Auswahl von CRM Software
Ein Referenz-Vorgehensmodell zur methodengestützten Beurteilung und Auswahl von Customer Relationship Management Informationssystemen
ISBN 3-86537-054-3

Cuvillier Verlag Göttingen
Nonnenstieg 8 • 37075 Göttingen

Göttinger Wirtschaftsinformatik

Herausgeber: Prof. Dr. J. Biethahn • Prof. Dr. L. M. Kolbe • Prof. Dr. M. Schumann

Band 47: Dr. rer. pol. Andreas Lackner
Dynamische Tourenplanung mit ausgewählten Mataheuristiken
Eine Untersuchung am Beispiel des kapazitätsrestriktiven dynamischen
Tourenplanungsproblems mit Zeitfenstern
ISBN 3-86537-084-5

Band 48: Dr. rer. pol. Tobias Behrensdorf
Service Engineering in Versicherungsunternehmen
unter besonderer Berücksichtigung eines Vorgehensmodells zur Unterstützung durch
Informations- und Kommunikationstechnologien
ISBN 3-86537-110-8

Band 49: Dr. rer. pol. Michael Range
Aufbau und Betrieb konsumentenorientierter Websites im Internet
Vorgehen und Methoden unter besonderer Berücksichtigung der Anforderungen von kleinen
und mittleren Online-Angeboten
ISBN 3-86537-490-5

Band 50: Dr. rer. pol. Gerit Grübler
Ganzheitliches Multiprojektmanagement
Mit einer Fallstudie in einem Konzern der Automobilzulieferindustrie
ISBN 3-86537-544-8

Band 51: Dr. rer. pol. Birte Pochert
Konzeption einer unscharfen Balanced Scorecard
Möglichkeiten der Fuzzyfizierung einer Balanced Scorecard zur Unterstützung
des Strategischen Managements
ISBN 3-86537-671-1

Band 52: Dr. rer. pol. Manfred Peter Zilling
Effizienztreiber innovativer Prozesse für den Automotive Aftermarket
Implikationen aus der Anwendung von kollaborativen und integrativen
Methoden des Supply Chain Managements
ISBN 3-86537-790-4

Band 53: Dr. rer. pol. Mike Hieronimus
Strategisches Controlling von Supply Chains
Entwicklung eines ganzheitlichen Ansatzes unter Einbeziehung der Wertschöpfungspartner
ISBN 3-86537-799-8

Band 54: Dijana Bergmann
Datenschutz und Datensicherheit unter besonderer Berücksichtigung des elektronischen
Geschäftsverkehrs zwischen öffentlicher Verwaltung und privaten Unternehmen
ISBN 3-86537-894-3

Cuvillier Verlag Göttingen
Nonnenstieg 8 • 37075 Göttingen

Göttinger Wirtschaftsinformatik

Herausgeber: Prof. Dr. J. Biethahn • Prof. Dr. L. M. Kolbe • Prof. Dr. M. Schumann

Band 55: Jan Eric Borchert
Operatives Innovationsmanagement in Unternehmensnetzwerken
Gestaltung von Instrumenten für Innovationsprojekte
ISBN 3-86537-984-2

Band 56: Andre Daldrup
Konzeption eines integrierten IV-Systems zur ratingbasierten Quantifizierung des regulatorischen und ökonomischen Eigenkapitals im Unternehmenskreditgeschäft unter Berücksichtigung von Basel II
ISBN 978-3-86727-189-9

Band 57: Thomas Diekmann
Ubiquitous Computing-Technologien im betrieblichen Umfeld
Technische Überlegungen, Einsatzmöglichkeiten und Bewertungsansätze
ISBN 978-3-86727-194-3

Band 58: Lutz Seidenfaden
Ein Peer-to-Peer-basierter Ansatz zur digitalen Distribution wissenschaftlicher Informationen
ISBN 978-3-86727-321-3

Band 59: Sebastian Rieger
Einheitliche Authentifizierung in heterogenen IT-Strukturen für ein sicheres e-Science-Umfeld
ISBN 978-3-86727-329-9

Band 60: Ole Björn Brodersen
Eignung schwarmintelligenter Verfahren für die betriebliche Entscheidungsunterstützung
Untersuchungen der Particle Swarm Optimization und Ant Colony Optimization anhand eines stochastischen Lagerhaltungs- und eines universitären Stundenplanungsproblems
ISBN 978-3-86727-777-5

Band 61: Jan Sauer
Konzeption eines wertorientierten Managementsystems unter besonderer Berücksichtigung des versicherungstechnischen Risikos
ISBN 978-3-86727-858-4

Band 62: Adam Melski
Datenmanagement in RFID-gestützten Logistiknetzwerken
RFID-induzierte Veränderungen, Gestaltungsmöglichkeiten und Handlungsempfehlungen
ISBN 978-3-86955-041-1

Cuvillier Verlag Göttingen
Nonnenstieg 8 • 37075 Göttingen

Göttinger Wirtschaftsinformatik

Herausgeber: Prof. Dr. J. Biethahn • Prof. Dr. L. M. Kolbe • Prof. Dr. M. Schumann

Band 63: Thorsten Caus
Anwendungen im mobilen Internet
Herausforderungen und Lösungsansätze für die Entwicklung und Gestaltung mobiler Anwendungen
ISBN 978-3-86955-399-3

Cuvillier Verlag Göttingen

Nonnenstieg 8 • 37075 Göttingen